Also by Jasper Joyner

A FLAMBOYANCE, A CHAPBOOK

JUNIPER LEAVES

Library of Congress Control Number: 2024902100

ISBN: 978-0-9995386-6-1

ISBN: 978-0-9995386-4-7 (e-book)
ISBN: 978-0-9995386-5-4 (hardcover)

This book is a memoir in tradition with the term biomythography, first coined by Audre Lorde, a storytelling style that combines myth, history, and biography to create an epic narrative that embodies significant themes in which humans view the world. This story includes the author's memories of past experiences. Some real names and characteristics have been changed, some events compressed, and some dialogue has been added and/or recreated.

A version of the poem, "san.ko.fa." was featured in *Killens Review of Arts & Letters* Spring 2024 issue.

Copyedited by Cydney R. Humphrey

Front cover design by the author

Printed by IngramSparks, in the United States of America

First printing edition 2024

For information about special discounts for bulk purchases, requests for live events, or any other inquiries regarding this book, please go to jasperjoyner.com or contact Jasper Joyner at jaz@jazjoyner.com

Pansy

A Black American Memoir

Jasper Joyner

For my family
To my people

Table of Contents

INTRO

I won't be telling you my birth name. She's dead to me.

I do not hate her. No. She's cute or whatever, it's just that...*she*. She served her purpose. Carried me through childhood (girlhood, if you're nasty) within various countercultures of the infamous southern city of Memphis, Tennessee. Sputtered out of me like an upchuck on my first day of third grade when my first-ever friend, who hadn't known she'd been my first friend, asked, "What's your name again?" at lunchtime. This friend hadn't been there when I'd whispered my name hours ago in homeroom. And, often, that was the case. Her bashful entry, so delicate on the ears. Like a sweet kiss, perfectly inoffensive yet memorable. I never forgot how sweet she was; how sour I felt holding her, even when my hands were full of other things.

She was always kind. Rarely got mad when I'd inevitably announce I hated her shortly after the various discussions—within my mind—of her existence.

"What do you mean you hate your name?" My mom would ask, flabbergasted! Like it was the first time she'd ever heard such a thing.

It wasn't. It never was, except the first time, which was *ages* ago.

"Too girly!" I'd declare, all scrunched up and befuddled.

Mad as all get out about a thing I couldn't quite explain beyond its aforementioned *girliness*. For a while, I didn't even know what girly meant. Didn't care that my predilection for hair styling and obsession with the color pink made me a mighty fine candidate for "girly."

It wasn't some elusive girlie or boyishness that made her and I worlds apart. It was a more complicated thing than that. I didn't have language for that dissonant feeling of a wrong name bestowed on you like a funny-fitting shoe. You simply wanted to take it off. Too uncomfortable. You'd rather go barefoot, but there's too much dirt and debris on the ground, and ain't nobody tryna sludge through all of that with no protection. What if there are nails?!

She's retired now, thrown up the old jersey in the proverbial Name Hall of Fame, and I thank her for her service. She's beautiful. She always was. But I haven't been called by her in years. I bask in the unfamiliarity of her. A distant whisper of a soft kiss. No hard feelings, unless you asked my body...

My body is less forgiving than I am. When I say that I am fine, you might wait for my silence and listen closely to the cries of my own body. It would tell you that I am hurting, that in moments in which we fought, I'd disappear.

They disappear often, my body would say.

My body might tell you that sometimes the pain it feels does not belong to me, that my ancestor's pain has found home in my bones, and so we all live together. Sometimes there is no space to breathe. They tell me to try. They speak to me through poetry. I learn to listen. They say that I, like many of them, come in a more ambiguous shape. That, once before, there was no shame in shapes like ours. But today, I need armor to exist as I am.

My ancestors tell me that I will be confused by what's required of my existence, because though Somebodys have made rules against our living and tried to erase the proof of our people and told us that there are no other genders but The Two, they will also try to destroy the proof of our gods, who show us we have been here, forever and always.

It's by design, they say, and it will take me years to understand this. So, this will not be a story about my armor, though it is vital to my existence. Armor is needed so that when I am greeted in this world, I am not called a liar without even opening my mouth. So that the alarm bells do not sound, alerting beasts that I am one of *them*, in need of elimination. I'll work like hell to protect myself. I'll replace makeshift bandages with permanent top surgery. I'll remove some of my own flesh. I'll grow a beard and relax my own vocal cords and take my own father's face to be free of this dangerous siren. But this will *not* be a story about my armor.

This will be a love story. With the rockiest of roads and pit stops at everyone else's doorsteps but my own, until finally, I understand the constant shape of me. I'll draw you a picture of it, and I will color outside of the lines. It will be messy. But it will be beautiful and true.

My name now? Jasper. Sometimes I go by Jaz. It means "bringer of treasure" in Persian. A gemstone symbolizing nurture, protection, tranquility, and wholeness, characteristics I hope to represent one day or today. Whichever comes first.

Anyway, nice to meet you. I hope that upon reading this story, you will see why a soft whisper of a kiss of a name doesn't suit me at all. Not now, not then, not ever. Here I am, whole. It is my only way to exist. Curling, curvy, hard then soft, square and wavy. Still feminine and masculine in ways both aren't often called. Still flowery and effeminate and pink, and sometimes green, blue, always Black. On my best days, full of love and on my worst, timid to the core. A pansy, if you will. A soft and vibrant pansy, hence the title of this book.

PART I

No one can stop you from being yourself.

Not even you.

PLACES, PEOPLE! PLACES!

Memphis, TN, 1998

I'd like to introduce you to a little thing I'd like to call "trout."

It's a round, leavened dough with a signature grid pattern, typically eaten around breakfast time. Sometimes butter-smeared, drizzled with maple syrup in its many perfect, tiny squares. Maybe you'd prefer honey, a little whipped cream if you're saucy. You can't really go wrong. Not to be confused with the freshwater fish of the salmon family, typically found in North America and Eurasia. My vegan siblings and I knew very little about this pescatarian delicacy. But the word "trout" was so fun to say, so distinct and enthralling a term that we simply could not reserve it for a *fish*.

"What's a *trout*?" Momi would laugh, staring directly at a plate of it in my brother Andrew's hands.

"This!" Drew doubled over, shoving a plate of waffles her way.

"Child!" Momi rolled her eyes in that way she did specifically for shenanigans like these.

A very specific genre of antics by three very goofy children—myself and my younger brothers, Drew and Andon. Momi liked to call us the Word Patrol, because no word was safe from distortion, nothing safe from being renamed. The world was our Scrabble playground. Often, instead of conversations, my brothers and I had words, separate from sentences or full thoughts, obscure sounds and shapes in our mouths that we played with like toys. This was true whether anybody else liked it or not. Cause if anyone, and I mean anyone, twisted a word by accident, or with earnest intention, here we were, the doggone relentless Word Patrol, dragging that word into the ground. We didn't care if you were our Daddy telling us not to be afraid of the snake in our backyard that had us shaking in our light-up, knock-off Payless *Adeedas*. As soon as you twisted your southern, Black mouth into the shape of "afred," emphasis on that soft "e," we would cackle to the heavens above so loud we laughed out all fear and forgot the snake was there.

"What is so funny?" Our Daddy smirked, amused by our ridiculousness.

He would surmise from our repetition, "Afred, afred! Afred!" brought laughter. Nothing made us laugh harder than the scoop of a word, except a bundle of words specifically crafted for some outrageous joke. At ten and six, Drew and I knew nothing of any four-letter words. Our parents raised us without cable or any real access to TV for a reason. But when we saw Bernie Mac, with his signature slurred Chicago drawl, joke about being too old to "fuck" for 45 minutes straight on a bootleg copy of *Kings of Comedy* in my cousin KeKe's room, we laughed and laughed and laughed like we knew. I loved how comedians played with words. How the way they said something could make or break the humor of it, the punch of its delivery. We'd sneak while our parents watched *Saturday Night Live* and crack up at how Rachel Dratch's Debbie Downer made even the most solemn facts hilarious. We'd copy our favorites, insisting, "More cowbell!" at random noisy intervals around the house a la the Will Ferrell sketch, featuring the week's host, Christopher Walken. Yet, outside of these playful word games and jokes, we didn't speak much at all. Maybe that's exactly why our laughter would be so loud, and our jokes about these words so, so long. As to stave off inevitable silences like rebellion, because without these moments, my brothers and I had nothing. It was just me, the second "daughter" to Philip and Joanne, and them, the two youngest children and my parent's only sons. We might have been under the same roof but outside of our words, we lived in completely different worlds. Like that sunny Sunday in Spring '98, right after church. All of us, sans Andon who wasn't born just yet, piled into the family minivan to some undisclosed location deep in Germantown. The whiter, fancier part of the Memphis area. Daddy pulled up to a lot full of quaint little boutiques. Beside us, Grandmother Joyner (my Daddy's mom) and Aunt Treacy (his sister) exited her silver Nissan Sentra, dressed to the nines, beaming a little too hard for my liking. Something was up.

We greeted each other and Grandmother asked,

"Have you seen the window you'll be modeling in?"

To which 8-year-old me squawked, "*Modeling*?!"

Now the exaggerated curls and matching yellow dresses my sisters and I wore that day were starting to make a whole lot more sense. Especially since we never had to dress up at the casual, new age church Daddy was the music director of. Even more telling were the very un-dressy khakis my brother wore, instead of the three-piece suit Grandma bought him weeks before. He would not be joining us.

"Grandmother set up a modeling session for you girls! You're gonna model in that window," Auntie Treacy said.

She pointed to the front of a frilly, lacy, old fashioned-looking boutique with fake flowers in the window and three pedestals of varying heights. Just for "us girls." Huzzah. What a *great* surprise. I'd already established myself as a picture-hater, with my signature mean mug in just about every photo. I never smiled because I hated my smile, and I always thought I looked strange in photos. Like someone I didn't know.

"What about Andrew?!" I demanded to know.

"We're going on our own excursion." Daddy relayed calmly, grinning annoyingly.

Drew behind him stuck out his tongue, "Ha, ha!" He laughed, as he pointed at me because this is the exact moment you rub injustice in your sibling's faces. Dems da rules.

I frowned at no one in particular. Scrunched up the oddly crispy skirt of my dress.

"Hu, hu." I mimicked half-heartedly as I walked away.

Furious. Fuming. But I had no time to fester because within seconds, Aunt Treacy grabbed my hand and ushered me inside.

"I've got some pretty girls, don't I!" Momi grinned inside the shop, and, like a reflex, because we've danced this dance before, we all said,

"Yes, ma'am."

Pretty. I knew I was supposed to be pretty. I knew what "pretty" was supposed to look like, and that Jalisa's light skin and Jessica's light eyes, and my long hair were all pretty, pretty things. I knew that we were all on the "right side" of thin, that Jess was dangerously close to crossing that line. But oh, thin made us so, so pretty. My mom would tell us so all the time,

"See, Jess takes after the Palms! She's gonna have to be careful!" She and my aunties said.

We all knew this as well as we knew the alphabet, but I felt strange about all of it. I didn't want this thing I was supposed to want, this "pretty." My mind drifted out my body like it did sometimes when I felt this way, disconnected, detached. I'd go somewhere else like an old memory, or a daydream, or nowhere. This time, I went to the first time I tried on this very dress.

"You don't like this one, either?!" Aunt Treacy let out a snort of a laugh, looking down at the yellow floral frill of a thing wrapped and zipped up on my body.

I shook my head. I'd always shake my head, often before some general statement like, "I don't like dresses," to which Grandmother, Auntie, or my mom would quickly say, "Yes, you do!"

I tugged at the sides of the dress then turned to look in my grandma's mirror. Behind me, I heard her say,

"Child, you really look just like your father."

Uh oh. Here, always, would come the waterworks. Anytime someone would remind me, as family often did (on both sides!) that I looked like the spitting image of my Daddy, I cried. Not because my father was hideous. He was a beautiful Black man, but that was just it. He was a man, who was a boy. And that ain't pretty at all. You know, the thing I was supposed to be. Any time anyone would say I looked like him, I'd think I'd failed at this "girl" thing, which I knew, at a very young age, I needed to succeed at. In my mind, looking like my dad was a curse that meant I'd never be a girl in the right way, and I didn't know why this bothered me so much. Maybe because I didn't like being called a girl. Or because when I'd fall asleep at night, I was never a girl in my dreams. Or because secretly, I always referred to myself as a boy. A thing I knew never to talk about out loud. Maybe looking like my dad was the final nail in the coffin of my unavoidable fate, and I was not ready to admit to everyone that I was, in fact, never a girl in the first place. But then I wasn't sure what to do but cry and to know that I hated it. Standing in this window only emphasized that hate.

"Like adorable little mannequins!" My grandmother cooed, gently nudging me up the stepping stool to the post where I'd belong for the next hour.

I frowned as people pointed and tried not to think about what they might be thinking while grinning at me in my silly dress. I tried not to wince when they entered the shop to tell me and my sisters we were the cutest little things this side of the Mississippi. I wondered what Drew was doing. What fun voyage he and Daddy were on? I imagined myself there, the second boy, making a quick stop at Home Depot with Pops, his favorite store those days. It was a store I didn't enjoy, sure, but it sounded like a theme park compared to my current situation. I wished to be wherever they were, or wherever wasn't here. My mind wandered again, flew by old memories, and stayed there. Lingered.   To   playing   pretend.

After Momi let us stop homeschool for the day, or after hours-long string quartet practice with Daddy, or symphony rehearsal in the city, if he was feeling especially kind, my siblings and I would play pretend. As soon as either parent left the room, Jess would bark orders like a power-hungry showrunner, "Pick your character and stick with it!"

And we would, quickly.

I always played some boy. Boy warrior, prince, male cow, male crow, boyish president, boy, boy, boy, boy, boy. My siblings never made a fuss of it. Jess would just roll her eyes and shoo me away and I'd quickly start being free. I'd deepen my voice faster than she could say, "Action." Move my body in all the ways Momi called "unladylike." Happily, naturally. I could sit with my legs apart and joke loudly, not quietly like girls are supposed to. And Drew would copy me, and I'd laugh because we were being boys together and it felt right and nice and good. At dinner time we'd arrive downstairs in our usual roles once more, Drew over there, me over here, in my assigned seat at the dining table, my parent's second child, their little girl.

"Smile!" Aunt Treacy chuckled at the three of us in vain.

I glanced at Jess, whose smile was plastered in a way that looked almost painful. Jalisa, on the other hand, the natural model, could have been in some kid's fashion magazine. I tugged again at my custom-made dress, sewn by my grandmother's best friend, a tailor out in Winchester.

"Look over here." My mom said, snapping a quick photo of all of us.

Thankfully, the last one before Daddy and Drew returned.

"Are we going back home now?" Leesie asked.

Momi nodded, "And you girls can help me cook!"

This was commonplace for us. After church, "the girls" and our mother would make dinner, and Daddy's to-go meal for his weekly piano gig later in the evening at the Peabody Hotel. Daddy, Drew, and later, Andon—until allergies took hold— would march out into the wilderness of our four-acre lawn for yard work. Everywhere we turned, we were met with rules for boys and girls. I hated that there were rules, even when I didn't mind doing the things the rules required. Like helping Momi in the kitchen. I loved cooking.

"You are going to be such a great mother one day." Momi grinned when I handed her the salt.

My stomach would quake the way it did in moments like this.

"I don't want to be a mother." I'd tell her.

"You say that now!" She laughed.

Dismissed. *Silly girl.* But I was serious, I *didn't* want to be a mother. I didn't ever want to have children, something my mom said I could never know at such a young age. But somehow, as soon as I learned where babies came from, I knew the thought of my body holding another human felt wrong—not *this* body. And I knew well enough to know not to talk about my little "dreams" and unacceptable feelings out loud. The ones where I looked more like how I felt inside, before I'd look in the mirror. The ones where I would meet my future self: a handsome, studly person, not at all like the "woman" I was supposedly growing into. The thought of my body growing, changing, bending into a body like my mother's didn't add up to me, but I wouldn't dare twist my mouth into those words out loud.

So instead, I'd say, "Yes ma'am."

No point in disagreeing. Besides, I could get my frustrations out later when me and my siblings would hit up Grandma Palm (Momi's mom's) house. There, we had cable, and our cousins, and the ability to cuss, but only when Grandma's stories were on. Or her "wrassling". Unless Grandma wanted company watching her shows, we were free to roam around Frasier with KeKe, Ashley and them. Laughing at silly, silly, things that never had to make real sense—I wished we lived in that giggle fest forever. Instead, Momi eventually picked us up. Jess would go to her room, me and Leesie to ours, and the boys into theirs. Where boys go. And soon, words didn't hit like they used to. Like an overused elixir, they'd lose their punch between us. It was gradual, over the span of several years, so subtle you might have missed the shifts if you hadn't paid attention. We still laughed together, but it had stopped being our solace. It just wasn't substantial enough to counter the real-life experiences we continued not to share. I witnessed something different growing between my brothers. Found in two-person huddles, in giggle fests over things rather than words, in conversations that had no laughter at all. For some reason, those hurt the most to see. Maybe because I'd never been able to get past the surface of laughter with them and could only guess how things truly were, like when I overheard Andon tell Drew he tried weed for the first time, or when Daddy scolded Drew for failing in some way only namesake sons can—this happened too often. Or when later, Pops took his namesake on Jazz Fest trips only a father and First Son could enjoy. When he got home, Drew'd run upstairs with Andon close behind to have a moment only two brothers can. I knew because I'd tried, just once, to enter their world. Leesie and I clocked 15-year-old Drew one Saturday afternoon mistakenly rocking short sleeves, raising his arm just so to reveal the ink blot on his bicep in the semi-shape of a lion. He got it in his friend's garage, he'd told me, "And don't tell nobody!"

I told no one. Leesie told no one. And only when no one was around, I leaned in and said from my heart, "You know you can talk to me, right?"

"Yea, okay." He'd laughed, because that's how we connected.

Nothing more came of it, so I let him be. Maybe he was right to only laugh. By then, I was well on my way down a path so rigid and respectable, that any advice I might have tried to give him probably would have sounded like a joke. It's funny how different folks respond to the roles they have been given. I answered quickly with a pen in hand, ready to sign on the dotted line, as long as it meant that one day, I'd feel at least a little okay. Do girlhood. Be the right kind of girl, and bam! Success. I told myself that was enough for me, for a long, long time.

My body never listened.

17

I don't like that water mane. Water don't stay still.

A Black man, overheard in Memphis, TN.

JAZ IS SHORT FOR JASPER

New York City, Summer 2014

We dare you. Open your coffin in the daylight and slither into the mighty world of macabre erotica with Provocateur-in-Residence Marc Dennis. Enjoy the sexiest (and weirdest) science lesson of your horny little dreams. He'll talk post-mortem photography, the strange secret about Rosemary's Baby, and of course, highlights from his hottest vampiric tales.

This. This is the fire blurb I send to the loveable man child™ also known as my superior, Dan, whose favorite thing to do these days is call me a "cool dude" because when we first met, I wore an "I Miss Pluto" t-shirt, and I was the only person he'd ever met who volunteered their pronouns.

"I might fuck it up!" He'd tell me.

I'd blurt, "He/him is also fine," to assure him I was totally chill, on account of the wince forming at the corner of his mouth. To be clear, he/him actually wasn't "fine" at all. "No worries! As long as you try."

Because I am not difficult; I am not *one of those* queers, persistent about how they like to be addressed. Affirming themselves regardless of your discomfort. No, I am not one to ruffle feathers—especially not at my new job—so, Dan decides to fuck with me heavy almost instantly. I'm elated.

"Anybody ever tell you you're a cool dude?" He asked me later that day.

Dan moved to Los Angeles from England when he was 10 so every ten words had an odd curve to it that made your ears perk up in confusion. It was weird and endearing. Charmingly odd. It was Dan, in a nutshell. He loved my blurb.

"You're a witty one, Jaz." He said, patting me square on the back in that way that said, *You're a fellow dude, my dude.*

I'm affirmed in a very dude-ish way I'm not even willing to admit to myself. I loved that he loved my writing. Especially since only weeks before, I had been the Office Manager of this fine establishment we will call *Take Off NY* and was now full-time assistant editor of the Stuff-to-Do department. It had taken me seven months waiting patiently for an editorial opening, then weeks to convince our stylish, though obnoxious, Editor-in-Chief, Kerri, that I had the stuff by writing dozens of practice blurbs the magazine later used for zero dollars and zero cents. I was new enough to feel like an outsider of this "professional writer" thing, so I valued Dan's opinion. Dan, who strolled into daily pitch meetings, holding a skateboard, rocking holey, vintage t-shirts at age 32.

At the end of the day, neither Dan nor my opinions really mattered though. It was Victoria, our Deputy Editor, who had the final say come galley day, or what we in the biz called the day we close out edits for our weekly print issues. Victoria and Dan were milk and Red Bull—they did not mix. The week before, she made Dan rewrite an entire feature because he decided to go rogue on the angle despite what we decided in our weekly issue meeting.

"This perspective doesn't quite work." She said, shoving Dan's edit back to him. Dan had this thing about switching up last minute as a sort of rebellion against the "corporate machine." It meant perpetual backlash from the higher-ups.

"What the hell did they hire me for, then? What am I, a fucking puppet?" He'd said, kicking in his chair and trudging out the building, eventually returning with bagels or donut offerings I gladly enjoyed, and forgetting about said fury by the time we finished up galleys late that evening.

But alas, all was forgiven once those galleys closed; that's the thing about working for a weekly magazine. It's like the Men in Black flashed their neutralizer over the whole office and we collectively forgot what it had been like *before* galleys kicked our asses. Galley days for Dan and me were Thursdays, and, not to brag, but we held the record for the latest close, often being the last of the editorial team to bounce besides Victoria, who was like Olivia Benson if Olivia Benson had grown up in Louisville, Kentucky in the 60s—always, *always*, about her business. I liked her because she reminded me of the white women I grew up in Memphis around; still white, but less scary because they were raised knowing not to try it. Dan did not appreciate her pragmatism though.

"She's uptight, man," Dan complained over delicious, steaming $5 chicken from the Peruvian spot around the corner.

"I mean, she's chill as long as we don't have a ton of errors and shit," I replied with a shrug, mouth full.

I was still getting the hang of telling Dan about himself. Read: I was still a total wimp about hurting his feelings, or *anyone's* feelings for that matter. I liked to tell the truth, but preferred a soft and gentle, often meaningless response like, "You're good." "Don't worry." "You've got this," as my titular goal in conversation was to make sure others felt good after leaving my presence. But that day I didn't even need to drop a, "You're good," at all because shockingly, he was! No major edits, no rogue angles. Finally, *finally*—Victoria handed us our galleys without a single red mark on them at 8:30pm!

"Let's get drinks. Celebrate!" Dan nudged me.

I smiled behind blurred vision, still lacking focus from staring into a computer screen for too long. I was tired, hungry for a quiet, companion-less meal. But then I remembered, *Take Off's* offices were in Chelsea, about a forty-to-fifty-minute train ride on the A to the G to the Clinton Hill apartment I so reluctantly shared with four other twenty-something creatives like myself. Before that, I lived in my little sister Jalisa's two-bedroom apartment's living room she shared with her college bestie since she'd successfully convinced our parents that Pratt, an expensive private university over 1000 miles from home, was the only place she could be for the perfect architectural education. It was an impressive feat I'd never dared attempt, proven by my recent NYC move despite an over decade-old promise to myself to move to this city straight out of high school. I'd be the first to tell you New York City had been my dream location since I was 10 years old. But when Ma told me she'd sleep better knowing I was just a short three-hour drive from Memphis for college, I quickly shelved my life-long NYC dreams and packed up my three sad little bags for Vanderbilt in Nashville, no matter that I didn't even want to go to college at all.

"*And* Jess is there, too?! Now, that's perfect right there!" My mom raved.

I'd beamed because everything was worth it when I got my mom to smile like that. Almost had me feeling good enough to forget all those dreams I was ignoring. And it was fine now! I was finally where I wanted to be. As soon as I got my first full-time gig as *Take Off's* assistant editor, I dragged myself and those same three bags down Willoughby to Classon Ave, and up to the fifth-floor walk-up into my new mouse-infested, constantly messy, crowded apartment. A small price to pay for a dream well-lived, easily remedied by going out often, even when I was tired, even when my social meter was shot, only returning when tipsy and carefree. So, when Dan asked if I wanted that drink, I ignored the fact that I didn't, and recalled that furry, quick creature I'd spotted that morning on my way out the door.

"Sure, I can do a quick drink." I agreed, grabbing my backpack.

We headed a few blocks down to a Latin-themed bar with several different country's flags at the front of it, and I smiled politely as the bouncer joked, I didn't look a day over 13. They always think they're the first to say it.

"I swear I'm 23." I laughed, all five-foot-three inches of baby-faced me.

"You're lucky, dude, I've looked forty for like ten years!" says Dan with a funny dose of self-awareness. He ordered us a round of pints and chips and guac. Then his glass flew towards mine in an aggressive swoop.

"Oh!" I slammed my glass towards his, startled.

We clinked like two Viking warriors after battle. Manly. Ridiculous. While I am not a man, apparently, I liked when men treated me like I am. Even if they are dude-men like Dan.

Dan grinned, "You fucking killed it today, dude."

"*We* killed," I beamed, enjoying how complimentary Dan tended to be. And happy to be out of the office before nine. But also regretting saying, *we killed,* a phrase that nearly shocked my senses on the way out my mouth. I said things that felt wrong all the time.

"And I read some of your blurbs man, good fucking job," He praised.

Mind you, Dan was supposed to read *all* of my blurbs. That was literally a part of his job. But I thanked him anyway, and the compliment train continued.

"Yeah, dude, you should write a book." I didn't think he was serious.

Funny story: I *had* written a book. It was a young adult fantasy novel about a girl who loses her grandmother and embarks on a magical adventure as she goes through phases of grief.

"Whoa dude!" He bellowed.

I nodded, "Yeah, it's a nerdy lil' fantasy for kids but—"

"You want a round of tacos?" He interjected.

Oh good; new topic—so I wouldn't have to delve into the fact that said book, called *Juniper Leaves*, had been the catalyst to this recent move to my dream city. I finished it over the summer, and, the moment I was done that past winter, I bought my one-way ticket for LaGuardia and never looked back. But Dan didn't need to know that. It was the first book I'd ever written, and it showed. Oh, did it show. So, it was good that I wouldn't have to tell Dan I'd been on the brink of self-publishing because it had been over a year of querying with no success. The thought of that embarrassed me, and I preferred presenting as someone who would soon be an author with a well-known publisher, equipped with all the prestige and honor that comes with that. I didn't want him to see that I wasn't actually proud of this little book at all. That this book carried so much shame, a bucket full of all my personal doubts. So yeah, it's good. It's good he didn't ask.

I returned to him then, shook my head *no* before he ambled toward the bar. I sat there alone in my bow tie (I was down with a serious case of Dapper Dyke Syndrome). Of course, I also wore suspenders, and I tried not to stare at the Michael B. Jordan knock-off darting his eyes at me. *Oh no, he's walking my way.*

"Hey ma, you fine as hell."

Okay. *Ma?* This was what I mean about not being seen how I wanted to be seen. Yes, I did bind my already flat chest, and yes, my hair was short, and no I didn't wear makeup over my albeit baby face, and sure, I wouldn't start testosterone for months but still. *Still.* I fenced in a string of disoriented thoughts behind gritted teeth, lowered a questioning brow and hoped he'd call it a smile.

He filled a loud silence with a question, "What's your name?"

"Jaz." I answered.

I wanted to say, *"Are you sure you wanna talk to me? Me?!*
And not any one of these lovely straight women in this straight
bar waiting for their very own Michael B. Jordan look-a-like to
swoop in??

He laughed a laugh that made it seem like I'd just told a joke.
I had not. It was a flirtatious laugh, with a little chuckle at the
end of it right before he—wait for it—licked his lips.

"Jasper, actually." I corrected myself.

I had to add this correction. A new thing I did, as of late,
after several mistaken assumptions that Jaz stood for something
more feminine than Jasper. Still, I was baffled that looking like
a lesbian extra in the bar scene of *But I'm a Cheerleader* wasn't
enough. I didn't want to have to say anything. I didn't want to
have to tell this man that I ain't nobody's *ma*. But I knew I
looked like a woman to him; it didn't matter how much I
butched myself up. And it's not that I didn't like men—I'd had
my crushes. But even then, I was still me, a trans masc
somebody. Nobody's *ma*. But why would this man know that?
Why would he even for a second assume that I was anything but
a young woman when, in 2013, barely anyone—even the gays—
thought anything about folks who weren't men and weren't
women at the same time. I felt wrong for even feeling frustrated.

"Jasper. I'm Jared," said Jared.

Wow. Not even a flinch. I felt like that would have been a
great time to pay attention to gendered stereotypes. No?

"Hi, Jared."

Jared grabbed my hand and raised it to his lips and, *oh my god, oh my god.* Ew.

"What's up!" Greeted Dan with tacos and two shots of tequila stuffed in his grasp like the white savior in an ill-advised B-movie.

"Y'all together?" Jared asked us.

"Yeah, dude!" replied Dan.

"We're not, like, 'together.' We're friends—" I stammered as an attempt at damage control. Dan caught on.

"Oh shit! Yeah, no Jaz's super *gay*, my friend. They're dry as a desert for dudes." *Oh Dan.*

Cue facepalm but somehow with my whole body. And an extra cringe at how grateful I felt for him getting my pronouns right this time. Of all the times, this was a wonderful time I especially preferred. And I remembered why I called Dan a friend, a complicated friendship we had indeed. *My pocket buzzed.* Saved by the bell. I checked it while Dan complimented Jared's watch and the two bonded, quickly, as dude-men so easily do.

Hey hey! Me and some friends are hitting up Cubby Hole later. You should come!

It's Heart. Phoebe Heart, but I, like most people, simply could not believe her last name was so perfect, and so this was what we called her. She was the first friend in NYC I'd ever made. We met on OkCupid and though I'd never tell her this, I thought our first meeting was a date. It's fine though—we were better as friends, which was what I continued to tell myself. I knew I needed to go see her, because Jared and Dan were having far too much fun, and Jared had, *alert, alert,* just grazed my right shoulder. I was reminded why I never went to straight bars. Why I rarely told folks my pronouns unless they revealed theirs first, or interacted with anyone who was not expressly queer outside of work. It was because in the wrong spaces, folks' assumptions swallowed me whole, and I wasn't sturdy enough to bust out unscathed.

"Hey, I'm gonna go. I'll see you tomorrow?" I said to Dan, who'd been downing an entire, though small, taco in one bite.

"Aw, really?!" I could tell he was genuinely upset, "Tacos tomorrow?" He asked, mid-chew.

"Definitely!" I told him. I meant it. I exit, more excited by the minute that I'd be able to breathe more freely soon.

I feel more deeply since I learned how to read
poetry

YOU A WRITER, BUT YOU DON'T READ?

Memphis, TN - 1997

Child! How you a writer but you don't read?

Well. She had me on that one. I sat there like a lump on a log, notebook in lap, with my warm pen right on top of it 'cause, *baby*, I'd been writing. I was always writing. When I wasn't writing story after story, poem after poem—my first novella at 7 years old—I was narrating some off-the-cuff tale to Jess or Leesie or Drew or baby Andon or anyone who'd listen—or at least not tell me to shut up. And not once had any of them had the nerve to point out my stark aversion to opening somebody else's book.

But Aunt Treacy? Oh, she had the nerve. In my mind, Aunt Treacy had the audacity of five bullies, but that's what everyone thought of the person in the family who pointed to the truth. And how could she not have noticed? My bibliophobia was impossible to ignore against my sisters' obsessions with books.

Now, I *wanted* to read more. When Aunt Treacy bought Leesie her third, first-edition Harry Potter book, and she read it in a record half-day sitting, I grabbed it right off the shelf when she was finished.

"Isn't it good?" Jess asked me, passing me by in our quiet nook at home, noticing I was somehow midway through it, not knowing I'd been skimming. Trying to find one sentence in this book with words I could grab hold of.

"It's *okay.*" I shrugged, slamming it closed. Rolled my eyes at her 'whatever' because I knew *she knew* I was full of it. But I didn't know how to tell my oldest sis, the one who already knew I was the dweeb of all dweebs, corniest of all corn balls, that I couldn't read five words without them all becoming one big bundle of nonsense off the page.

"Child! How you a writer that don't read?" Auntie interrogated me with every bit of fervor.

"I read! Sometimes..." I argued, voice lowering with every word.

I wished I'd never answered that first question. The one before this reading question. It'd been a trap. I'd known it the second Grandmother Joyner asked.

"What do you want to be when you grow up?"

I was six. I wanted to be magical. I wanted to fly. I wanted Daddy to let me stop playing violin and take up electric guitar or drums. I wanted to get really good at yo-yoing and be able to teleport to anywhere in the world whenever I wanted, but always, always, return to Momi before dark. If I'd said that, I would've heard laughter.

"What do you want to be? What's your grown-up job gonna be?" Auntie pressed.

Of course, Jess knew to say, "I wanna be a teacher!"

I knew she'd said the right thing because her words were met with unanimous coos from the adults. And she continued to say it every time she was asked—I found this quite impressive. It made sense. Daddy was a full-time musician and Memphis City School music teacher. My mom had been a teacher before she and Daddy got together, and even then, she'd taught seminars at Prepaid Legal, as one of their top salespeople and occasional conference headliner. But how did Jess know to say it in the first place?

Was she just hip to the game or was that what she *really* wanted? It was hard to tell—and I needed to know—but in the meantime, I took her lead. Now, I couldn't make myself say I wanted to be a teacher, too. Nobody loves a copycat, a lesson I'd learned long ago as a second born. I had to think of something equally as studious. A doctor? No, no, those hospital segments on *Sesame Street* were my least favorite. Magician? Not studious enough; only very fun to think about.

It had taken me two whole years to learn that being a writer could actually be a grown-up job. I'd always thought of it as a thing I *needed* to do—had to do. Like eating, waking up in the morning, going to bed at night. But once it clicked that writers could also be respected adults, like teachers, like doctors? Oh, that was it right there.

"I want to be a writer." I paused. The rest fell out of my mouth, "And a magician on the side." Versatile.

But had I known of the follow-up question...*How you a writer, but you don't read?*

I'd thought about it before and then pushed the thought out of my mind 'cause I couldn't be bothered with the frustration of trying to figure that out. I'd been too busy finishing up my first novel, that I admit shared a shocking resemblance to *Alice in Wonderland*. Might have known that had I read the dang book.

I did bring up my reading woes in class, though.

"Momi, I feel like I'm reading in circles." I'd complained. I was homeschooled along with all my four siblings until third grade. I later learned that after Jess' very racist kindergarten experience at a fancy private school my mom had *had it up to here* and decided she'd teach us herself.

Her least favorite comment from me was,

"I can't read this!"

It was the "can't" that made her teeth grit. "Can't" in the Joyner household was a non-sequitur. A useless jumble of letters that would get you nowhere fast. My mom tightened her upper lip, and the top would curl up just so, and I'd think she were mad if it weren't for the twinkle in her eye.

"Child, every one of my children can read! Try again."

So, I did. I tried again and again. Still, words weren't words to me unless I wrote them myself. Not that they looked much like words to anyone else but me, but that's the magic of writing your own story. You know in your head that you wrote, **The princess left her secret village to play with her friends.** When what you actually wrote was, **Th prencis lef her secrt villy to play wit hur frens.**

I was fine with this, content with reading slow as drying paint in Momi's classes or writing a story after class to make myself feel better. Learning at home meant I didn't have to keep up with anyone but myself.

Until my parents rocked my world with the twist of the century. "This August, you'll be starting your first year at public school!"

I learned the news from the bellowing voice of my dad at the helm of the dinner table. He loved a grand announcement, so he'd gathered us all into the kitchen in the middle of a Saturday when he happened to not be at one of his many weekly music gigs. After he spoke, Momi started off a slow clap, chuckling in that way she did that made everyone else laugh. Meanwhile, I wondered, *what's funny?* I scrunched up my nose at the rancid scent of change. Public school? With...other children? In...public?!

I was almost eight. Accustomed to bright and early morning meditation before my first "class" in our playroom-slash-classroom, surrounded by siblings I didn't have to "get to know." I was mortified at the thought of all those new faces, new voices, new interactions. Now other people would be witnessing me read? My greatest nightmare?!

I begged my mom, "Can I at least get my eyes checked?"

A last-ditch effort to smooth over this thorn in my side that was my reading struggle. I had three months to figure this thing out before I made a complete and utter fool of myself. I felt like glasses could be the remedy, the missing key. Like I'd put on some glasses, and all of a sudden—there it was: the flawless reading comprehension of a high school senior! No such thing occurred. I mean, yeah, I got glasses. My astigmatism was so bad I'd get motion sickness from the blur. But as for my reading, not much changed beyond bigger words on the page. It had been too late for excuses, anyway. I started school in .2 seconds and still couldn't read a full page without starting over at least four times.

Then, it happened. All too soon. Sooner than I expected. My biggest fear slapped me in the face on an unassuming Tuesday afternoon, directly after lunch as if those evil reading gods picked the time knowing I got nauseous when nervous. We were playing a reading game I'd like to dub *Low Key Child Torture*, but my teacher, Ms. Brown, lovingly called *The Reading Train*.

Choo, choo folks, chug- a-chug along the reading train-n-pick up where the kid next to you left off. You'd better be paying attention because if you miss it, the horn will sound, and everyone will know—you've failed! You failed, you little dumb, dumb idiot,   you   failed! (At least that's what I'd heard when she ticked off the rules before we began.)

"A good is something you can touch with your hands." Cadence recited from *USA and Our Neighbors* like a seasoned actress. Then D'Angelo, Marcus, Anna, and the rest of her row tapped in, no big deal. Effortless. My index finger glided along the thick textbook paper, guiding my gaze as I mouthed along with each kid. But then the voices got closer. And closer. My palms sweat. I cleared my rasping throat. My stomach whirled like a 7/11 Slurpee maker, and I wriggled in my seat like that would distract from the noise. Marjoree, the red-headed Black girl who always bragged that the Vice Principal was her dad, sat in front of me. She read like a college student. Fluid and flaunting, all confident, like she'd memorized each sentence before class. Maybe she'd been practicing.

"Helloooo!" sang Ryan as he pressed a pointy finger into my left shoulder. *Oh no.* Had it already happened? Had I missed my turn?

"Um..." I stalled, eyes darting up and down the page.

She could have stopped anywhere. *Wait.* What if she'd turned the page and I was too panicked to notice? Too focused on the *knock, knock* of my own heartbeat. Snickers reverberated from the back of the room. Tingles like fire ants scattered across my back.

"People who..." Ms. Brown nudged, "People who buy goods..."

She spoke softly, like a gentle alarm, gracefully waking me up from my frozen stupor. I turned the page, my finger drifted across like a marker on a possessed ouija board until, finally, I saw the words.

"Pee-pol... who... b-eye goods and... ser-vice-es are called..." It started with a C... "Con. Consum. Eers."

"Good." Ms. Brown murmured in the background.

I scratched my shoulder and hoped it'd make the full-bodied anxious itch disappear. It didn't. I kept going. "A con. Sum. Er. can buy many things." I paused.

I looked up at Ms. Brown, who gestured for me to keep going. More snickers. I wanted to stand up and shake off the invisible ants staking claim on my body. I wanted to slam the book shut and run out of the room.

"One...Ex. Ex.... Amp. Lee." *That can't be right.* The laughter grew.

"Example." Ms. Brown nudged.

"One example of a consumer is..." I don't remember how I finished. Only that Ms. Brown lied to me so sweetly when I was done, "Good job."

I almost breathed a normal breath before remembering— that *really* just happened. Then, the bell rang for gym class like a rescue siren, and I scurried out so fast my shoes squeaked. Oh, was I traumatized. I was like that for a while, suffering fits of terror any time the reading train rolled around again. I rushed up the stairs to my bedroom after school, pulling out my journal and writing furiously, drowning out embarrassment as Leesie sat serenely, cross-legged on the bed beside me, reading a thick, thick book. I felt like something was wrong with me.

I'd told my mom as much. "You do not need to be in any special class with other kids who don't know how to read. Actually, you're quite brilliant. You know you were reading circles around most children at three years old!?"

I knew she said what she'd said because she loved me. I knew her intentions were nothing but good, responding sincerely to her child's insecurity with conviction. But this was not what I'd needed then. I needed to know that how I read was nothing to be ashamed of, but that it was, indeed, different. Different from my sisters, different from what many U.S. public schools preferred, even Memphis public schools, which were very much behind due to poor funding.

I wanted to feel okay for how I already was, not to be told that there was nothing to need to feel okay over. This was a common refrain between my mom and me: me, wanting to wear my brother Drew's old cargo shorts to school. My mom telling me, "Girls don't wear shorts like that." Me wanting my hair braided like Lil Bow Wow's, my mom opting for "more feminine" hairstyles instead. In all the ways I knew I was different, my mom was like a baseball bat, knocking back all my curveballs, constantly redirecting me on to acceptable paths. Respectable paths. As if to protect me, as if it is protection to be steered away from parts of yourself. Human parts that are not wrong, even though we're all taught they are.

It took me 5 years, hundreds of hard-earned C-pluses and a state-of-the-art Microsoft Windows XP to discover the term "dyslexia." I had all the signs of it. "Sounding out" barely worked for me. My spelling skills were a joke. Reading was torture. Never knew my left from my right. I had a really tough time grasping instructions and I hated school with a passion. *Oowee,* I hated school.

"I really feel like I have it. I took a quiz online and everything." I told Momi. Cue trading my full-sized violin for an extra tiny one I could play after my mom once again stated,

"Child. You are brilliant, you understand me? There is nothing wrong with you."

It didn't help that she'd gone and got me and my sisters' IQs tested at some learning center. She announced it all proud as we sat in the back of the big blue Ford minivan.

"All of you got above average scores!" She cheered, "Jess, you had the middle score, and Jalisa...you're a certified genius!"

I might have been a C-student, but it didn't take a genius to know I came in dead last. I wish I'd known not to care. I wish my mother knew that my so-called high score had nothing to do with having a learning disability. I had many feelings on the matter I could not articulate, many of which I learned to keep inside after the fifty-leventh attempt at intervention with my parents.

I began to think of school as a joke. Resented how so-called above-average IQs never meant a thing to my report card. I had no respect for testing, which seemed like an arbitrary waste of time that, proved nothing more than, *oh wow, you're good at taking tests.* I also did not like the bland array of subject matter offered to me in most schoolbooks. Seemed like poop-flavored icing on a nasty ass cake. *What do a group of white British boys stranded on a mysterious island got to do with me?* I'd wonder.

I had a point. Memphis, currently the Blackest city in the United States, was even Blacker in the 90s yet the majority of public-school curricula featured books by white authors, starring white male protagonists. What did that do for young folks other than tell us our stories didn't matter? That the school has highlighted what was relevant, i.e—not your Black ass. But my immediate rejection evaded the bigger issue: I did not consider that books served many purposes, one of which was to expand your mind. That even books that had nothing to do with you could teach you a hell of a lot. That when my sisters were on their fiftieth book of the year their creative juices were flowing, their little minds growing. Meanwhile, I worked overtime trying to *seem* as well-read as the best students in class. Shout out to Spark Notes. Oh, don't worry, I had tactics—many! I knew there was no space for my doing poorly in school. Not with two college grad parents who'd told us our two post-secondary options were college or bust. My mom let me do one more year at home in 4th grade, but come 5th, I had to step it the fuck up. I had to do well in school, prove my mother right, prove to my sisters, who couldn't give two sticks about this one-sided competition, I was smart!

So, I found my ways around my reading. I read slower, like *slow*. I started reading out loud when I was alone, often in a British accent because it forced me to really take in the sounds of the words. I'd always do the extra credit because *baby*, I was not going to do well on nan one of those tests. And it worked! By high school, I could pull out a solid B+ average on my report card if I worked my ass off. I was okay with that B+; I earned that B+. But still, I remained a writer who didn't read until after I graduated high school.

It was not something I was proud of. It was more so a fear I overcame very slowly over time. After high school, when I was on nobody's time limit, I began to dip my toe into the land of books on purpose. I started to read books that had caught my eye years ago, but I'd avoided anyway. Then, books recommended to me by college professors, friends...When audiobooks became more popular, I'd read along while I listened. But my rocky journey still showed up in my lack of trivial knowledge, my vocabulary, my confidence, until recently, and I still struggle. I still mourn all the time I wasted avoiding books, but I am not angry with how my brain works. I read every day now, like my life depends on it. Racing, racing. Forever catching up. Oh, the trials of a writer who didn't read.

Still, I was lucky. I got plucked out of my own little world, kicking and screaming in my own ignorance like a snail out of moist earth because the writing gods don't play that, *"I don't read."* A jerked awakening, like smelling salts, for me, was simply a matter of time.

Comfort can be dangerous. Comfort provides a floor but also a
ceiling.
Trevor Noah, ***Born a Crime***

FOLLOW THE SCRIPT

Brooklyn, NY – Late Winter 2013

It's 7am. Shady clouds float pompously over demure Brooklyn trees, and I hop out of bed—see little sister's rollout couch—with enough energy to jumpstart the sun.

I'm moving. Sure, just five blocks and 4 minutes down the road to a rat-infested 5-story walk-up to live with four, 20-something roommates I didn't know. *Don't matter, I'm motherfucking moving*! Out of my little sister's two-bedroom apartment, away from the constant reminder that I, baby queer and self-proclaimed "aspiring writer," was still so parasitically attached to my family. I love them. I do! But as of February 2013, I was truly, truly on my own.

I was proud, because it had only taken me six weeks in New York to find a temp-to-perm PR firm job that paid enough to cover my new expenses.

"So, what you're saying is if they paid you, like, a dollar less an hour, you wouldn't be able to move?" Jess asked me on one of our almost daily 3-way calls with Ma.

"I mean...yeah. But! I also have $500 left in savings from working at the Peabody." I reminded her, because she seemed to feel that a college grad being paid $12 an hour to be somebody's Public Relations Assistant was a scam. But in oblivious pride I'd said the thing most CEOs like to have everyone think: "I gotta start somewhere!"

I had no space among endless excitement to agree with her. Not that I didn't usually agree with most things my older sister had to say. Jess, the ever-responsible eldest, helped me develop a loose budget that even included entertainment the week I started my new job.

"See, if you set aside about fifteen a week you can still go to your lil' movies." She laughed.

My ears perked up at this. The day after I'd landed in New York, I wasted no time scrounging up a sizable chunk of my savings from my summer Peabody hotel job to buy a bike so I could ride off to the nearest movie theater at least once a week. The thought of riding under the sun to sit in the dark alone, watching someone's creation, was my kind of poetic contrast. I watched many of the art films I'd never had access to in Memphis, or even Nashville, and it was amazing. New York life was amazing. And nothing could convince me any different, because this New York dream was over a decade in the making.

Ever since I'd seen my first episode of *Sex and the City* at ten years old, I knew: *New York is where it's at.* Now, my mother fully disagreed, hitting me with a rotation of the following:

"What are you making for dinner today?"

"When do you think you'll come home next?"

"Does ___ stink?" (Insert any location in New York City or any of its five boroughs).

Unlike Ma, I hadn't been forever traumatized by my last NYC visit two years ago, when she attempted to exit the subway doors and they'd begun to close, and she'd stared longingly at the rest of her family, frozen as the train she was trapped in zoomed off to another stop. She'd been lost for hours because her phone hadn't worked, finally stepping out into acid rain that stained her pristine white, cotton blouse. Sniffing that acute fresh, wet trash smell New Yorkers knew all too well. I understood her disgust. I understood anyone's disdain for a city like New York. A city that indeed, stunk. I never thought New York *didn't* stink, only that it was *my* kind of stink. My kind of chaos.

"All at once?" Leese asked me, staring down at my beat-up suitcase beside my new fold-up utility cart. Inside it lay a trash bag full of food and knick-knacks from my first few weeks in Brooklyn.

"Yeah, why not?" I shrugged.

48

Looking around her apartment once more, I noticed a newly installed bit of artwork on her walls, an abstract painting I assumed was by one of her talented Pratt friends. Her place was coming together. She'd only been there one year before me but somehow when I arrived, she already had an air of audacity in her walk. New York could have that effect, especially on a 20-year-old certified genius architect major. Knowing Leesie, she'd say I just wasn't paying attention.

"It's only five blocks." I shrugged, when she asked if I was sure. Then off we went, carrying everything I owned with wooly coats on our bodies down a busy Brooklyn sidewalk.

Me with a large suitcase and an air mattress, and her with my utility cart, which, in Memphis, would have looked strange rolling down the street, but, in Brooklyn, turned no heads. Perhaps what had turned some heads though was my big, red, kinky afro, crinkling past my shoulders under a black beanie like a boundless flame. A hater might have called it clown red.

I called it, "Fire!"

"I meaaaann. It's super bright, but you pull it off. Kind of..." Leesie shrugged in that sarcastic way she did, and I scrunched up my face, only smiling when I knew she got my message. *Shady.*

Heart complimented me the moment she'd seen me later that day. But because she was white, I'd still needed confirmation I wasn't walking around giving Black Raggedy

Ann. Not that I didn't trust her—I'd never met a white person who didn't love my hair for the simple fact that I had some, and they'd been blessed with the opportunity to stare *real* close. But she still didn't quite have the authority to give me any green light. Unlike Black folks, who knew damn well bright red was no shade for a bean like me with cool undertones.

"One more floor." I told Leesie, who thwacked the cart up behind me, step by step with a grunt. I dropped my suitcase and dug around in my black, oversized jumpsuit for the new set of keys, shoving the jammed door open to the wafting embrace of mac and cheese and weed.

"Sup." Waved a dark-haired white guy whose shoulders naturally slumped like he'd been ducking in a cave for the past eight years.

He'd later explained this with his near decade staring into computer screens as a film editor. He was the only one of my four roommates at home at the time, so I used our privacy to reiterate at peak volume, "I've got my own place!"

Leesie laughed and rolled her eyes, not to be shady but because I genuinely believed for her, this was instinctive.

She responded, "You need furniture."

I looked around my bare little room, my three pieces of luggage crowded in the very middle of it. I had a bed, all I needed to do was to roll it out and plug it in. But everything else?

"Should we go to Target? Then celebra—"

Buzz, buzz. Hushed excitement as my pocket vibrated. A simultaneous buzz came from Jalisa's handbag. Ma and Jessica—always a duo—called us both. Leesie won our staring contest. I answered as her prize.

"Hey Ma, hey Jess," I said, putting my phone on speaker, ready to shout my new favorite proclamation if not for the cumbersome blanket suffocating the air. Something was wrong.

"Drew's in the hospital." Jess said, because my mother couldn't get out the words.

"He's. He's not conscious." My mom had spoken like sadness and shock were fighting in her throat.

My 19-year-old brother, Drew, four years my junior. Found unconscious on the floor of his bedroom by my mom, who'd been calling him to cut the grass for too long.

"They found spice in his system. And weed... Something called fentanyl..." Jess said.

My mind crowded with unsolicited predictions, attempting to answer my confusion. I said nothing out loud. *Why, how, what if...Drew.* But. This felt too familiar to have never happened before. The Deja-vu of my fears for my brother all crammed together, all the times I could only reach him through Andon, the times I knew I could not help him because we spoke different languages. When he longed for Pop's approval and couldn't get it. When he said he didn't want to go to college, but we, myself included, pushed him to go to some random university he'd soon after dropped out of. Because we expected him to follow a script like we all did. Like I did. Drew hadn't known I'd admired his rebellion and commended his bravery for seeking freedom in ways I'd never had the courage to.

I was so far away from home, my script was basically obsolete anyway. But what had gotten me this far? It wasn't more freedom; it had been the script. It carried me through high school and Vanderbilt, and now, some stuffy New York PR job. I felt dirty and ashamed of the rules I followed just to give myself permission to be free. And how, somehow, living within the confines of my journey, was still a sort of box people like my brother rejected. Why did some of the world's freest people have to be the most respectable? And was that really freedom, in the Nina Simone sense of "no fear."

I hated it. Any happiness left in me disappeared. My journey to this very special day had been tinted an ugly shade of blue, a lot like the pen I signed away so much of my life to. And what would my life have looked like had I been more like Drew? What is traded when you chose the path of rebellion against all the things we—Black respectables—are supposed to do? I wanted to yell, "You were right! It's all fake. You can wake up now!"

I looked Leesie in the eyes. Searched for some sort of rope to grab hold of to pull myself out of this quicksand of thinking. I needed to be a present part in building the support raft my family would surely work to build. We always did. At least there was that, our promise to each other to send those rafts, no matter how far one of us swam out into the sea. We stayed silent for a while, waiting for updates, sitting beside my luggage on the otherwise empty floor of my new room.

He lived. I should say that now. He lived and is living and is very much alive. He'd told us it was a mistake. "Bad weed." I wanted to believe him. But part of me knew that sometimes, the path of least resistance is the safest, and on other, freer paths, it takes a toll. No wonder I'd stayed on mine for so long.

Period

I was

always

That Girl

but

never

that girl

no

not even then

OH, WHAT A FRIEND WE HAVE IN JESUS

Woodstock Middle School – 2001

Shortly after graduating fifth grade, it was announced that I'd be ditching Memphis proper, miles away from my recently proclaimed best friend Megan, to a faraway middle school in Millington called Woodstock.

"The teachers are cool," Jess assured me, since she'd been there a whole two years already.

The problem was, I did not care about things like cool teachers, and "fun" learning curriculums. Like, what's "fun" about learning?

"But what about my friends?" Okay, fine, *friend*. But I had to ask.

Jess and my parents must not have realized how hard it was for Meg and me to become friends in the first place. And best friends at that? It was a feat! But I was at least looking forward to riding a bus for the first time. The head-in-the-clouds sort I was, my main reference for this had been the earnest hope our driver might be a bit like Miss Frizzle. As you could imagine, I was rudely awakened.

"You're not gonna like the bus. It sucks." Jess said.

"Don't use that word." My mom interjected as she always did for all ugly phrases like *da bomb*, "Because people are dying in the Middle East."

Jess sat with me on my first day, which was cool, but she had the window seat and I sat on the outside across from an eleven-year-old white boy with a full beard named Conor.

He smiled at me. Wouldn't stop staring. I had no plans to talk, but one of my covert stares hadn't been covert, and our eyes locked.

"You know deez?" He asked me.

Uh oh.

Not "Hey." Not "Hi, my name is..."

Jess interjected, "Don't listen to him."

I ignored. Actually, I pressed him again, "What?"

Yes, yes, I did. I know. One of the most owniest of owns was about to commence on my behalf.

"Who's deez?"

Damn, damn, damn. I should have listened to Jess. The whole bus had somehow heard him; I didn't know how, laughter erupting. *So, this was sixth grade, huh? I hated it.*

I soon learned Conor and I shared a homeroom. *And* periods second, third, fifth, and sixth. Thanks to his big bro, Brett, Conor had come to be known as the resident cool kid around Woodstock Middle. He proudly trotted around school wearing Calvin Klein jeans or Ralph Lauren shirts sent in from his brother. And he always, *always* wore a fresh new pair of Nikes.

"My brother works at AOL." He shared, totally unsolicited. But he knew we all cared because of AIM. This Brett character was a legend. "Me and my brother wear the same size. It's crazy."

Cue: Oohs and Ahh. Me? A hater? I wouldn't have called myself a hater. Even though I rocked whatever Payless knockoffs I found at the back-to-school sale instead of Nikes. Or, instead of looking eighteen at eleven, I looked eight. Or, instead of crowds surrounding me in homeroom to check out my new kicks, no one knew my name. Okay, being harsh—Ms. Baum knew my name just fine.

When my family visited New York the year before, I'd wished they'd left me behind. What an otherworldly city. I saw girls holding hands. Momi pretended not to notice, but I saw. I admired a short Black woman rocking a durag and tank top beside a taller, more feminine woman with long flowing locs, walking down a busy Brooklyn sidewalk together. Eerily similar to my auntie and her roommate, I remember thinking, who were never seen without each other. Who, if they thought you weren't looking, would get mighty close to each other. But gayness didn't exist in Memphis. If it did, you didn't talk about it. My other aunties and uncles always called my auntie's roommate her *friend*, and we all accepted that, even though the adults knew damn well what was up.

In New York, though? Two women holding hands in broad daylight was gay as hell, and clearly not a problem. No one cared. When 9/11 happened and I felt like my dream city might have died under the terror, Conor's brother said he was staying. That he loved the place too much to go, and that it needed strong people in it to keep it alive, I knew. *I knew.* New York had to be something special. So no, I wasn't necessarily hating on Conor. But perhaps in some roundabout way I was mad envious of Brett, for all his existence represented. Especially since I was recently madly lonely after having just left my very best friend in the world, Megan. A girl I had held hands with—in the privacy of her bedroom, of course. I thought about her a lot—not because I *liked*, liked her. Stop it, no! I told you...not in Memphis—but because I hadn't been ready to let go of our friendship. It proved difficult, because the more weeks went by at Woodstock, the more it felt like our friendship only existed in my memories. We spoke less, and when we did speak, she always had something annoying to say about her raggedy new friends that she'd somehow made overnight.

"We should all have a sleepover! Like, maybe we could, like, all do each other's makeup?"

No, Meg. I hate makeup. I hate your friends.

"Maybe!" I lied instead.

"Do you like school better now that you've been there a little longer?"

"I mean..." We shared a laugh, though, inside, I wasn't laughing.

I dreaded the thought of sharing Megan with her new friends who, instead of watching taped recordings of *Bill Nye the Science Guy* or playing with her neighborhood cats, preferred doing each other's makeup and talking about boys. I pretended us growing apart had only been the distance. The main issue with this whole "new school" thing was that there were less chances for our sleepovers. This was bad, because Megan and I only told each other secrets in person. It was an unspoken rule we made during our very first phone call, when I'd heard my dad breathing heavily on the other line when Megan had been about to tell me about her dad cheating when she was six.

"Wait." I commanded like a premonition. Awkward *almost* silence hovered between us for what felt like minutes as I affirmed my dad's breath on the other line... I knew it was him. Pops would sit on the phone sometimes just as a power move, and he'd stay there for as long as he wanted. But I couldn't even allow him to come between mine and Megan's secrets.

Finally, "Five minutes." He cleared his throat, "Quartet practice will begin promptly thereafter." *Click.*

Never again. Only covert operations moving forward. Sometimes, back at Brownsville Elementary, if my mom was in a good enough mood, she'd let me ride with Meg back to her place, and even if I only stayed for a few hours, it had been such a sweet reprieve. Now, we were too far away from each other for impromptu visits, and I hadn't realized what a void losing those visits would feel like. So, I was back to being mostly silent again. I couldn't relay my dreams to anyone else but my diary now— the dreams where I was never, ever a girl.

"Like, never?" She scrunched up her nose at me.

I'd grabbed her Dandy bear and squeezed it for a little extra bravery, murmuring, "No. Not really." She was the first and last person I'd told in about twenty years.

"So, are you, like, a *boy* in your dreams?" she asked.

I shrugged. She nodded, "That's cool."

That was it. Never any judgment between us. I missed that; I missed us. It hadn't felt right telling Meg secrets anymore, let alone my dreams.

"Oh my god, I *have* to show you this note I got yesterday!" Megan said, yanking me into her house from the front door and dragging me up the stairs to her room. She dug around in her backpack and pulled out a piece of paper folded into the shape of a frog. She opened it, revealing a blue gel-pinned heart beside her name. My heart sank at the sight of it.

"From Kevin!" She blurted like that name meant something to me. My confusion gave way to remembrance.

"*Kevin* from PE, Kevin?!" A tall, blonde, Nick Carter-lookalike who used to mime Michael Jackson moves in between exercises. My heart ached when she nodded again.

The note said:

Megan, I like you. Do you like me?

Yes. No. Maybe.

What was my face doing? Why was I frowning? Why was I mad?! I blinked hard. Looked away. Nothing worked; still mad.

"Like, I didn't tell you or anything 'cause I'm, like, embarrassed, but I kinda have a crush on him. But like, I didn't know he had a crush on me!?"

I rolled my eyes, "Kevin is so annoying."

I hadn't meant to say it. I hadn't planned to speak. Kevin used to call Megan and me the String Bean Twins because we were always together and had worn green on the same day, *that one time.* We used to laugh about how annoying he was! I looked at her, infatuated beyond belief. I didn't get it, didn't like it, and had no idea why, which only made me angrier—to the point that I didn't even want to look at her in her gapped-tooth grinning face. I used to love that grin, but now, all I wanted to do was rush home, up to my room, find the diary entry where I'd written about us moving into a West Village apartment together with just us and our cats and *Tear. It. Out!*

I didn't stay the night. Momi picked me up early on account of me feeling "sick," and I didn't see Megan again for a long while. The next day, a Saturday, Jess, Leese, Momi and I hit up the library to stock up on books since Leese had just finished the fourth Harry Potter book and was fiending for something to take its place. I came along for a change of scenery, I liked the library for other reasons than books. I loved how the children's section always felt like a magical, colorful land of make-believe. I adored how children's books *looked*. So enticing, inviting, damn near begging me to read them. I liked to flirt with the idea and maybe, just maybe, check out a book if I hadn't made the mistake of opening to the first chapter where there would, in fact, be words.

Later, after my sisters power walked into the place like two middle aged, tracksuit wearing ladies in a shopping mall, I dawdled in the children's section, expecting nothing, only to find something quite special, indeed. Lying on one of the multicolored round tables with little yellow chairs there gazing back at me; four preteen, white girls lying side by side, mid-laugh on the cover of *Are You There God? It's Me, Margaret.* One of the girls, dressed in orange with thick, dark hair, wore the most inviting smile, like she had something to tell me that might change my life. I *needed* to know, so I turned to the first chapter.

I read, and read, and read some more—reading struggles, where? Not in between those lines. That was the thing about not reading much, you found one book that you could actually get through, and it becomes your gospel, even if it doesn't deserve your praise. Maybe if I'd read more, I'd have compared its ideas to others. Instead, I embraced this witchcraft as I breezed past the first chapter in only a couple hours; a record for me.

This girl Margaret and I had a lot in common. Both flat-chested, quiet, and awkward. Both our parents were not very religious. My parents had never made much of a fuss about Jesus. We went to churches where Daddy played or musically directed, or Momi was curious about, or family and friends invited us to for various reasons. We'd rarely gone to only one place for more than three months straight.

My mother was as spiritual as they come; the truth-is-within-you, we're-all-made-of-stars sort of spiritual. I embraced the magic of her platitudes; enjoyed believing that I was *such* a magical being that I didn't need to learn another magic trick from the kit she bought me for my eleventh birthday, because *the magic is already within, sweet love*! But her magical lessons did not fare well outside of Joyner Manor (what both my parents called the Joyner household), especially not in Shelby County where even the most "liberal" were staunch Christians.

Her magic did not mix well with her and Pop's remnants of religion—my father, a former Baptist, my mother, Church of Christ, though she'd rebelled against its teachings since childhood. Still, its remains could be found in their rules; enrolling us in Vacation Bible School, and all the ungodly things their kids could not do with said "magic." The contradiction was impossible to ignore. As far as I was concerned, nothing I believed could be applied outside of my home. But then I found Margaret. I told myself she would be my entry into a normal, magic-less life.

Margaret spoke to God all the time. He was, arguably, her best friend. It didn't matter that her mom was Christian, and her dad was Jewish, which also felt relatable. She had a personal relationship with God that was special to her. I'd never thought about God this way; had never considered the fact that I could *talk* to Him the way I'd talk to a friend. I'd actually always been afraid of God—a guy who caused floods, killed babies, witnessed every little thing you ever did or said, and could hold it against you! But Margaret made Him seem approachable. Chill. Yeah, chill God, I was into chill God. And I didn't want to envy her, but the more I read, the more I did. Because this girl knew exactly what she wanted out of life, and it was all the right kinds of desires. She knew she loved being a girl. She knew she wanted a boyfriend, and boobs, and, of course, a loving relationship with our Almighty Lord and Savior.

I didn't even know who I'd be in my dreams that night! And I couldn't figure things out with Meg, anymore, she was too busy with her new friends and new crush and new makeup to be worried about me. I didn't have any other friends to talk to, and I didn't talk about this kind of stuff with my siblings—we were close but not *that* kind of close. I had nothing to say to my parents, they wouldn't understand. I might get in trouble for admitting some of my deepest, darkest thoughts. So, I did what my new favorite person Margaret did—Instead of just journaling everyday like I used to, I started writing to God.

Dear God, I need answers. What am I supposed to be doing with my life? Why do I feel like I'm not a girl? Why don't I have any friends? Why?!

Two weeks went by. Still no friends, no real answers. Still very, very awkward at school. But then something holy happened.

"Family. This Sunday, we'll become members of Greater Faith." Daddy announced at the helm of the dinner table.

I cheered. Clapped! Praised! I...was the only one. We'd skipped church for about three months because Daddy had an early Sunday music gig, but it had just ended. Usually, I would have loved this lull. But lately, because of my Margaret shenanigans, I hated the deprivation and needed to step onto some holy ground.

"Greater *Faith*?" Jess winced.

"I would like all of you to have the Black church experience." Daddy grinned.

I didn't get it. We'd been to both my grandmas' churches many times before. I mean, yeah, we were usually in children's Bible study, but they were still Black churches. They felt familiar, like going to a family reunion where your uncle gets a little carried away with his pre-lunch speech. So, I'd assumed my dad meant something similar. I'd find out later he meant a giant prosperity church, a newer phenomenon for folks from my parent's generation. But I didn't care what church we went to, I just knew that we were about to go somewhere consistently for the first time ever. This *had* to be a sign from God.

I'd never seen so many people congregate in one church. At least two thousand Black folks, all ages, dressed to the nines, hats for days. I saw more sparkles on some of the men's shoes than I'd seen in the sky at night. But when we entered from the 2nd floor, no one looked back at us. No one waved. Not like at my grandma's church, where mid-sermon drifted lemon pepper perfume from the church community room, signifying we'd all talk around food very soon. You knew you'd get some and candy from elders who knew your name and age, but you didn't know theirs. Not at Greater Faith—every single eye was dead set on that stage. Right into the eyes of Apostle Adams, head-to-toe in orange. He glowed and I gawked, even though they say it's not healthy to stare directly at the sun. I didn't care, Apostle Adams fascinated me.

He even got this otherwise antisocial crowd to speak to each other, "Look at your neighbor! Tell your neighbor," He belted, "Tell your neighbor, 'Neighbor'!"

"Neighbor!"

"Your blessings are on the way!" He'd proclaimed.

"Your blessings are on the way!" I shouted to no one along with two thousand other people I knew believed it as much as I did.

Hundreds of Saints waved $10, $50, $100 bills and checks. Dozens across the room praised their way down the aisles, others splayed out on the floor with the Holy Spirit, something I was quite familiar with from my grandmothers' churches but felt far more theatrical here. I could tell they were ready for their blessings. Momi whispered something to Daddy, and he pulled out his checkbook. Scribbled something down. Dropped it in the bucket and passed it down to each of us kids. I fumed, red with shame. I didn't have anything to give. The next week, I came with two quarters from my four-dollar allowance, minus my two-dollar deduction (I hadn't made my bed a couple times, and practiced violin less than what was required). I eventually started giving pretty much all my allowance, even though they said ten percent was just fine. It was only the beginning of my relationship with God and I needed to prove how loyal I was. Each week I learned something new about God that made me want to straighten up and pay more. It didn't take long for the pastor to confirm my assumptions about the gay stuff—just two weeks before he uttered a word I'd never heard before: *homosexual.* "God loves all his children, amen?" He started, unassumingly, as he always did.

"Amen!" said the church.

"But God made Adam and Eve for a reason, amen? God didn't make no Adam and Steve!" He paused for uproarious laughter from all God's saints.

I too, laughed, because everyone was laughing. Both of my parents were laughing, and my mom was not one to just laugh at anything. She'd made a chore of turning to us kids and dramatically rolling her eyes any time she didn't agree with something Apostle Adams said.

"The man is the head, amen?! But your woman, now, your woman is your neck!"

Cue long, drawn out eye roll.

Apostle cited King James versions of 1 Corinthians 6:9 and Romans 1:24-32, "Homosexuals will not inherit the earth."

At first, I was confused but referred to context clues: Adam and Steve = gay = bad. *Say no more. Got it.* But then I panicked. I'd done a few Adam and Steve-ish things in my day. Mostly in my head, but God's all-knowing so I figured He knew? I didn't have space to disobey Him anymore, not even in my diary, let alone my mind. I figured I'd keep my dream stuff, and that I didn't want boobs or a boyfriend, and the time I kissed Megan to myself from now on. But then I got stuck. What on earth would I replace my thoughts with to keep them from coming back? Well, I did what any reasonable eleven-year-old child of God caught in such a predicament would do: I copied

Margaret's dreams. Not exact copies—copycatting outright was still a well-known faux pas, but I used them as foundational. I took everything she desired; from boobs to my period, a boyfriend, and I made it mine. I willed it into my mind. I made her truths my mantras.

Still, I knew this wasn't enough. I needed to do something major, transformative to prove to God that I was serious. Like the final period to this whole new chapter I'd written for myself. So, the next morning, I asked Momi if I could be baptized.

"You are made of stars! You *are* God. You don't need to be baptized."

Yeah, yeah, yeah.

"Ugh. Come *onnn*. I know all that already, that's not what I'm talking about."

"I'm telling you the truth!"

I didn't have time for this; the longer I waited, the more God would think I wasn't serious. Who knew how he would punish me for that? Like Apostle Adams said, God is a gracious God, but he's also a jealous, wrathful God.

"I don't want to keep living in sin!" I yelled. I hadn't meant to yell, but she had to understand—I was fueled by a holy passion to be born again. *I needed this.*

"Child, there is no such thing is "sin.""

I scrunched up my nose at such a statement. If there was no such thing as sin, why did I feel so dirty? Why were we going to a church where 'sins' and 'sinners' were mentioned in every other sentence throughout a two-hour sermon? Why did she get to be saved, but not me?

"But you're baptized." Oowee. Winning retort right there. I knew I'd won. She laughed, unable to stop herself.

"The least you could do is let me have that same security." I said with all of my eleven years.

There were only a couple dozen people in the church pews the evening I was baptized, including my family. As a true Christian, it became my task to convince Jess to join me.

"Yeah, I guess." She shrugged after our symphony practice at Audubon Park Baptist Church.

She shoved me away after I hugged her harder than I ever had. She had no idea she'd just chosen to save her soul thanks to me. I was getting really good at this. I didn't even judge my parents when they shared a somewhat shady glance I couldn't decode when I shuffled out in my long, white baptismal gown. I needed to focus; I was about to experience the rebirth of a lifetime. I couldn't tell you if I believed in hell, I'd been told not to all my life. But I did believe in and fear consequences, unanswered prayers, and punishment for being wrong. I was even wrong that day, when I spotted myself in the mirror and wished, for just a second, that I'd actually woken up looking like *dream me.*

I hoped I could help save Jess from anything bad she might have done in secret, because I had secrets that I could let go of now. I could start fresh; be more like Margaret. The Apostle looked unreal up close, as if molded out of red clay, not a wrinkle or ruffle, even when he smiled. I chalked it up to how Godly he was. Clearly apostles didn't get wrinkles. The water was warmer than Luke, and the Apostle held me under for what had felt like five straight minutes. His words were muffled underneath, all I could hear was my heart pounding. I asked God that he'd bring me back in time to hear, "Amen."

He did. My first answered prayer of many as a saved child of God. I resurfaced like a new me, all that trash inside me washed away. I was a girl now, the best eleven-year-old, boy-loving (respectfully), boob-having Christian girl you ever did see. I didn't need Megan anymore. I didn't need any friends—except the Christian kind—because I had God, the best friend there ever was.

My first order of business as the new me was to go to school with my head held high, ready to make the *right* kind of friends. There was this one girl, Shanese, tall and Black and pretty, whose little brother played football with Drew. Every practice, I saw her on the other side of the park at the swings, surrounded by three or four other cute Black girls that hung onto her every word. We were always separated by a bridge, and sometimes, I'd hear the faint tunes of B2K coming from her portable radio as she danced with her friends and I watched from afar.

At lunch, I sat adjacent to her, next to her right-hand girl Jenay who *had* said two words to me, once complimenting my shirt. I said, "Thank you," which had given me the push to sit there. I noticed Shanese had this deep caramelly voice that made everything she said drip with *cooooool*. I watched her smear roll-on sparkling lip gloss from the beauty supply store over pretty pink lips.

"This is the best one." She said, raising the tube of lip gloss to her minions. Dang, now I needed roll-on sparkly lip gloss from the beauty supply store.

She was rocking a cool ass airbrushed tee with her nickname, "Ne Ne" on it, tied up real cute at her waist, revealing the teensiest bit of skin—but not too much to get docked by our lunchtime monitor, Vice Principal Lee.

"It looks really good on you, Ne." Jenay said.

I would have thought nothing of Jenay's compliment. I would have let it go in through one ear, out the other. If it hadn't been for what Shanese said next.

"That's so *gay*, "

That's so gay as a response to a sincere compliment! She giggled as she spun the top back on her lip gloss and dropped it in her plush-monkey purse.

I glitched. Frozen.

"Oh my god, no it's not!" Jenay said, giggling too, as if she hadn't just been insulted with one of the most damning words in the English language.

"Whatever. *Gay.*" Shanese retorted playfully.

There it was again! They all laughed, and I took one tasteless bite of my peanut butter and jelly sandwich, wheels turning in my confused brain as I watched this mind-boggling moment unfold. How were all of them having the greatest time throwing around this word I'd tried to run away from? And then it clicked: they weren't saying gay as in "gay," but "gay" as in whatever thing you wanted it to mean at the time (which could also mean *gay* gay). Brilliant. A menacing gay to slight thine enemy. A lighthearted gay for the road! Playful, meaningless but somehow weighted and full of depth. Ah, the versatile, all-encompassing slur. Old me would have sweated at the sound of it, but new me? I could do nothing but embrace it, champion it. I loved it. I *had* to use it. If I refused, I was only proving myself to be so *very* gay. I was even more convinced of its power as the week went on. "Gay" as a multi-purpose insult spread like wildfire. Every cool kid used it. New me used it often; if I couldn't think of anything to say, "Gay!"

Conor nudged me on the bus. "Gay!" Laughter. Wonderful.

Jenay complimented the same shirt she complimented the first time. How epically... "Gay." Laughter. Perfection.

It was the best conversation starter, like the secret password into the coolest club. So cool that even Shanese talked to me now. By Friday, she invited me to sit with her girls *on purpose*. The next week, she liked me so much she invited me to cross over the bridge into the cool part of the park while our brothers practiced. I told God about my progress.

I'm making friends! Finally! Thank you, thank you! I think I'm gonna be popular.

I just knew God was smiling. He was so proud, He rewarded me with a sleepover at Shanese's house. Megan, who? I didn't need to go to her little sleepovers, or meet her annoying new friends, or respond to her last phone call. I was becoming popular. Pop-u-lar, okay?! Here I was, legitimately cool for the first time in my eleven years and I felt...

I felt strange. Sad. *Why was I sad?* Cramped, like I'd thrown on a shirt two sizes too small. That was my fault though, not God's—never God's. Clearly, I hadn't been praying enough, or the right way. I was doing everything else exactly how I was supposed to, I'd even asked my mom to buy me a training bra.

"What?! *You* want to go shopping?"

My mom hadn't been able to believe it either. Other than the one-time Aunt Treacy had taken me to pick out my very own suspenders (unironically inspired by Steve Urkel from *Family Matters*), I opted out of all shopping trips with the quickness. There was something about the florescent lighting in a department store that left me nauseous. I hated browsing the isles, hated turning my head to see Momi holding up some lacy, frilly, floral, nonsense talking about, "How about this?"

Then *I* was the asshole for shaking my head as if rebuking a demon. I could never picture myself wearing anything the mannequins rocked and hated dressing rooms.

The thought of prancing out to hear my mom and sisters go, "Now *that's* cute!" to me in an article of clothing I felt unlike myself in made me cringe. Momi knew this about me better than anyone, but I wasn't *that* me anymore. I was this new, *girly* Christian, a *better* me who dreamed of growing boobs big enough to wrap in pink knit bralettes. I wouldn't wince at first glance like I usually did.

I power walked, nearly jogged to the frilliest frill, and picked it up and asked, "How about this one!?" and Momi laughed at my eager little face and replied, "That's just fine, but make sure you get your size."

I smiled while she explained bra sizing to me. *Girl talk, we're having fun.* We left with one training bra and a sports bra, and I wore the sports bra to bed as part of my religious practice until Momi warned,

"Make sure you don't wear your bras to bed. They stunt your growth."

I hopped out of bed and staggered over to my underwear drawer every morning, fastening my too-big bralette over pancake-flatness for three months straight. And one day, it'd wrap me tighter than before, tugging around my rounding chest, nipples poking rudely under thin fabric, and I'd stare in the mirror at an answered prayer and fight the urge to cry melancholic tears. I wouldn't know why, but I took no time to dwell— I was almost twelve and was wasting precious moments not thanking God. The God who blessed me with exactly what I said I'd wanted. I should have been ashamed. I grabbed my notebook and wrote like I was running out of time.

Thank you, GOD, for boobs! Thank you for my friends. Thank you for everything!

Tear drops accented the page. I wanted to rip them out but didn't. I could not disrespect Him like that. And I needed to leave them as a reminder to myself how good things were. How good God was to me, how lucky I was. On the way to symphony practice one weekend, my new boobs throbbed like two pulsing wounds. I winced at the thought of these blessings. Days after my twelfth birthday, I met Aunt Flow. Who knew such a painful broad brought so much celebration? Momi raved all about her while I sat flinching under the sweltering, greased up teeth of her hot comb.

"This is wonderful news! What do you wanna do for your Women's Day? We can go to a movie? Or maybe we can finally go to that restaurant that opened a bit ago, I was thinking..." She nearly sang her words.

She let the hot comb sizzle on the nape of my neck as I contemplated womanhood, which seemed ridiculous to twelve-year-old me. Laughable, but I wasn't laughing. I knew Momi was serious, and that womanhood was no laughing matter—I could get pregnant now. Getting a boyfriend was the last unanswered prayer on my list, so I was closer to that can of worms than ever before. Closer than Margaret, yet, I felt nothing like the beaming, bubbly girl on that cover.

I never stopped not being a girl in my dreams and never felt like a girl in real life. I still found myself sometimes wishing to hold Megan's hand. I'd call myself gay and apologize to God. I apologized to Him for sleeping in my sports bra on purpose, hoping my chest would stop growing. I prayed He wasn't angry with me for all the things I still thought that I wouldn't write or say aloud. Like that I thought Shanese was pretty. Or that I once dreamt about kissing her. That in the corners of my mind, I often wished to wake up as this person in my dreams, or the one I'd met there, who told me they were me from the future. Who showed me that this life was worth it so long as I became them. I hoped He didn't think I was ungrateful. The *last* thing I wanted was for Him to see me as ungrateful. Because I was so, so grateful, to seem so very normal and okay.

does He love us?

well, does He?

and

i think the question on the tip of everyone's tongues here is

does He

the Christian He

the one they say is white

exist

enough to have a say at all?

DOES GOD LOVE DYKES?

New York City, Spring - 2014

Feel it: The *thump, thump, thump* of electronic bass over *212*, bouncing off the walls of a dark, dark, dark dance floor. Azealia has the grrrlies by their necks. Dancing. Drinking. Talking like their friends can hear a thing. Can't hear a damned thing, but good music. So good.

Casey, in front of me, nods. We clink our overfilled glasses and mine spills ever-so-slightly down the corners of my mouth. Oh, the sweet hot fire that is tequila. Mind you, we've been dancing this whole time. Or, not dancing so much as moving our bodies to the vibration of the music, however they flow. We set our glasses down on the counter not too far from us before returning to the floor. Our hands are free now, free enough to feel the sweat on the creases of our tops. Theirs, a denim vest with the arms cut off. Nothing underneath, of course. Mine, a ridiculously thin white tank top offering all sorts of low-cut peeps of skin on either side of my chest. Still a-cups. Still mine, for now.

"It's so fucking hot!" Casey says to me, but I don't hear.

They say it again and then, "Fuck it!"

I keep dancing, smiling, tipsy and grand until I see them unbutton the last three buttons on their already deep-v vest. That's right. Take. It. Off. Bare chest flouncing in front of me as they glide a damp hand through their sweat-drenched sandy brown, slicked back fringe. Grinning. *No,* cheesing. Effervescent, and I'll bet the homos surrounding us got an eye full. My eyes were on theirs, living in the freedom of the moment, cheesing just as hard. Before I know it, my flimsy muscle tee is in the corner of my deep hammer-pants pockets. This is pure joy. This is happiness. This is what I call a good time. Two guys, one Black, one Jewish but tan and fluent in Spanish—from Miami—so the grrrlies, myself included, think they're brown, having fun on a Friday night at a queer club in lower Manhattan with their shirts off. Where I'm from, fools might say we were two dykes praising the devil in hell. Depends on who you ask, I guess.

"Look." Casey mouths, nodding to their left.

I follow their gaze to a dark-skinned woman draped in gold, glowing in the dark. Crown unbothered with tresses to display the godly shape of her whole head. And that gorgeous face. Where there was once music, all I hear now are the things her eyes are saying: "Come get me. Don't be shy." And I'm not shy—not on a dance floor, and certainly not when met with my soul mate. Because this woman *is* my soulmate; I am in love. I have been in love six times this month. It is the last week of

May—in April, I fell in love four. Woke up four times beside four different lovers I'd envisioned four different, very vivid futures with. None of them becoming reality, but that never mattered to me. These days I thrived in short-term memory, quickly forgetting what heartbreak feels like—

"Hey." Her name is Eva.

Our hands clasp, I pull her in. She turns around, grinds her body on my spirit, and I am so far gone. Casey laughs.

"I'll leave you to it!" They tell me.

Top still off, Casey turns and pumps fists with a boi we ran into early on, whose name I always forget though we run into this fool at every queer event. Eva and I keep dancing. Our lips meet. We're lost in each other. Casey understands. Casey always understands, and we will talk about this tomorrow.

"You wanna get out of here?" I ask Eva, nothing but a wisp of air between her ear and my mouth. We hold each other, dancing like a ballad plays but it's very much a trancey Kaytranada beat.

Her eyes narrow but her mouth curves upward, wantingly, "Yeah."

I find my white tee in the depths of my pocket, throw it on, and we're off. Booze evaporating. Adrenaline, lust, *love* overtaking. We float on a flying nimbus to her Flatbush flat, hitting up the bodega across the street for curly fries and wings.

"These are literally the best." She tells me.

I believe her. We kiss and walk and pause to kiss and finally, make our way into her three-story walkup. I don't notice her roommate chilling in the kitchen, laughing audibly at something she watches on the tiny screen of her Android. Even though we have to pass her to get to Eva's room, a luscious land of cool blue cloaked in living flowers. *I always knew my dream girl had a green thumb.*

"What?" She asks.

"Oh," I giggle like a fool, "did I say that out loud?"

I don't repeat myself. Her bed is soft, not firm. Her skin, like silk. We go on a voyage across each other's bodies, and we care so little about our destination, but we get there. Oh, we get there. And I am in love, again. We fall asleep in each other's arms and I wish to stay here forever. I know that when the sun comes up, I am Cinderella. A single Brooklyn pauper with no lover to my name, once again. It always ends this way, no matter how hard I try. No matter how many paragraphs I dedicate to our time together in my journal, or if I happen to get her number, of which I often don't ask, so as to not kill the fantasy. Texting something three days later like...

Hey, I had so much fun with you the other night

And by then, anyway, I have moved on to a new love. The cycle continues. It is my perfect formula. Never enough time to get lonely, or enough time to think about my feelings under feelings of this love. I like it this way. I tell myself I like it this way.

"See you." I say, knowing those words mean close to nothing. My life will go on without this love.

Heart calls and asks, "Do you still wanna meet before?"

She often sounds winded due to her constant movement, typically rustling and rummaging through her own things in search for a specifically important item like keys or a phone. At least we could rule out the phone. I hear a fumbling noise on her end.

"Sorry. I'm looking for my wallet. It's a whole thing."

Ah, wallet this time. We opt out of morning coffee since we're both running behind. I power walk to the G to later transfer to the A and hop off at 14 St and 8 Av to make it to The NYC LGBT Center. I'm greeted by a white lesbian with an undercut behind the front desk. An eager grin plastered across her very gay face. I check my black Casio; five minutes till 12pm. Smooth sailing. I love when the subway's on my side.

"Do you know where the Dyke March meeting is?" I ask.

Of course she does,

"Yeah, totally! Right around the corner. You'll see a sign, can't miss it." She points to my left.

I turn the corner. As promised, there's a big purple Dyke March Committee Meeting sign plastered on the first door I see. It's my third meeting in my second year on this committee. I sit in the middle row of fold-out chairs and place my pleather wallet in the seat beside me for Heart. I wave to Casey who seems to have recruited another, quite affectionate, dyke committee member last night. We have much to discuss.

"What's up dykes!" Says the committee head, a 30-something red haired business-y, chapsticked white lesbian named Sharon, "Seeing some new faces, love that *so much*."

There were about thirty of us. Half my age, half 40-plus vets with a world of tales to tell. About a quarter of us not white, six Black, including myself.

Five of us younger dykes would all become a crew. Heart and Casey, and a dark-skinned Dominican femme named Sofie, a brown Ecuadorian woman named Abby, and me. Only Heart wasn't here yet so I waited, impatiently for my right-hand dyke and number one homegirl. Don't worry, I wasn't totally spaced out. This dyke took notes (also see: all dykes take notes). It was a fascinating sight, actually. As soon as Sharon pulled out her iPad, and, assumedly, found her notes app, it was everyone's cue to rummage around for their own pen and paper or notes apps to begin jotting down their own bullets and takeaways.

Sharon continued, "Next Thursday is our raffle! Can you believe?!"

Break for sapphic applause.

"So we've got two slots still open for the second shift at the front table. Any takers?"

Casey and their new Mx. Right Now shoot each other knowing glances. They raise both their hands without Casey moving their other arm from around this person's neck.

Laughter ensues.

Sharon types something, "Perfect! Casey and...?"

"I'm Myra by the way! She/her." She grins so hard her face crinkles. A blanket of silence covers the entire room. Casey wriggles in their seat as if trying to muster up the courage to explain what exactly just happened. The girlies were verklempt.

"She, her?" Says a confused, older white trans woman named Samantha in the back of the room.

"It's like, her pronouns." Casey explains, squeezing Myra who just seemed to realize the gravity of her very basic introduction.

"I mean, aren't we all she-hers?" Snorts a respectable half Asian dyke in her late thirties.

And Heart is nowhere to be found as the beginning of the dyke wars quietly, begrudgingly begins. When we joined weeks before, neither of us mentioned our pronouns. I quietly claimed they/them but only if someone asked me, otherwise I'd grin and bear any she/her thrown my way. And I never assumed a non-woman like me was actually, *openly* welcomed in the Dyke March Committee. Maybe that's why I kept it hushed. Even though I wholeheartedly, even now, identify as a dyke. A dyke of the non-woman variety. It felt like something I needed to keep quiet. I just hoped that I'd run into other people like Heart and Casey and later the rest of my crew who got it. *And if you got it, you got it,* I thought. Giving don't ask don't tell. But no. This moment, this utterly uncomfortable moment, was much deeper than that. We were the Dyke March Committee for fucks sake. This had to be a discussion. I didn't think I'd have to "come out" this soon. But of course, I would.

"I'm not." I blurt. There's that silence again.

I try and fill it with, "I prefer they/them."

Someone very out of touch guffawed. In walked Heart. Waving in oblivious bliss as she pranced over to the seat I'd saved for her. She had no idea. She asks me with a raise of her eyebrow.

Sharon answered with a, "We don't really have to get into the weeds of this today, folks, this is a really big topic?"

Casey disagreed, "No, I feel like we should."

Sharon, "Huh."

Casey swivels around to Samantha, "Do you feel like you have to be a woman or a lesbian to be a dyke?"

86

Casey was bold. Sharon looks like she'd rather die. Heart looked like she'd been smacked by a gust of wind. Mind boggled.

Samantha's face went red, "A dyke is a lesbian. Is a dyke not a lesbian, am I missing something?"

Oh my god. I was not prepared to argue with dykes on the meaning of dykes today but,

"A dyke *can* be a lesbian, but a dyke can also be a nonbinary person or trans guy or gender queer whatever who loves women and femmes. Just not a man."

I didn't know about "cis" then, otherwise I would have added it. But the majority of this crowd wasn't hearing me anyway. Casey, like a ride-or-die, joined in, "Right. Like I'm a trans masc guy but I'm a super dyke."

Heart seems to have found her footing. She chimed in, "What's wrong with dyke being a gender-neutral term?"

The collective shit was being rocked out of the old school dykes in the space with every new exchange. We were *this close* to Dyke March weekend, just a few measly events away. It was supposed to be business as usual. Now it was nothing but. Things were officially different in a way none of us expected. I understand the palpable confusion enveloping the space now. But I don't welcome it, nor did I feel welcomed by it.

Sharon, whose head was about to explode, stammered, "Ya'll. We have way too much to get through. This is like a *very* divisive subject I just don't think we can resolve today."

I don't know what came over me,

"But is this not extremely relevant? As the committee isn't it our job to be clear about who's welcome and who's not?"

Sharon responds, "I hear you. Definitely, but we have like an hour worth of logistics to get through and people have things to do after this. How does everyone feel about finishing this discussion via email?"

Via email. Like a fucking chain letter. Like a casual thread among friends. Something about her question made my blood boil. And don't think for a second I didn't notice her epic dodge from sharing her own thoughts on the matter. I felt strange. Off. I felt exposed. Too exposed to grasp full hold of anger.

"You know what," Casey stood. *Oh my god*. Casey, "I don't really feel chill about finishing up the meeting, anymore."

They gathered their things. Myra, the quiet catalyst of this whole debacle, stood with them, grabbed their hand. Then me,

"Yeahhhhh."

Heart, who'd been there no more than 5 minutes, stood too. We left.

"So where should we go now?" Casey cackled when the LGBT Center door closed behind us. None of us could help but to laugh and laugh. None of us had any idea what would happen next, but I know I felt good somehow with our choice to walk out. It was, actually, quite dyke-y of us.

"That was *wild*," Heart stressed in the most epic late-to-the party whirlwind sort of way.

We enter Think Coffee, the 8th Ave location. I got a hibiscus tea, and we sat in the back at one of the round wooden tables big enough for four.

"Four rebel dykes, getting tea and or coffee, "Casey declared.

"We should start a podcast," said Myra.

"What the fuck happened before I got there?!" asked Heart.

We laughed again at how bizarre this morning went. But I understood the rift. The older dykes grew up fighting a whole other fight. Just to be able to be women loving women out loud. And here we came, the youths, shaking their shit up before they even got to enjoy it all the way. I could see how that'd feel disrespectful. Myra explained she'd been sharing her pronouns ever since she started working at the feminist center back in 2012. We all nodded, all different levels of intrigued at this new reality she'd just welcomed us into. I liked it. Feared it. The thought of telling my very straight, very white lady co-workers at my PR firm that I actually hated being addressed by "she." That I'd quietly, legally changed my name in the third week of work and I'd, yes, like to be addressed by that now. I'd grown comfortable compartmentalizing. My mother didn't know, nor Jess, and well, pretty much none of my family but Leesie who was so close to me physically and mentally that I simply couldn't keep that part of me hushed. But even to her, I didn't make any announcements, just acted in ways that required further questioning. I'd never lie when asked, and it'd usually become a discussion. But why did I tell her not to tell anyone? I mean, I was more open now than I'd ever been. New York had been that freedom for me I always hoped it would but it was a freedom with time stamps, only available to me when I clocked in and out of certain spaces. Myra was onto something, something special. Something that if she hadn't brought attention to, we all would have simply avoided. It was so much easier not to ruffle feathers. It always is.

"Shout out to Myra." I said.

"Shout out to Myra!" Heart repeated, raising her mug of chai. We all did it then, the four of us, rebel dykes, raising mugs of tea and or coffee in celebration.

Then that evening in bed, I texted Casey.

Wanna come with me to cut off all my hair tomorrow?

I knew to text Casey because Casey was down for literally anything and everything. Heart might have asked me questions, and I was too fragile for questions. I knew that my big, fiery red locks sparked certain expectations about my being that I want,

90

nay, needed to nip in the bud. And it's not that my long hair was a rouse *to me*. I considered it just as queer as anything I rocked. But I knew what long hair meant on a person like mine. Pretty, like girl-pretty. Even though I called myself a pretty boi, I knew long hair to most people in this colonized world meant "girl." "Woman." Time for a change, a shift. A bold new marker. I needed someone who knew that when I said I wanted to do something as impulsive as cutting off twenty inches of slow- growing kinky curls, their only response was,

Yessssssssss.

Sunday, Casey and I met early for bagels right around the corner from their Dominican barber. I didn't give myself time to consider my PR firms' dress code. Didn't care that there was no turning back. That this hair cut would be an irreversible step into obvious dykedom. But who was I kidding? I was a dyke. I am a dyke. I was a dyke when I applied to this stuffy job and I'd be one when I left. I didn't care to care, not anymore. That Monday my Subway ride felt like a slow walk to my own execution. My heart pounded like a scared rabbit's foot. I shuttered at the breeze from the trains open doors, hitting my bald sides with a sensation so unfamiliar. I entered my office. *I did it. I did this shit.*

"Hi...Umm, hi, I lo-wow! Hair cut?" Here she go. My 25-year-old high powered girl boss manager named Katelyn. I would expect nothing less.

"Hey! Yeah, needed a change." I say, grinning my 'lil corporate smile.

"Yeah, that's a...change. For sure."

I expected this. I set my backpack on the empty seat beside me and turned on my computer for a long day's work of data entries and requests to find this Timex watch or that shade of Shiseido blush in our product closet. And this day? Was so, so long. There was barely any variation in shock because there was barely any variation in white woman, but the chorus of insidious "surprise" grew tiring real quick. And it wasn't just my hair folks accidently winced about. It was the sweater vest, the black skinny jeans, the Doc Martins. All things I'd worn before, but that hit different under a classic high-top fade. As far as they knew I went from respectable Black business lady to dykey office delinquent overnight. I felt more alien than I ever had, even though nothing really had changed. I hated that my long hair had all that power. That it could not also be dykey. That there are certain ways you must show up that are shorthand for safe. But something about this othering felt liberating too, felt...rebellious. Until,

"Can I chat with you for a quick sec?" This was the CEO speaking, which wasn't saying too, too much with the size of this little firm and how shortly it had actually been a company at all.

But still, I nodded, walked over to her office with her in front of me and we stopped at her door, and she blocked me from entering,

"Real quick, no big thing, just a quick reminder on dress code, yeah? Love the new look. Very cool. But it's not Friday. Let's just keep it business caj. Good?"

My heart dropped, and I got angry at my own shock. Because why was I shocked?

"Oh yeah, totally!"

I turn around, I make the walk of shame all the way back to my sad little desk. I was angry, I was embarrassed, and angry for being angry and embarrassed. I opened Indeed.com. I scrolled furiously. I landed on a new position at *Take Off NY* for Office Manager. I saved it. I spent the next hour ignoring email requests from my manager to update my resume, instead. I updated my name. I listed my pronouns. I wanted to scream. I applied, instead. And I still went to work the following day, and the day after that, with my new haircut and my only clean pair of slacks, and shirts that were much frillier than I currently preferred. And for one week I heard nothing. And felt worse, and worse. Because now when people used my old name it felt like daggers in my side, when before, when I was very much okay with hiding, I could so easily ignore it. I wished I could bury all these feelings again. Oh, sweet compartmentalization. But on the second week, I got an email for an interview. I called out sick on Thursday to go to it. Nothing again, for two weeks. Every day was harder. Another day passed and then a whole new Wednesday. I was growing claustrophobic. I needed to shake things up, decided to have lunch outside. And as I nibbled my soggy homemade pimento sandwich in the office courtyard, I got an offer notification on my phone. My affirmation. I could be me now, full time. Finally, Jasper, dyke extraordinaire, on and off the clock.

It was not the world that was my oppressor only, because what the
world does to you is if it (oppresses) you long enough and
effectively enough, you begin to do it to yourself. You become a
collaborator, an accomplice to your own murderers, because you
believe the same things they do. They think it's important to be
white, you think it's important to be white. They think it's
shameful to be Black and you think it's shameful to be Black. And
you have no corroboration around you of any other sense of life. All
those corroborations which are around you are in terms of the white
majority standards. So deplorable, they frighten you to death. You
don't eat watermelon. You get so rigid you can't dance.
You hardly move by the time you're 14.

James Baldwin in conversation with Nikki Giovanni, 1971

LIKE A KICK IN THE FACE

Memphis, TN – Fall, 2005

Life, in the shape of a size-10 Doc Martin boot attached to a gaunt, pale-bodied Christian punk screamo singer atop a makeshift stage inside an indoor skatepark, kicked me in my mutherfuckin' face.

But first, a lot of other things happened.

One of which includes my starting tenth grade at a new high school after leaving Craigmont, a place the whites of Memphis claimed was quickly "going downhill" after (Black) kids from North Memphis got bussed there.

I didn't leave because those kids got bussed. But I cannot lie to you, other than sadly exiting my soprano spot in their epic gospel choir, or their expressly great track team, I was quite happy to hop on out that bitch because Black kids from North Memphis could see right through my charades like a camera through cellophane.

By charades, I mean the sort of scaffolding wall surrounding my jello-soft interior, of which I'd just adopted post-middle school after the harrowing realizations that I was, in fact, very, very weird. I'd accepted it. Tried for years to avoid it but there was no lying to myself anymore. Now, words like transgender or queer hadn't blessed my vocabulary just yet, but I knew 'gay,' and the way it left my mouth still felt like the worst kind of slur so I rebuked it like any good Christian would. Called it 'weird,' instead.

My walk, like a butch robot, was 'weird,' not a clear sign of my dyke-itude. My sturdy cadence, though paired with a pitch sometimes only dogs could hear, did not help either. And neither did my style, of which I couldn't possibly pretend was hitting the way it was supposed to had hit. Not at a place like Craigmont High where North Memphis girls somehow figured out a way to make a white button-up shirt and khakis look fresh. All I had to do was speak, and the Black kids at Craigmont could read me up and down like a scroll.

I saw what cool was at Craigmont very fast. It was night and day different from Woodstock Middle 'cool,' so, none of my Woodstock cool transferred over. And I'd worked so hard for it! Still, not a bit did. And at Craigmont, it'd be foolish for me to even try. Not that I didn't try. Nobody said I wasn't foolish. But the mix of imitation and raw me-ness mixed up into it came out like the silliest brew of out-of-touch nerd.

One sentence out my mouth and the Craigmont kids could clock every bit of my person. They'd know my parents looked down on their parents. Could have probably predicted that just that weekend before, my Daddy had been on a rant about young Memphis thugs overtaking his band class, sounding like Uncle Ruckus. They could hear it all in my voice, all in the bend of my words that didn't quite bend like Memphis, because they'd been expressly trained not to.

And so, my performance of Craigmont 'cool' didn't just fail flat, it made me seem *fake*. And fake is bad. Like bad, bad. Fake is worse than nerdy, which is worse than corny, because corny and real still have a lot of potential to be fun, and fun is always good.

Now, real means a couple different things, depending on who you ask. But in Memphis when I was in high school, it was all pretty straightforward: Real recognize real. Real recognize fake. If you know, you know, and if you don't, tough.

And Real Ones were always Black or brown. Always the heart of the city they come from, born and raised, the 'culture' part of the town that tourists come to see, and developers ironically push out when they have the chance. They carry the story of their city in their twang. You spot it in the strut, note it in the references, the slang, the likes, dislikes.

There is no once removed to a Real One, no uncanny valley where the realness should be. Not like with my hollow attempts. My cousins on my mom's side are Real Ones. Around them, me and my siblings got to be the corny exceptions because we never felt the need to act fake around them. They got that we had no control over how we were raised. By two boujee Black parents who trained Memphis right out of our tongues to the point of no return. However, that didn't mean they didn't drag us about it constantly.

Stiff head ass, Keke would laugh.

Corny, boujee head ass, said Ashley, whose boisterous laugh would crack me up despite myself.

Getting dragged came with the territory. Everybody knows this is a price you pay as a corny kid around Real Ones. As long as you don't front like you're something you're not, Real Ones will respect it. Because they know speaking white people's language is how you make a come-up, it's how you find a job that pays more than the city's average, how you save up enough to move to another city where there's more chances to thrive. And you'll probably thrive, because it's easier to thrive when you know how to talk that talk. Everybody knows that, just some of us don't want to, or can't, or never had the chance to, or rather stay Real.

Now, I'm not saying you lose part of your Blackness for success. This is not a boujee Black vs hood Black critique. What I'm saying is American success is a rocky, white road, and to travel down it you gotta be fluent in the language, in the movements.

Some Black parents, like my dad, are generations deep in it. Fluent. Then there are *exceptions* like my mom, who somehow break through barricades separating classes after winning rigged games they were never 'spose to win. She was the first in her working-class family to graduate college. And that's with 9 siblings and a single mother after her dad passed. The first to get a college-educated type job—a teacher. The first to marry a third-generation middle-class Black man (mind you, Black middle class and white middle class are two very different things).

But me? Let's just say if (white) success is your first language, like it was mine, odds are you'll grow up a lil' cornier than your Black counterparts. It is what it is. As long as you don't play like you're still a Real One, when you're so far removed from your city's heartbeat its funny (by no fault of your own, of course), you'll be fine. Either accept it or live the tortured life of an ashy Black conservative. We all have our plights.

Anyway, back to sophomore year, 2005. Millington High School to Craigmont High. Where were we...

Right, yes, yes, how the whole 'me' part of *me* just wasn't hitting. Not for myself, and apparently not for the rest of the Black Craigmont High population. And so, instead of hiding awkward, teen, closetedness devout Christian girl, (GIRL, okay?!) delicateness, I wanted out. I couldn't deal. I wanted nothing more than to hide in plain sight while I figured this thing out, and you can't hide around Black people who know what truth looks like.

So, Millington High School, which was about 50/50 Black and white at the time, seemed a better option. Plus, most Black people in Millington were different. Instead of being Memphis or Shelby County natives, most of them were army brats, just arriving from places like Guam and Korea. They had no context for my particular brand of weirdness (see queerness) and therefore I could hide in plain sight around them, too. As long as I avoided the few Real Ones during my two and a half years there, which was fairly simple since they were the minority, I was good to go. And it felt nice. To blend in with a bunch of other nerds who were just as miserably insecure as me. I didn't stand out at all.

But then I discovered Tokio Hotel. Or, more specifically, Bill Kaulitz, the ever-pale, makeup-donned German lead singer of Tokio Hotel. I'd never seen a more gorgeous, mysteriously androgynous creature in my entire life. One look at him and I knew, I was doomed because every wrong thing he was, I wanted to be.

But that, my friends, is not how you blend in. At all. Didn't matter. I didn't care. I needed some way to express myself that felt more real and free than this caricature of a "good girl" I'd been rocking. Plus, this was Millington. I figured I had more space to experiment without getting dragged.

So, what does a closeted queer who knows nothing of the terms "closeted" and/or "queer," but just listened to a torrented version of *From Under the Cork Tree* by Fall Out Boy for the fourth time this Monday morning wear to feel good? You rock a black and white checkered zip-up hoodie you once saw Pete Wentz wearing on *TRL*.

On your feet are some knock-off vans because your mom refuses to pay more than twenty dollars for "flat, boy shoes." And your mom won't let you shave your sides so you secretly die the under-part of your relaxed, scene-grrl swoop purple, the part your parents won't spot unless you dramatically flip it up, revealing your forehead, like you do constantly when hanging with your new, partially white, partially Black, very emo friends.

And you are not gay. Not 'queer.' You aren't even a little bit strange. You're emo. Maybe a scene kid, sometimes. And no one bats an eye because they've just seen the *I Write Sins Not Tragedies* premiere on *TRL* so none of this get-up phases them one bit.

I had this one good friend named Kelsey. A mixed emo kid with scraggly, bright yellow curls the color of Hayley's from Paramore. She had a blood-red jacket she always wore that looked a lot like my checkered one, so when we walked together, we looked like a two-person punk band called Checkered Blood.

Kelsey was tall and commanded a room, and even though her black eyeliner was thick and her smile a little naughty, she had soft and sweet sad-girl eyes. I think this is why my mom let me hang out with her.

Kelsey was like no friend I ever had. If the dirty boy in *Charlie Brown* was a house, it'd be hers. The tannish film over everything felt grungy—good grungy. And besides the subtle, though consistent, desire to puke at the smell, I liked going to Kelsey's house. It was like going to a punk house, and that made me feel so cool.

Kelsey's mom, a white lady, was a nurse and rarely home, and her mom's also white boyfriend didn't give two fucks about whatever we were up to. He spent most of his time playing Xbox in her living room, sometimes alone, other times with this other guy named Toby. He didn't say much, barely even looked up, and that was perfectly fine with me. We could do whatever we wanted. Invite our friends, like this one Black anime-obsessed guy named Curtis, who I rarely saw outside of class because his parents were somehow stricter than mine. And we could leave Kelsey's place on a whim. Whenever the mood struck.

I could even smoke if I wanted at Kelsey's house. This fact titillated me. I loved that I could do it. And no, I did not. I'd just watch Kelsey smoke and felt very cool about it every single time. I liked to be around people who smoked weed. I liked to be around people who could tell their parents to shut up, who could drive their mom's boyfriend's car without a license to pick up Hot Cheetos and Snickers from Wallyworld around the corner, who could dye their hair all over, not just the undersides of their swoop.

Kelsey made me feel cool by association. The fact that she never did her homework, that she'd write gay *Fruits Basket* fanfiction during English exams—all of that only made me love her more. Because while Akito and Yuki made out in her notebook, I was furiously writing and erasing question B in hopes this grade would boost my chances of getting tapped into The National Honors Society. While she was getting caught smoking weed in the courtyard after school, I was at one of my many extracurriculars (show choir, student counsel, jazz choir) counting down the minutes till we'd meet again. We balanced each other out.

Kelsey strangely liked how my family would eat dinner at 6pm sharp. I liked how the only way we'd eat dinner most days at her place was if we threw together some ramen concoction in her kitchen by ourselves.

My favorite thing about Kelsey had absolutely nothing to do with her bad girl demeanor at all, though. Nope, my favorite thing about Kelsey is that, she too, was a devout Christian teen. I'm talking down-on-your-knees-for-prayer-before-bedtime-Christian. And since none of my siblings gave a flying duck about religion, and my mom had already made it very clear that I didn't need to do all this, I didn't have too many outlets to express Christian fandom. It was great.

Me and Kelsey could talk about how hot Hayley was, and how we couldn't wait to swoon at her feet come the next Warped Tour, but we could do it without being gay because, duh, we were Christian, and Christians aren't gay. Definitely not emo Christians. *Are you out of your mind?*

But of course, we were both very, very gay. Still, every one of our crushes from Gerard way to Ciara were shrouded in innocent emo giddiness. Our favorite thing was to hit up Christian screamo shows at the local indoor skatepark. She first invited me to one when I told her I got my parents to baptize me in middle school.

""That's *so* cool. I was just baptized as a baby, like I didn't even get to choose." She said.

Compliments from Kelsey were like shots of adrenaline. I'd get hyped up every time. I loved how she went up for me finding Christianity on my own. She'd say it made me cooler than anyone who was just born into it. I'd sit there, chest puffed out to Timbuktu. Then she'd point to a blurry picture on her flip phone of some cute screamo band, because Kelsey was cool enough to have one of those at 15.

"I think you'll really like these guys. The main one, Bryan, is like, very screamo, but he'll be saying shit like, "Thank God I didn't die, you know?" It's tight."

I loved when she cussed. I couldn't even say "dang" at home without my parents talking 'bout some, *Aht, aht, too close to the other word!*

We'd spend hours furiously bobbing our heads to local Christian screamo bands off Kelsey's burned CDs. We also loved bands like Emery, The Devil Wears Prada, Underoath. I liked how she never put the bigger bands on any pedestal. Very punk rock.

"Dang, they are tight!" I'd agree, wishing quietly the cop in my head would have let me have 'damn' this one time.

I even rocked an Underoath shirt Kelsey gave me to one of the local shows. Well, that along with the slightest bit of black liner and a serious emo swoop that drooped over my right glasses' lens. *Baby.* I felt grown.

The skatepark was in the whitest part of Shelby County I'd ever been in—Bartlett. It's the part of town my parents wouldn't let me practice driving because the cops over there are known to pull over a young Black driver in a heartbeat. But that night, beside my tall, pretty much passing friend Kelsey, surrounded by all those punk rock white kids, I could get away with more.

There I was, the Black exception. Feeling mighty special about it, too. That's how you get seeped in. You walk around feeling like the coolest kid around, cause these white kids who get to do whatever the hell they want accept you.

"Let's head up front," Kelsey said.

When we got there, it wasn't too crowded yet. There were a few booths repping local bands and shops scattered around the outskirts of the warehouse-turned-show-venue. Some sold jewelry. Others, mixed CDs. In front of us were two huge doors that led to an outdoor area with a taco food truck and a few fold-out seats.

A smattering of teens our age, and some kids who looked no more than 21 but were not at all high schoolers walked around. Slowly, of course, because cool kids walk real slow. This was a tough thing for me to learn, as I, to this day, walk like Freddy Krueger's on my case.

I'd tense up when I saw another Black person, constantly afraid they might be a Real One who would clock my game immediately. *Gay. Corny. Wack.* I knew that at any one of these shows was at least one group of all-Black punk kids who didn't try and opt out of their Blackness or weirdness to be part of the scene. They were a fearless group to me, of which I surely didn't see myself fitting into, because I knew they could see that I was not like them. I was not *fearless*. I was hiding. Surrounded by folks who were supposed to be my cover. Kelsey and I were the only non-white folks in our crew. I liked it that way. I couldn't tell you then why I liked it, or why I liked that in the right lighting, Kelsey looked like one of them. And I didn't even want to know why I felt this way. It was honestly much easier to just avoid, avoid, avoid.

By 8:30, it seemed like every emo kid in Shelby County was packed into that space. Every style of platform black boot and loafer you'll ever see in your life was planted firmly in front of that stage. Finally, the DJ turned up the background music playing in surrounding speakers. It was a song I recognized by Cool Hand Luke.

Setting up on the small stage in front of us was one of Kelsey's favorites, a local band called Follow. She'd gotten an autograph from the lead singer, Bryan, on the top of her hand and, in true Kelsey fashion, managed to not wash it off for over a week. By this time, we were a can of sardines, packed in the middle part in front of the stage, staring up at Bryan as he tuned his guitar with this stoic, albeit gorgeous, squint. I liked his face. I liked most emo-boy faces. Gentle, tortured. Perfectly framed in black liner and spikey and/or messy hair.

As if out of nowhere, Bryan yelled into the mic, "Ya'll ready to fucking party?"

That can of sardines started vibrating like a washing machine. We became one organism, waving, rocking, bopping to a continuous beat and right behind me. *Unh!* My first hit of the night. Right in my backside.

We were smack dab in the middle of a mosh pit, and there was no turning back now. I looked over at Kelsey. She shoved back. *I guess that's what you do*, I thought, so I shoved too, which you might have guessed leads to more shoving. Those first few shoves were nothing compared to when Follow sang the first note to their very first song. *Bam!* The party really started. Somehow it was always the biggest, tallest white boys jabbing my back and sides. Every single time. But there was no escaping, no, this was a sea of white rage, as far as the eye could see. I was trapped.

And by trapped, you might think I feared it, hated it. No, no, don't misunderstand. Yer boi was having a blast—the time of my life. Every hit was the sweet, sweet pain of a punch towards my salvation. I'd made it. I was officially an emo kid, and nobody could tell me any different. And I was in the trenches. I was shoving back! I was surrounded by kids who lived and breathed this life, and *I* was one of *them*. Finally, not just cool by association. I was so excited I didn't even notice the inch-by-inch shove closer and closer to the stage, to the point that Kelsey and I were literally up against it, the front of the stage folding into our stomachs with every hit.

I threw up my hands and waved them in the air while my body rocked here and there, only bringing them down to shove back the hardest hitters. I was a bobble head of excitement, grinning big up at Bryan who seemed to be feeding off our energy, screaming louder and louder and even more incoherently into the mic than how he'd started. Living.

He started jumping. We started jumping. He threw up a fist at the part about Jesus and we and all these white kids joined in. This single organism was very much in-sync. And then, he kicked me. He kicked, a classic, straight-out kick into the air, only it wasn't just air. Because my face was directly in front of his foot, and so I, ever so graciously, caught the end of his swing. Right in between the eyes. Down went my glasses. Black went my vision. I don't even know what happened in the next few moments, only the part where I tapped back into life, with Kelsey's arm around me. A small hollow ring around my silhouette as folks watched me hobble to my feet.

"I'm okay!" I promised and before I closed my mouth after that 'y' the kids swarmed all over again, recreating that pit as if it never left us. Kelsey was able to squeeze me out in the milliseconds between the re-swarm, but my glasses? Lost in the abyss.

"There's no way we're gonna find them in there!" Kelsey yelled over the music, which never stopped by the way, "Should we wait until it stops?"

We squeezed through the crowd and watched from afar. Then waited beside a jewelry booth that sold these things called gauges that I'd never seen before. *Note to self: gauges are cool.* And I, the true emo kid I was, nodded my bruised little head as hard I could to every song until Follow's set was done. Couldn't see a thing. I found my glasses in two parts—luckily salvageable with a bit of tape until my parents took me to the eye doctor a month later. But to me, it was all worth it. Because after Follow hopped off stage, the lead singer sauntered over to me and Kelsey and said,

"Yo, was that you up front? You okay?"

I died.

Life was the Doc Martin boot of a pale-bodied Christian screamo singer and I was a bruised ego, ready to be healed.

They say dreaming is free, but I wouldn't care what it cost me.

Lyrics from the Paramore's *26*

MY KICKSTARTER

Brooklyn, NY – Fall 2014

"Your tripod is lopsided." Says Jalisa, looking like a dollop of daisy in all white atop a furry bean bag chair. Poised in her spacious Pratt dorm room.

"Damn, okay."

I get up from the rolling office chair by the window where I've determined is the very best place to shoot. I loosen my too-tight bow tie and tugging suspenders before adjusting Jalisa's EOS Rebel Canon on the tripod she's so kindly loaned me for the next hour.

"How's this?"

"Yeah, that's fine." She nods, returning to a thick art history textbook.

I would be in my own place, if not for the family of mice currently asserting dominance in my bedroom. Plus, Belle, my roommate, had guests from out of town and who was I to ask them to simmer down for an hour so I can shoot a pitch video for my Kickstarter campaign. She was kind, and wouldn't mind, but I was nervous and also using politeness as an excuse to avoid admitting defeat to those damned mice. Also, Pratt's dorms were especially chic which made sense to me since it's an art school and most kids who went there, not including my sis, had old-money rich ass parents. It only made sense for me to take advantage of such aesthetics in this very important, pivotal moment in my life in which I begged strangers for money.

I didn't want to do it. Not at first. Well, not even then as I read and reread and attempted to memorize the script I wrote for this campaign video. But it'd been one year, over 75 query letters, two requests to read, and no offers. Yet, I still believed, perhaps naively, that someone somewhere would spot *Juniper Leaves* and simply have to invest in its success. But in the meantime, I delved into the demanding world of self-publishing, and it seemed so freeing. So affirming and empowering in a way traditional publishing wasn't. And I, the ever-dreamer, constantly painting nuanced realities in my favorite shade of rose, focused quite intently on the immediacy of it. Imagining the thought of funding and publishing all within the next six months. It sounded so wonderful. So perfect. Perfect, mainly, because this book had been nagging at my spirit ever since that night in 2012, a week before college graduation, that it came to me in a dream. I wrote its first draft the summer before I moved to New York. Now it was beginning to feel like the most poetic torture devise. I decided Kickstarter could be my knight in shining armor, saving me from this thing I once called a beautiful dream. And for a whole month I obsessed, as I did most things, on nothing but this very campaign, from the first paragraph on my Kickstarter page, to what I'd wear in the video.

I even reached out to one of the first grrls I'd ever been on a date with via Facebook. A sweet Persian illustrator named Aspen who was going to Memphis College of Art when we met on OkCupid that closeted summer of 2010. She's the only person I knew who could do the artwork for my book, who was also kind enough to accept being paid *after* my Kickstarter succeeded. I was that confident, or stubborn, to believe it would succeed. I'm not sure which, because I wouldn't allow myself to consider a reality in which this campaign failed. It could not fail. I wouldn't let it, because I needed every penny of the $3,600 I asked for.

To pay Aspen back.

For e-book distribution.

To pay an editor.

To market the book.

To print the first 150 copies of which many would go to my Kickstarter supporters.

I thought it was more than enough, but only if I got every single dollar. There was no way I could fund *Juniper Leaves* on my *Take Off* Assistant Editor salary of $35,000, of which most went to rent and bills, and dates I always paid for, and quickly increasing credit card bills, the rest to food and the occasional movie date with myself. And, oh yes, I could not forget my, quite frankly, thriving social life. Well, definitely thriving compared to any other point in my existence. But even there, I found ways to skimp on spending or drinks, or found gratis entries a la media passes and popular friends.

Amid all this planning and dreaming and obsessing I hadn't once looked at my actual book. It's as if my dreams for it lived outside of it now in some far-off land of dreams deferred. It was its own entity and my hopes for it, a whole other thing. Still, I knew with every bit of my being that the *idea* of *Juniper Leaves* was something quite special. A story about a Black queer teen girl who discovers magical powers amid grieving her late grandmother. It had legs! But then there was the fact that I knew nothing, really, about writing a book. And the insecurity around that, and the fact that despite my own knowledge I'd written it anyway and I knew, I *knew*, I had blind spots. I wished for guidance, for those nuggets of wisdom you only get from living life doing the thing you love for a long enough time. I settled with the idea of it though. The idea of this special something existing that first lived in a dream, that could reach other people with similar dreams. *That*. That was enough to keep me going. I hoped and prayed that someone, somewhere, who knew more than me, would believe in my work enough to help me cultivate the real thing into something great. Because I admit, even then, as I worked tirelessly on that Kickstarter campaign, I didn't believe I could do that. Not on my own. And right or wrong, the fact that I believed it made it true. Anyway, I had no time to dwell on silly shortcomings. I had a Kickstarter campaign to promote.

"You think I should send the link to Open Heart?" I asked Leesie.

Open Heart, the spiritual center my parents had been attending since I left for college, of which my dad had since become music director and my mom, a significant member of the board. I'd visited a few times over the years and every time felt a bit of shock at how wildly comfortable and at home I felt. Ma always made a point to say,

"It's not really a *church*."

Because it was more like a fellowship of genuinely empathetic, kindhearted quirky folk who gathered weekly to bond over how much they love their fellow human and the earth, and also disagreed with organized religion. And because everyone was so welcoming, and I'd actually witnessed not one, not two, but three queer couples there in the times I'd visited, it seemed like the perfect place to tout my new book.

"Probably. And I can send it to my friends, too." Leesie offered.

I quickly posted on my Twitter account. Sent out the press release to several of my media contacts I'd connected with over my short but budding professional writing career. I drafted a pitch email to Afropunk I planned to send that Monday, in hopes they'd feature my Kickstarter since I'd been writing for them over the past year.

And they did! But they made me write it under the guise of their "Gender Bent" section to make it seem like someone else did. I didn't mind. Whatever it took. I was the marketer, the public relation specialist, the fundraiser, the talent, whatever I needed to be to make this campaign succeed. And after just one week of the 30-day campaign, we hit 20 percent.

Then something happened that shook up the whole situation.

Janet Mock retweeted my campaign! I texted damn near every number in my phone.

This was no small thing. Especially for a tiny Twitter profile like mine, with under 900 followers. A co-sign from a trans icon?! Stunned wasn't the word. More like, ecstatic. Nearly speechless. In rolled a dozen more supporters; $10 here, $50 there, $100! $250, $150! For days, my campaign grew and grew with folks who found me through Janet. But soon the hype faded. Days passed where not even one person shared my campaign, let alone made a donation.

"You still got it though, have faith!" Ma said on one of our calls.

I can't lie, I got frustrated glaring at my campaign, frozen at around 65%. I resented people with larger followings who were good at social media, who didn't even need a celebrity co-sign. And all those other Kickstarter campaigns that reached their goals in a few days. A few hours! So many of them seemed to thrive in a way mine couldn't. Plus, I knew a YA novel with a Black queer protagonist was a rather niche subject to get behind, by a Black transmasc author no less. I was starting to feel like it wasn't just niche but irrelevant to most people. Like what on earth did my little book have to do with them? Why should *they* care? Why should anyone? Then, an email. No, *the* email blinked into my inbox:

Hi Jaz,

My name is Pam Plemons and I'm the creator of Black Lady Savage, an online and offline press centering queer and trans people of color. Janet Mock just tweeted me the link to your Kickstarter and seeing the info about your book, I wondered if you'd be interested in submitting it for consideration for publishing by Black Lady Savage Press?

Pam mutherfuckin Plemons. The brilliant Black queer woman author I'd followed on Twitter since having one, who's online blog I read religiously, *that* Pam.

I'd opted out twice to submit my essays to Pam's highly regarded blog out of pure intimidation. BLS only accepted the very top tier of prose and I simply didn't think I was ready to measure up to their standards. I would have never reached out to Pam about *Juniper Leaves* on my own. Not that I was a newb to rejection. I'd submitted to dozens of publications since moving to New York, many of which were quick to reject me. I figured it came with the territory for all the fools like me who chose this writer's life. It was the high regard with which I held BLS as to why I never reached out. I wanted to come correct. I considered Pam to be the epitome of Black queer greatness. I couldn't *believe* she liked the sound of my book enough to want to work with me. I was damn near frothing at the mouth with excitement, but also buckling at the knees with nerves. *Pam-gat-damn-Plemons wanted to work with me. Me?!* Passing up this opportunity seemed a highly irrational choice.

"Me?!" I screeched again all up in Heart's face that evening. Nursing a rum and ginger but mostly forgetting it because I was too dang excited.

"That's amazing, Jaz!" She cheered.

I smoothed back a clump of rebel strands stuck in her looped earring.

"Thank you. Oh my god, I'm a mess." She smiled, apologetic and sweet.

"So, what's happening with you?" I asked, as if we hadn't spoken hours ago.

I wasn't expecting an update on her current fling with some white woman fifteen years her senior who I found to be quite banal, actually. But I'd never tell that to Heart, even if she asked. I wanted her to know I supported her no matter what, because the thought of not having her around was too much.

In walked Casey, "DYKES!" They roared to a room full of them. All the dykes cheered.

As Heart, Casey and I headed back to the courtyard, Casey said, "So tell me 'bout this fucking book deal, dude!"

I loved how proud of me my friends were. I replayed the whole scenario—my surprise, the spirited ardor of relaying the news to my mom and Jess.

"See?! This is your destiny! Everything is coming right on together!" Ma said.

"Yeah, dude, I'm so happy for you." Jess said.

And then I showed Casey my initial email exchange, of which I'd spent way too many sentences gushing over Pam's work before officially accepting her offer.

They laughed, "Nah but of course you nerded out. I would too!"

And then I show them Pam's response.

Okay: I'm estimating about $3000 for the entire editing process (developmental, grammatical, and copy). I would LOVE to get this book ready to go on sale before Christmas. That's a tight timeline, but I'm a jump in and get it done sort of person. It's part of my genius. ;)

You have an artist who is doing your cover art already, yes? What fee have you agreed on?

"I haven't responded yet cause it's hella late, but I think we're gonna talk contracts tomorrow." I said, once I saw they'd finished reading.

I was instructed to pay her team before any edits began, before they'd even read my book. I didn't think much of it. If anything, I preferred it, wishing to stall on reading my poorly edited book as long as humanly possible. I would receive 35% of all book sales, electronic or otherwise. This was nearly half of what Amazon's self-publishing program offered, at 60%. However, fresh in my mind from researching traditional publishers was the mere 20-30% they offered to authors on a regular basis. I figured the exposure I'd get from BLS press would make up for the amount I'd be missing as a self-publisher. And plus, if anyone was going to own my work, I wanted it to be a Black queer woman. But the look on Casey's face...

Their head cocked to the side, chin raised, said, "Wait."

I frowned, not because I was upset but because I was confused, "What?"

"Your Kickstarter is how much again?"

"I'm trying to raise $3600. $600 for my artist but she's been really cool about possibly getting it later if anything ends up being over budget."

"And Pam wants *all* of that $3000?" Casey asks.

"Casey." I hated where this was going.

"I mean, it's a super small press, probably like 2 people on staff. I get that they don't have the funding." Heart said.

"Literally neither do you." Said Casey, "Like I'm not trying to kill the vibe it's just a little sus, no?"

"Anyway, enough about me and my shit, where's Kati?!"

I changed the subject to Casey's new main squeeze. They laughed and rolled their eyes and I smiled because it was over. Finally, no more questioning my dreams. I felt strange and uncomfortable and tired. Tired of inching towards the cliff of a years-long hope, so close now I could see the light. I erased this conversation from my psyche. I decided Pam's email was a sign that my campaign must, must succeed. And I moved on, I had to. The next morning, I submitted $755 to the campaign from my only credit card that wasn't currently maxed out. Brought the campaign up to 98%. I had to do it. I had no choice. The thought of losing Pam's support on this book... I couldn't even think about it.

body

sex drive always high

off this perpetual puberty

every year

a new body

every year

a new mind

I am so   becoming

still becoming

new

HORRIBLE BOSSES AND CROSSES TO BEAR

New York, New York – Summer 2015

The award for not giving a flying fuck goes to...drumroll... Dan Dearden! Well deserved, artfully gained, brilliantly, effortlessly unworked *so hard* that it couldn't possibly go to anyone else. I imagine his award speech would begin with a joke,

"Who, me? Guys, I'm hurt."

All to uproarious laughter from the entire *Take Off* staff who, despite doubling over at each of his witty gags, despised his impressively low work ethic and lack of attention to detail.

And I, admittedly, admired this about Dan. Me, someone who instead of strolling in late on most days, power walked in about one hour early to "prep" for any of my upcoming stories and blurbs for the week, all tightly wound like a wind-up toy. Unlike Dan, when I moved, it wasn't some whimsical flit followed by laughter and delighting eye rolls. No, it was feverish typing at my desk computer, or floundering to the printing room to get some info read for none other than my oblivious boss, Dan.

I'd never been more simultaneously annoyed, impressed and inspired. And I never thought I'd be so sad to see him go. We'd become friends, as close as our differences would allow. But trust, I knew Dan going was a matter of when, not if. There's only so many late mornings, error-filled galleys, and overall nonchalance one corporation can take. *Take Off*, in particular, gave him six months, with a nice little warning in between.

"Can you believe this shit?" Said Dan, huffing at a typed warning letter from our Editor and Chief, a punchy white British lady named Kerri.

I...could. But I wasn't sure how to respond to the guy I'd known to stomp out of a room when given a tough critique from one of our other editors. To avoid sparking some kind of scene I said my favorite vague indeterminate response,

"That's wild."

But with all this reality staring me right in my face, I didn't want to see Dan go. I enjoyed our inside jokes. The way he called me "kid" like the older brother I never had. And most of all, I liked that in this nerve-racking editorial position, that thousands of other new writer hopefuls vied for, I often felt okay. Because I knew that before anyone got on my ass about my shit, they'd go to Dan who inevitably did something way shittier.

Once he left, all of that changed.

Ariel replaced him within a week. She was a Columbian-white twenty-something woman who was nice enough, and immediately great with my pronouns, which is saying a lot at *Take Off,* where it seemed co-workers jumped at the chance to address me as "she." Let's just say my fingers were tired from pinging John, David, Mary and Sue every other weekday,

Friendly reminder, my pronouns are they/them. I'll also accept he/him.

Oh! Thank you, so sorry!

Cool, see you same time next week.

Most significantly, though, Ariel was a brilliantly diligent editor. Smart, savvy, well-read. A true perfectionist. Nothing like Dan, and with her brilliance came the magnifying glass over my own work that I'd yet to experience in my short but thrilling writing career.

"Jaz, did you read this over for grammatical errors because..." She trailed off.

Handed me a blurb I'd banged out an hour ago that I had in fact re-read for grammar, but not out loud (which is the only way I could know for sure I read it right). I felt uncomfortable reading aloud in public so often I'd skip it, which was never a good idea. I studied the blurb she gave me. I'd forgotten a period, and misspelled "their." *I before e except after C. C'mon.*

"Jaz, we're spending a lot of extra time on grammar. Something's got to change," She told me after two weeks of the same.

I'd already been on pins and needles with this new editor, and thanks to autocorrect so many of my usual errors were nevermore, but even with sharper eyes, I wasn't up to par. Nothing gets past Ariel and her well-trained journalistic eyes. I couldn't keep running from this glaring flaw. Couldn't keep being a writer who couldn't spell. The nerve! But I also couldn't tell her that I struggled with this sort of thing since childhood, that I'd trained myself beyond a lot of my own grammatical barriers, but that a learning disability made this sort of thing difficult. What a bizarre, ridiculous excuse for a writer.

Then there were the ugly whispers in the back of my head that said I'd clearly chosen the wrong profession, because amidst Ariel's very valid critiques were my dubious interactions with my new publisher. There wasn't a night I didn't lose sleep expecting an email from Pam that she'd changed her mind about working with me. I was so afraid she'd realize I was a hack of a writer. I thanked my lucky stars that she didn't ask to read my book after offering to work with me. And she still didn't ask before we signed our contract, and I sealed the deal with the $3000 from my campaign. No, it wasn't until we were official, and I closed out my Kickstarter, and announced to my 73 supporters, "*Juniper Leaves* is on the way!" that she emailed me to send over my book. I panicked. I knew she loved my idea. Had to, why else would she reach out? And I assumed she'd read the sample of it I shared on my Kickstarter profile. It was the best chunk of my book, hand-picked by me. But she had no idea, not really, of what lied within those 300-sum pages. She didn't know that I struggled with grammar or phrasing, or book structure, because I hadn't read enough books to know what the hell I was looking at. Or that the two friends I had read my book had returned it with the sole critique that it was "great!"

Boy, were we both in for a ride. I sent Pam my book the second she asked for it. Yes, that very second. Not even waiting an hour, or a day, or three days, so I could reread what I'd written. No. I know. I know now how impatience is the shadow of preparedness but no, no, no I simply couldn't wait to prove to myself that this was all real. I was finally a legitimate writer with a real, live publisher interested *in me*. I wanted to know, finally, from the mouth of a writer I admired, that I was worthy of calling myself a writer, because I didn't actually believe it myself. What a silly, silly, mistake. And by silly I mean life-altering. It all began with Pam dragging me from here to next week.

Hi Jaz,

I was not expecting this work to take such intensive edits...

At first, I was annoyed. Had Pam not read my Kickstarter pitch, which began with the words *My book is in need of extensive edits...*? I'd been very forthcoming about its flaws. It's the main reason I was raising money in the first place—to hire a diligent editor. Like, that was the *whole* point. Had she read my book first maybe she would have seen what I meant. Maybe she wouldn't have wanted to work with me at all, which was fine, because I was planning to self-publish anyway. But then I breathed in sweet humility. Because still, everything she had to say about my book was right and needed to be said. Her commenting on my need for edits was only fair. I knew it was true, so why be upset? Why wasn't I just letting Pam Plemmons, editor to tha gawds, do her job?

"Do you think it sounds like a lot?" My friends asked about the many red marks across my *Juniper Leaves* pages.

"I'm just glad to have a mentor finally, you know?" I said, because that feeling overwhelmed any other. That and the fact that this was all happening at all. I had email proof that *this, my dream,* was real now. I could tell my supporters, *this* was real. I proudly shared an update on Kickstarter:

Great news! Thanks to you and 73 others, Juniper Leaves: Quirky YA Fantasy Book has been successfully funded. Congratulations! Now you can visit the project's comments and celebrate with your fellow backers.

After I sent it, I refused to think about my book's flaws, or all the reasons I did not deserve a mentor like Pam and instead, celebrated. Drank. Took shots to remove the worry and planned to party in a place with loud music that might drown out ugly thoughts. My friends supported this plan.

"We're going to *the dungeon*!" Casey yelped over three-way with Heart and me.

A fitting celebratory location for a queer like me who had just woken up to the end of a new-ish fling the night before. My longest yet, at three months. I believed it ended because the person, named Avery, a very cute brown femme with stubble and an adorable smile, was too keen on my eager request to see them later that week after saying I could fully see us dating, like *really* being "a thing." I was ghosted. Anyway, what better day to visit a queer sex dungeon in the basement of an unassuming, upscale Cobble Hill brownstone? Avery, who??

"Let's get there around eleven." Casey requested, for a party starting at 9, "there's gonna be a cool demonstration at midnight."

And so, Heart and I arrived at 11pm sharp because even though we liked to party, we were still nerds who partied. We waited thirty minutes for Casey and their current main squeeze, Lucia, to arrive. They had an agreement.

"We can do whatever we want but it has to be together." Lucia explained.

The big, tall dyke-bouncer at the door was strapped under tight acid wash jeans, and a dark blue tank top. Beside them was a table with colorful bracelets where a pretty femme with blue hair told us, "Red means Taken/Not Looking. Green is 'Ready to Mingle.' Orange is 'just looking.'"

We all wore green.

"I'm nervous." Heart blurted, grabbing my hand. We looked like a couple, and I liked it. I squeezed her hand back, "Me too."

I felt jittery joy rush up from my toes to my cheeks. I was warm and tipsy, two whiskey shots in already from the bar around the corner. Drinks weren't allowed in the dungeon, for obvious reasons, but I assumed most folks weren't one hundred percent sober by how boldly they moved in the space. Clothed and unclothed. With and without harnesses, or strap-ons, or pasties. And not one cis man in sight. I know because in the event's email flyer they warned against it. This was a comforting notion for me, who had a perplexing relationship with cis men, especially the ones who could not understand how a body like mine didn't want to be fucked. I'd since discovered I didn't just prefer topping but was nearly stone. And most of my interactions with cis men, since those two transformative encounters in college in which I didn't know my lane just yet, were often an awkward though appetizing spread of nothing but sides. Fun, indeed, but still far less freeing trysts for me than any and all I'd shared with other non-men. So, parties like these were special. It was nice to know we were all in sync, no odd, out of sync little notes playing around, making assumptions about our bodies. And in these freeing spaces I didn't care so much what my partners looked like as long as that spark sparked and that hit hit.

I smiled at some of the folks like us who were fully dressed as if at some divey Lower East side queer bar. Bashfully blinked at others who were scantily clad. Flaunting lingerie, topless with panties, or any assortment of see-thru attire. Then there were the extra bold; the exhibitionist donning nothing but frisky grins and (sometimes) shoes. Pussies and grrl dicks and all other varying crotches on full display. These folks, though few and far between, seemed to do the most mingling, like they needed to make sure everyone, old and new, got a good look. I admired them. They admired me for admiring them.

Though the clump of the four of us was still very much a clump, we were all in our own worlds now, exploring within our bubble as if at a sex museum. Beside the entrance of this basement party were several cages like columns. Showers lined concrete walls, some open with transparent plastic covers, others with opaque curtains where you could only see someone's silhouette. It didn't take much focus to make out the gasps and moans resonating under the thump of a heavy bass out of surround-sound speakers. On a small stage a topless DJ with half-dollar sized gauges nodded almost violently to their house mix, fingers moving fiercely on a MacBook Pro.

"They're cute." Heart said over the music, nodding up at the DJ.

"Very." I agreed.

There were cute people everywhere. Hot people, sexy people, people having sex, everywhere. There were also a couple private rooms the size of closets, where couples could close doors. But even those had little peepholes for voyeurs to join in on the fun. This was a place to be involved, it was your only option.

I caught on quickly that the front room, where the DJ was, and where we were, was the mingling, casual part of the space. Queers often looked at other queer's wrists here. Up then down then up again, then speaking. It was a ritual of sorts. But if you were not approached, and not the aggressive type, you stood around pretending to be busy watching like it was your job. The back room, partitioned with an open wall where a large door used to be, is where shit really got poppin'. That's where we were headed, like four baby deer searching for our mother.

The backspace was like a different world. A wonderland of carnal desires. The moans were louder here, along with the sound of whips and assertive commands. Right at the opening of the back space was a group of five hot and heavy queers. Well, more specifically, four topless folks surrounding one excitable and wanting naked person on a wooden bed. Each taking turns pouring hot candle oil on their bare bodies. One of them, a cute Asian person with short curly hair, motioned to us.

"Hi cuties." They said, wincing with sweet pleasure while someone poured oil on their nipple.

It was an invitation sort of, "Hi."

But the thought of getting naked already was far too daunting for me to grasp. Casey smiled back at us. Oh, they were *down*, down. But Lucia wasn't feeling it.

"We're just watching for now." Lucia said finally. The person shrugged and delved back into the scene.

Heart pulled away from me to take her phone from her pocket. She unlocked it and read something, and I pretended not to notice the smile blossoming on her face. She texted something and put her phone away. In the very back of the space a small crowd watched a gorgeous fat femme in spiky lingerie whip a scrawny, older trans man in a cage, spouting raunchy insults at him, even spitting on him to his utter delight. All his responses ended in, Madam Queen, which I loved. So enthralled by this scene, I jumped a bit when the DJ said, through a too-loud microphone,

"Everyone gather around for a presentation by our very own Lady Play and Mika Graft!"

So we headed back up and found an opening for us to stand to experience this scene. I saw Heart pull out her phone again, texting faster this time. I believe I heard an actual giggle. Then a contemplative look washed over her face.

"Hello, hello, my name is Lady Play! This is my sub, Mika Graft." Said the woman in pasties and leather tights in front of us, "Today we're gonna show you how to use nipple clamps...Spoiler alert—they aren't just for nipples."

Horny laughter all around. Sitting behind Lady was a fully nude Mika, a genderqueer sexy person with a very hairy nether region. The DJ played a somehow soft and chill House track. Heart's hand rested on my shoulder and I felt warm, but then I realized she was tapping it. She had something to say,

"I'm gonna head out."

Her expression, coy. I knew this coyness was residual. It was for someone else.

"Oh?" I said, unsure how to respond.

She handed me her phone. Pointed to the last text, from her on and off and on and currently off, almost girlfriend.

The text said:

Whatever you wanna do there you should do it to me. Right now

I wanted to cringe. I forced a smile instead, going, "Yooooo. Go get you some," over the noisy thud of my heartbeat.

Heart said goodbye to everyone as quietly as she could, and when the crowd cheered at Lady Play making out with Mika, she snuck out. I kept watching the scene, smiling like a clean towel over mess on the floor. I couldn't even tell you why. I was quite literally watching the sexiest thing I'd ever seen, but all I wanted to do was be the someone Heart left this party for. After Lady made Mika come an expressive five times, they ended the presentation and welcomed us to mingle among ourselves.

"That was crazy hot." Casey laughed, arm around Lucia.

They were beginning to envelop each other. I'd become the third wheel.

"Oh my god, get a room." I joked.

"Maybe we will!" Casey said.

A hand rested on my shoulder then and I turned to find a tall, older, sophisticated afro Latina woman with brunette hair that flew out and down past her shoulders.

"This ya first time here?" The woman asked me with a thick New York accent I couldn't quite place.

Casey flashed me a cheeky grin, like a nudge.

"Uh, Yeah..." I said.

I just know I looked nervous as my shaky voice sounded. This woman was beautiful. Her name was Fatima. She wore a see-through bralette top, boy shorts, high heels and the most intense bedroom eyes I'd ever seen. I shooed Casey and Lucia, who were now engulfed in their own steamy lust filled air.

"You good here—" Casey asked between Lucia's kisses.

"Go, go!" I said, laughing.

They ran off into one of the private rooms.

I was alone now, with Fatima.

"These little 'parties' are white as hell." Fatima said with a sultry giggle.

"Right?!"

She was right. Separate from us, there was one other Black person. A few Asian folks held it down, a couple visibly Latine folks too, but everyone else white as the day was long. We sat on the bench and talked for what felt like fifteen minutes but was actually more like ninety. Fatima was 35 to my 24, a public lawyer and artist. Also a Harlem native who just started exploring Brooklyn for the first time in 35 years. Between laughter we kissed, we held hands. We acted like we'd known each other much longer than less than a day.

"Let's go somewhere." She whispered to me, kissing me so softly on the cheek. Shivers flew down my spine. I let her lead me out of the basement back onto Planet Earth with the rest of the humans, but us together felt otherworldly. I wanted whatever she was ready to give.

While we waited for a taxi, I texted Casey that I'd left. I didn't expect a response any time soon. Not when I'd just heard a very distinct moan from the private room they'd entered. I sweat as she touched herself in the back of the cab, stopping when she thought the driver might notice. I couldn't believe what was happening. How my night had unfolded. I embraced it. She whispered in my ear all the things she wanted me to do to her, promised she'd teach me all of it. And it felt different. Somehow more real than any of my other escapades. Like we saw each other too clearly to call this dreamy. We were too raw, too vulnerable to feed each other empty platitudes, for me to fall into infatuation like I often did. I was intrigued by this feeling. Scared of it and intrigued.

"I have so much to show you." She mused, her voice like good black coffee; incredibly strong and frothy, thick and hot.

She kept her promise. After three hours and a dozen little deaths we settled into her luscious satin sheets. Took turns nuzzling little kisses into each other's bends and grooves. I told her that I was from Memphis, TN, a place she'd been before, and she told me she was shocked I was from there with so many white friends. I laughed. I could do nothing but, because she was right to question it. I didn't tell her she was right. She knew that I knew. And I could tell by the smirk on her face that she knew my *why*. I changed the subject. I said, I'd only just started dating seriously a few years ago.

"I've never had a partner for real. Not really..." The second half was a new realization for me. I'd dated two boys in high school but I never *like*, liked them. We never did anything but kiss and I always thought of other things when we did that. And, of course, there was John, but that's a whole other story for another chapter (called Love Interest #2) ...

"Is that what you want?" She asked me.

I immediately thought of Heart, "Honestly, yeah."

It was an understatement. I wanted to love someone and for someone to love me more than I wanted water, food, sleep.

"Yeah you want it bad. I can tell." She said.

She saw right through me. So, I told her about Heart. Told her that I thought our first outing was a date, but for Heart we'd always been just friends. That she was seeing someone, a woman that didn't treat her well.

"It low key feels like we're already a couple, like it's almost weird," *Whew*. I was gushing.

But she did not respond the way I thought she would. No hand over heart, *how sweet*. Not at all—Fatima threw her head back with a laugh straight out her gut and said,

"You out here fiending off a white girl. With *blonde* hair?!"

Her response threw me. Laughter broke out of my mouth like a cough, and I laughed and laughed at the stark reality of my hurting heart. I *was* fiending off a white girl. A white girl with blonde hair and blue eyes, no less. But it wasn't even her whiteness that was the issue, no. The whiteness only symbolized how far from myself, a Black ass person from a Black ass town with mostly white friends in this colorful city, had been running from. It only offered Fatima a shorthand of my longing, of which she'd lived enough to know to flag so that people like myself might look within and then decide the necessary answer to the question; *Why do you long for this unrequited love?* I told myself I wanted Heart because she was the one for me. Because we made so much sense together and I never, not once, let myself explore why. Never questioned how, beyond handholds and longer-than-average glances, I could jump to the conclusion of her potential romantic love for me. Not once. Yet, and still, I wanted her. I wanted to be with someone who couldn't even see me full enough to know I was in love with her. *Why?*

"You're right." I said, as if stating the right answer to a classroom question, even though I quietly disagreed.

Her soft hand grazed my torso, and then she squeezed, "*Babeeee!* My advice to you; leave her alone."

I laughed, again not knowing what else to say. I shook my head and didn't know what I was trying to shake off. Fatima grabbed a hair tie from her dresser and wrapped sweaty damp tresses into a bun.

"I am telling you from experience." She said.

"Hmm." Is all I could muster.

Is this what conversations are like when someone really sees you? I didn't know if I liked this. Maybe I hated it.

"You know what? You remind me of me back in the day. Running from myself, insecure as fuck."

I'd never said I was insecure. I winced at this assumption. I grazed her shoulder with my fingers, trying to return to this present moment and not disappear. She smiled at me and looked away, off somewhere, "It's like, it started to look like I didn't love myself, you know?"

I nodded. I said nothing. Then she said nothing and we lay there, quiet and both living in our own minds.

"Yeah... "I finally let out like a long breath I'd held in.

She kissed me. I kissed her back, "You're so beautiful." I said.

"I know!" She laughed, head thrown back, throat bouncing with joy.

Her confidence against my own self-doubt felt like a strong wave coming over me. I was refreshed but left needing a change of clothes, of heart. It made me laugh because it excited me, as if it was a thing she just showed me I could have too, and it looks so funny and good in the light. We laughed together, until that laughter left us. Until I couldn't anymore. She then got up, grabbed a robe, and wrapped it around her glistening body. I watched her pick my clothes off the floor and tried to hide shock when she handed them to me.

She kissed me on the forehead and said,

"This has been amazing, but I prefer to sleep alone."

It was 5 in the morning. She called me an Uber and dug around in a drawer by her bedroom door. She pulled out a card while I waited. It was her business card.

"Call me if you want, but you better not be losing sleep off no white girl if you do."

I laugh because it's the easiest thing to do. But we both knew I wouldn't call her. Even when I'd let Heart go, like she said. Fatima was too real for me. I needed to figure out how to be real with myself before any other time with her could feel like peace. I would almost call Fatima on a Saturday months later, when Heart was still just a friend, but I was okay with it this time. I would press in her whole number but never hit *call*. I would feel too small and green to call up a woman who knew herself so well she could see through people who didn't have that same skill. And it was probably for the best that I didn't call her, and that I found a therapist instead, because before Fatima, I'd never noticed how much it looked like I didn't love myself.

There are no wrong questions, only wrong answers

I asked for freedom at a young age

before I knew its meaning

I'd been so good, I said to God

God said

freedom is for the afterlife

salvation is sweeter, if only you'd just wait

I said to God

no thank you

I'll find this thing myself

and perhaps there are

wrong

right answers

depending on who you ask

LOVE INTEREST # 1: MEGAN

Memphis, TN - 2000

Megan, oh, Megan. The sun didn't set if Meg didn't flash her gap-toothed grin my way at least once before fifth-grade lunch. And closing my eyes for bed at my usual 9pm simply could not happen if I didn't write in my journal the many special moments we shared throughout the day.

Today Megan and me didn't have to do the workout in gym class because we got into the science fair finals.

This morning Megan said she liked my shirt. I think I'll wear it again tomorrow.

Meg had a cool gel pen in class. She said she'd get me one too. She's really nice.

She was my first friend. My first *best* friend. My favorite person. I mean, okay, I had friends before her, if you agree that siblings and cousins can be friends. And I had tons of hangouts if you believe playing make-believe while homeschooled among one's two sisters and two brothers is no different than any a playdate among neighborhood kids. But if that's in fact a foolish concept to you, then, yes, I was friend-less until I met her.

I saw her first. I think. Because I was the first kid to enter Ms. Brown's class and my assigned seat was quite close to the entrance. I didn't know what to do with my hands, so I clasped them atop my desk and stared right at that door as our teacher greeted every one of her students with that gentle, calming smile. Megan was a little white girl with bone-straight, mousey-brown hair. I remember thinking, *Wow, she looks like Veda* (the main character from *My Girl*, my favorite movie at the time). I'd tried to draw Veda many times in fascination of her face. As if her face was anything to be fascinated by. But in Memphis, white kids weren't too common, and so seeing Julia's pale little mug and limp, mousey brown hair up close was new to me. Especially since white-flight was still very much persistent in early-2000s Memphis, in which many white parents opted for private schools or whiter areas like Germantown and Bartlett. Definitely not Memphis-proper if they could avoid it.

We didn't speak until lunch time. What a daunting ritual that is, school lunch. A gym-sized room covered in long benches and tables, enveloped in the scent of prison-grade lunch meat and government cheese. A bunch of rowdy or quiet, or loner, or popular children hustling into one space, hopeful or woeful of who or where they might be sitting next to. I quickly sat towards the entrance once again, braced for a quick escape. Equipped

146

with a smushed, vegan grilled cheese encased in a *Lion King*-themed lunch box along with an apple and a fruit punch Capri Sun. I faced the giant ceiling to floor windows, of course. *Perfect, I can see the road.*

"Hi." Is the magic word when your name is Megan Cleaver.

I didn't respond right away. Too obvious. Clearly it was more sensible to chomp a mammoth-sized bit of my silly little sandwich and wait till my mouth was full before, through chews, saying "Hi," back. She wore a lavender, floral print shirt under overalls and shoes that lit up when she walked.

So, I word vomited a compliment, "I love your outfit. And your earrings! And your shoes!"

Pretty much sounded like one big word.

"Thanks!" She laughed, "Your outfit's really cool, too."

She had an adorable way of speaking that turned "Rs" into "Ws," so it sounded more like, "Your outfit's weally coo, too."

I rarely smiled all the way. My go-to? A slightly curved mouth that didn't show what I felt were vampire-like fangs. But my teeth revealed themselves despite myself and my eyes, trying to dart anywhere but her face, twinkled at her with delight. And when she smiled back at me with that gap-toothed grin, I wanted to spew out my innermost thoughts. But I didn't tell Megan what I was thinking. That she would be my first friend. Though in hindsight, I believe we had the same thought. That

Friday she came to my home for the first time, and the next week I came to hers, and back and forth and back and forth again until we were best friends. Two years went by and we stayed close, even when I went back to homeschool in 4th grade or returned to Brownsville in the 5th but had a different homeroom teacher than her. Then came the summer of 5th grade.

"Are you sure you can't come to Colonial with me?" Meg asked, both of us depleting into her plush green pleather couch.

"I wish!" I'd screech, "My mom said I'm not in your district anymore." I didn't really know what that meant. I only knew that my family just moved from a house in Raleigh, to the annex of Millington/Memphis in house on a hill my parents built. Literally twice the size of our old place, and next door to horses, but no other children. I'd have to be bused to the closest middle school in Millington, TN.

"Well, one day we'll be in New York and none of this will matter anyway." Megan shrugged.

I agreed, grabbed a Dorito and sunk into the couch a little bit more.

Over my last few visits, we'd been watching the last season's tapes of *Sex and the City*. We beamed at the screen as rich and bougee white women found themselves in yet another glamorous pickle. I didn't care so much about the storyline, though something about Samantha's unbridled freedom intrigued me. No, it was New York City, the quietest, loudest most iconic character in *Sex and the City*, that kept me at the edge of my seat.

"We should get a studio like that one." I pointed at the screen as Carrie sat at her little desk in her West Village apartment.

"And we can get a bunk bed." Meg cheered. We both dreamed of living together, cooking for each other, prancing down the streets of Manhattan arm-in-arm.

Sex and the City is the first time I heard the word gay. It was, sadly, not when I saw my Auntie's studly "roommate" of eight years at varying family gatherings, or my older gay cousin from Cali whose wrist refused to erect itself. No, it was when Charlotte consulted her girls about the Pastry Chef she'd been eyeing, asking if he was gay. *Huh*. Everything clicked.

"Do you think you're gay?" I blurted out mid-show, to a gasp from my best friend.

"Do *you*?!" She retorted, and we laughed because it was the easiest way to cover our discomfort.

In my diary before this, I'd written about a girl. Not a girlfriend, because I had never known of girls loving girls, but a girl, who was my friend, who would live with me and hold my hand and love me and we'd do everything together. She would kiss me sometimes, but only on the cheek and we'd live in New York City. I knew after watching that episode, I would need to tear out those pages. Somehow, I knew that gay was not a thing that I could be. I wondered if Megan had pages somewhere like mine. Gay pages.

"No, for real." I pressed, when we'd both calmed ourselves.

At my house we had one TV and no cable, because,

"Children have plenty other things they can do than watch television." Said by both parents, more than once.

My favorite shows at the time were *Bill Nye the Science Guy* and this new show *Zoom,* starring just kids (that I secretly felt I could be great on). Only at my Grandma Palm's house would I catch something I knew full well I wasn't supposed to see on my cousin KeKe's bedroom TV, like a bootleg of *Friday* or *BeBe's Kids,* or one of Tyler Perry's plays. But the Joyner kids didn't speak of those. We didn't use the word "booty" even though it was the funniest word in the world, and we were deprived of saying "da bomb" because, "People are dying in the middle east." So, I longed for my visits to Megan's to learn one more word from a world that felt more honest to me than the one I'd been told to believe.

"I don't know." Megan shrugged finally, unable to look at me. It was okay though, because I couldn't look at her, either.

"Me either." I said, still looking away.

And she un-paused our tape featuring that utopia, where some people were gay and everyone was allowed to talk about it. That night Megan set out gummy bears and Doritos, and Sprite, *and* vegan chicken nuggets from the only natural food store in Memphis called Squash Blossom, just for me. Megan never made fun of me for being vegan, even though I realized how strange it was for me, a Black kid from Memphis to have never had barbecue.

"I hope these are the right ones," Meg said, grabbing a chicken nugget for herself to try, "I told my mom they only have them at Squash Blossom.

That's the name of the natural food store before it became Wild Oats, and then eventually Whole Foods decades later.

"You did!" I beamed.

The credits rolled and Meg hopped up.

She returned *Sex and the City* to its tape case and back into the cabinet in her comically large entertainment system where there were rows and rows of video tapes behind tinted glass. She pulled out a cover that read "Jerry Springer: Too Hot for TV" and waved it at me like the Cheshire cat. Nervous shudders ran down my spine at the very sight of "Too Hot" in the title. Meg put in the tape without saying a word, only a giggle. I wasn't smiling.

"Wait." I said, like a reflex before she pressed play. I swiveled my head around as if my parents would pop up from behind the couch and say, "Gotcha!"

But unlike my mom, who was typically four reasonable footsteps away at all times, her mom, who was older than most moms with kids my age, who'd met Megan's dad during a drug-laden 70s party, had retired to her bedroom where she'd be reading, or doing whatever the hell she did while recorded meditative drones welled well into the late-night hours.

"She wants me to have my own time, so I don't grow up resenting her like she did with her mom." Megan explained matter-of-factly.

Luckily her dad had a late Philosophy class at Rhodes College that day. Otherwise, he would have dropped in at least five times already saying a variation of,

"What's happening, cool kids? Oh! Don't let me interrupt ya', just leaning on the wall trying to soak in some of this *cool*."

Megan would look at me and roll her eyes and her dad, who 9 times out of 10 would throw his head back, open his mouth like your least favorite muppet and guffaw like he thought he was on some loveable sitcom. He wore blue-tinted glasses half the size of his pale round face.

"He used to do a lot of drugs." Megan'd whisper when he'd say something too weird like,

"Cool hair today, quite Africana. You know, I once taught philosophy in Ghana..."

Thank goodness I never once had a chance to answer any of his questions because he'd interject with what I'm sure he believed were fascinating stories from his heyday pre-1990 (the year his first child was born). Megan's younger sister (her *only* sibling) who looked older and towered over her by a good four inches, was at her own sleepover that night. So, we had the whole place to ourselves. Still, Megan had to assure me again because I was frozen as a statue with the look of terror in my eyes.

"It's fine! I promise." She shoved me. I let out a pitiful giggle.
"Don't be such a nerd." She pressed. She knew that'd do it.

"Oh my god, fine!" I motioned to the tape. She pressed play and it began.

Whoa. Jerry didn't waste no time. Right out the gate two thin Blonde white women danced around with their tits all the way out. A topless little woman came out dancing. The crowd cheered like a bunch of hungry animals and there Meg and I sat, frozen. Mouths agape. I glanced at her as quick as I could, my worst fear was that she'd look back at me, because then we'd both have to face what the other one had to be thinking.

This is amazing.   *This is amazing.*

Out came Jerry Springer's first, ever-infamous guests. A busty white woman in a denim skirt and tub top with brown hair who sounded like she'd stepped out of the pages of

153

Southern Comfort magazine. She told Jerry she was angry at another woman off screen who tried to steal her man. Queue The Other Woman ™, a Latina in a strapless dress, who rushed onto the stage swinging.

"Fight naked, fight naked!" The hungry crowd chanted. I gawked at this captured fever dream as both women obeyed! Dress, skirt, bra: everything off. For some reason they both allowed each other to strip before jumping right back into punches and blows, big men in black following them, readjusting their mics each time a garment fell.

I refused to look anywhere but straight ahead as the man in question entered, raising both hands to the crowd as if to big up himself. The Latina woman walked up and grabbed him and I must have blinked because out of nowhere, there they were making out as if no one else was around.

I grew hot, itchy, soaking with sweat underneath my armpits, tingly in the place I wasn't supposed to think about right now according to my mom's recent Talk. I'd felt this way before. During some of *Sex and the City*'s sex scenes. But I didn't know what to make of the feeling.

"You getting tired? I'm getting tired." I blurted out.

Megan finished my sentence with, "Yeah, same!"

Thank god. The tingling feeling was an eruptive one, urging me to do something about it as if I knew what could be done. It was like an itch and I refused to scratch. There's no way my feeling this way was a *good* thing. A thing that was even allowed. Besides, it really was late, and Megan's mom agreed to take us to the park early the next day. I needed my rest, okay?

Meg put away the video quicker than a hunted fly racing towards an exit. And she followed me up the stairs to her room. I played a game of changing into my night clothes without any hint of my skin revealing itself. Megan didn't get the memo, taking off her shirt revealing a training bra, and then frilly panties. The tingle wouldn't go away. It grew. I itched all over. Megan grabbed a pillow and threw it at me, perhaps trying to ease the tension, but I just wanted her to look away. It forced the giant night shirt I'd planned to pop over my head, to the ground.

"Fight naked! Fight naked!" She laughed.

I picked up my shirt, covered my chest and threw the pillow back at her in one fell swoop. This is, by far, the quickest I'd done anything, ever. I put on my shirt, finally. Right, then, the pillow hit me again. My cheeks were hot and prickly. I wanted not to laugh, but it bubbled out of me like an overflowing tub. I grabbed the other pillow off her bed and smacked her right in her face. No turning back now. Our pillow fight had commenced. And we laughed. And we giggled and laughed and laughed and fought the tamest battle.

Until, "Not too loud my loves," Her mother said over recorded Oms.

Her voice startled us both, so we jumped into Megan's bed, her first, then me on top of her. Not on purpose, it's just where my body landed, but now that I was here, we couldn't stop laughing.

"Fight naked!" I whisper-yelled on top of her as we pretended to wrestle.

Infectious laughter bouncing between us. I couldn't stop feeling good about us and this, and the moment, even though I knew I shouldn't. Especially when the laughter faded. I don't' know how or why, but it faded and we were left with just ourselves. Me on top of her, quiet, close, so close until we both let our lips touch. Stopping so quickly when I remembered we could not. Less than one second. But what a precious millisecond that was. And neither of us cringed, or shook our heads, or said a thing about what happened. Instead, we fell back on her bed and stared up at Megan's starry ceiling. Giggled a little bit more. Breathed in, and out.

"I'm really gonna miss you next year." I said, when we'd caught our breaths.

"I know. It's gonna suck." She said.

"You think we'll stay best friends?" She asked me.

And I let the question swim around for a moment in the depths of my mind. I didn't know what I was feeling, but it seemed both sad and happy, somehow at the same time.

"Duh!" I said. Wanting so badly for it to be true.

on reading and the signs

if

an earth sign will read you down

a fire sign will let it burn

an air sign will blow you away

a water sign will drown you in your own tears

how

would you like to feel?

LOVE INTEREST # 2: JOHN

Vanderbilt University – 2011

Vanderbilt is the Harvard of the South, and by south, I mean, "Girl, this is a football game. Where's your sundress?!"

By this time, I'd shaved my head under the guise of "the big chop" and didn't own one dress to my name, let alone a doggone sundress. But it was tradition, so at the one game I went to rocking a vintage Titans jersey I stood out like a sore thumb. Girls wore sundresses and boys seersucker suits—To every game, and it was strange *not* to, even in the year of our gawds 2009, the year I joined my big sis Jess who already attended this prestigious PWI (Predominantly Warped Institution). Not that I was following her. More that I was following my mother's hopes and dreams for me, her dear, albeit odd second oldest. She hated that I'd been going to Middle Tennessee State alone. I only went there because in a feeble rebellion, I applied to only NYU, and when I didn't get in, and realized I couldn't pull off a one-way trip there on my own, MTSU was the only place away, but not too far from Memphis that accepted my late application. But I hated it there. I hated it so much that I did so well in my classes I could transfer anywhere else. But I didn't go anywhere else. I took me and my fresh batch of student loans to Nashville, with my older sister Jessica, where at least I wouldn't owe anything else with Vandy's new financial aid program.

"If anything happens, I'm a quick 2-hour drive away!" My mom said for the forty-fourth time, even though Nashville is technically a 3-hour drive from Memphis. As if those extra thirty minutes gained now that I'd transferred from Murfreesboro to Nashville were truly that significant.

But life would be better, now. For one, I'd be around people. Free time at MTSU was spent mostly in my giant dorm I shared with no one, watching torrented episodes of *The L Word,* refusing to eat. If not there, I was in the gym, running lap after lap until I nearly collapsed in hopes of losing 15 instead of gaining. Mind you, anemia and fatigue were already plaguing my thin body before this. So much so that my period had stopped, and I wasn't even on birth control. Yet, come holidays, my family complimented me on the shape of my pain. And so, I'd return, motivated to disappear a little bit more all over again. Viscerally devastated any time I accidentally caught a glimpse at my still curving hips in a mirror. It's so much easier to disappear when no one else is around to find you. Not at Vanderbilt. As soon as I got there all that changed. Not because I wanted it to, but because not only was my sister *right there* but me and a few transfers clicked almost instantly during orientation. So, I couldn't hide out in my room starving on purpose because these new friends would drag me to at least two meals in the common area every day and would make very awkward comments if I called myself not eating. And I couldn't possibly leave my room at 3am for one of my doomsday strolls, nearing dangerously close to the edges of any a tall building because any time I left my room at least one of my new friends would pop out like a Wack-A-Mole to chat. And we would enjoy each other as much as a closeted, depressed Black weirdo, one funny, well-meaning rich Jewish girl, a shady Asian party girl and a waspy, sapphic, though wildly confused white girl could. Things were okay for a while, two years in fact. But then, two graduated, and one moved on after a dramatic, 2-on-1 fall-out.

And so, in 2011, I began senior year alone once again. Alone with many thoughts from a quietly homo summer that I'd spent driving my parent's van to Midtown several nights a week to date girls, hang out at Memphis College of Art, and go to OUTMemphis' queer youth meetings. Returning to Vandy felt like going backwards after that. The only thing sustaining me was what lied on the other side of graduation. A fancy degree to help me thrive in my dream city, finally, New York. I'd planned to go there right after high school, skipping college all together. I'd always hated school, and it made perfect sense to me that I'd run off and go be free, but no. I'd told myself I'd put it off for my mom. She needed me close. I prided myself on always being there for her. I did not want to admit that her convincing me was easy because I feared so much of all the things I said I wanted. I wanted to exist fully, but I also knew that doing that meant sacrificing some of the things that I felt I needed. Financial security, a nice place to sleep, love from my family that

I feared would wane were I to cash in on New York dreams too soon. So, college was my sacrifice. One last ditch effort to practice normalcy.

I started Pre-med like everybody else, then all sorts of random, uninteresting majors until Film Studies, because one special film professor, Jonathan Rattner, who became my advisor, saw me clear enough to know I simply wanted to create. Once I told him about the classes I hated the least, he pointed out to me that they were all in Vandy's small but diligent film studies program, and that, when it comes to being creative, it's always best to stick with what you love. "Love." A bit of an overstatement then, seeing that no class made me *happy* but at the very least, Film studies made me not want to quit college, and I needed that motivation. So back to classes I went, alone, indeed, but with a second wind motivated by a New York future. Well, alone until I met *him*: John. Early in the year. A gorgeous young Black man with the luscious timbre of a career baritone who drinks honey lemon tea before bed. He was *actually* pre-med with doctor parents and so much drive I was convinced he'd own his own practice within the decade. I worked the front desk at Hank Ingram residence hall as part of my work study. You know, a cute $7.25 an hour answering calls, and student's questions. Chill enough to half ass my homework. Unless distracted by a handsome man darting his dark brown eyes my way as he ambled down the stairs holding fiftyleven heavy textbooks. Backpack stuffed, too. An overachiever.

"Hi." He mouthed. I smiled. Or I was already smiling.

I didn't notice his roommate beside him, who, funny enough, had been talking the whole time. He gave his friend a nod and the friend exited the building. He lagged behind...

"Hey, do you live here?" He motioned to the building.

"Oh my god, stranger danger," I laughed, regretting my words immediately.

"No!" He chuckled, "I mean, I haven't seen you here before, I was wondering..."

"I'm in Barnard." I said, straight this time.

Barnard was one of the few residence halls on campus where I could nab a singles dorm. Not many spaces on campus had those, and after having my own room for a year for the first time in life at MTSU, I couldn't stand the thought of another roommate. Though someone like me, prone to months-long bouts of depression and hours-long, frighteningly macabre internet searches a la death and dying probably could have used one. John would know nothing about any of this. I liked that. I had a chance to reintroduce myself, no excess sludge from previous encounters weighing me down. He smiled.

"Cool, cool." He said.

I liked his face. We took a break in each other's eyes.

I returned first, "What's your name?"

"John." The word left his mouth like an invitation. I accepted.

My heart fluttered when he asked for my number. Flew when he asked, "When are you off?"

I agreed to meet him for a late dinner in the Commons after work. We exchanged numbers and I floated on a cloud for nighty straight minutes till I could sign out and hand over the desk to the next student worker. His dorm was on the fifth floor. I became very familiar with the abstract blue poster beside his bed and the red, goopy lava lamp beside his keyboard. And that his roommate, Ben, was never around...

"You're...the only one other than Ben who knows I do music." John told me in that mollifying murmur he spoke.

He made pop music based on his own poetry but refused to listen to other artists. We bonded over original poems, some made into songs.

"I don't want to be influenced by anyone." He'd argue.

"But, you're gonna be influenced regardless?! Why not be intentional about it and listen to songs you like?" I rolled my eyes to the back of my head with every bit of drama, as if I hadn't felt this same way not too long ago.

Secretly, I was amused by how stubborn he was. Openly enthralled when he sang. Flattered when he asked me to join him. We'd flutter between piano notes, our voices clasping each other on a musical journey. Much about him amused me. Most of all, his hopeless devotion to God. I understood him. I liked that he spoke about God so lovingly, so matter-of-factly, sometimes. I told him that I used to be a staunch Christian up until I turned 16, that over the years I began to ask the right, or wrong questions, that led me down a road of disbelief. I could not fix my mouth to tell him about those questions. I did tell him, though, that when I was 19, I'd stopped praying to God for good. He seemed intrigued by this fact, as if it was close enough in my past that he could still pull me back in. And I was intrigued, because I knew this loving way he spoke of a Christian God did not tell the full story. I liked to poke holes in his logic. I think he enjoyed challenging my doubts.

"I know it's not cool to be a Christian." He looked away from me. I reached for his arm. He pulled it away, laughing playfully.

"Nah, you on that Satan." He joked, pulling away but staring me down still. I'd laugh the hardest.

I told him religion was my issue, not the idea of a higher power, the Universe, something bigger than us all. He'd laughed at me avoiding the word God. I laughed that John so quickly called God a "He." We amused each other. But John also baffled me. He wasn't enchanted by bible stories, rarely translated them in the ugly ways I'd seen Christians do. Instead, he'd bask in their complexity, always happy to dissect lessons with me from one of his daily reads. As if that might sway me.

"Yooo, how can you roll your eyes at a story about love?" He'd laugh.

"Look, I'm not mad at it I just *can't*." I said again, that "can't" reverberating in my bones like a bell on a church clock.

"I mean, maybe you'll come back to it." He said, so hopeful. So sad.

We'd go back and forth like this. Circling around religion to distract from the giant love bug floating around his dorm room.

"I've never had a girlfriend." He confessed to me, impromptu one Saturday morning that I opted to "study" with him outside the Commons.

I'd been half-ass editing my senior thesis, an original comedy spec about a Black queer woman animal lover who takes up a job at the Smithsonian Zoo, of which I'd have a few students from that one strange acting class I took last semester to perform live (the biggest highlight of my college career). John was half reading some medical book for one of his final exams, but we were both woefully distracted by each other.

"I've never had a boyfriend. Not really." I responded.

I braced myself for the shock I knew would emanate off him, as it most certainly did. I presented myself like a little minx, fluent in all things sexual which was easy to do with him, a man who I assumed hadn't so much as kissed a girl before. Still, I wasn't much more experienced than him. Other than make outs, albeit some of them quite hot and quite gay, and that one time I had a one-night stand with a cis man, we were pretty much on the same page. But I didn't want him to know that. I liked being thought of as experienced, and I still wasn't ready to talk about my queerness out loud.

"How?!" He asked me, barely able to shut his mouth after speaking.

I wasn't sure how to answer him. I could have said that, yes, I had a "boyfriend" in high school. A closeted gay football player who I never once touched, let alone kissed. Or that I had that other boyfriend in show choir who I kissed often but felt nothing while doing so. Or that, since I was very young, I preferred the thought of a girlfriend. I believed such information would make his head explode.

"I don't know..." I said instead.

He turned his head right and then left and leaned in like he might whisper. Then asked, "But you've had sex before?"

I laughed at the boyishness of his delivery. He knew my answer already. It's like he asked me expecting a different answer because how on earth could I have not properly courted the man who deflowered me?!

"Would *you*? Have sex?" I asked back after coyly answering his question. This question was a popular thought in my mind when it came to him that, until then, I never had the nerve to ask.

"I don't know..." He hesitated. "I always planned to wait."

He twisted the wedding band on his right hand—jewelry meant to represent his celibacy. I couldn't explain to you why my heart dropped. I mean, I pretty much knew, by the simple fact that he read his bible every day, that he felt this way. But hearing it while at the same time vibrations bounced between us, from lip to lip, my hands to his fingertips. It felt silly... And we got quiet. Again, we circled. Circled and circled and swam and jumped and raced past our biggest questions to each other.

Do   you   want   me?
Do   you   want   me?
Should   we   be...
Together?

According to us, we were just friends. Good ole' pals. Perhaps becoming besties. But something in me and something in him could not meet Us where we really were. I knew what held him back. The fear of closeness for a devout man of God, waiting till marriage if all goes as planned. A tale as old as good sex. But for me. I truly didn't know. I could not bring my truth to words, not even for myself. I pretended the jitters I felt around him were simply what it felt like to be all of myself in front of another human, a feeling I hadn't experienced since Megan, that I'd never felt in my adult life, before John. It had to be that. I mean before John, I barely shared even a fraction of myself. Only the best, most respectable bits. But with John, it was impossible to hide. I laid bare to him from the very first time we set eyes on each other. Damn if I know how that happened.

One night dilly dallying at the Hank Ingram front desk, probably scrolling through Tumblr while I waited for the clock to hit nine, John careened over to me with a colorful flyer in tow.

"What's that?" I asked and he handed it over.

The Black Student Union was throwing an end-of-year dance party. I wasn't an active member of the BSU on campus but after a few rough years of debunking my own foolish ideas on being Black around white folk, I jumped at the chance to be around my people.

"Cool!" I smiled. It hadn't quite clicked yet.

"So, it's a date?" He asked me, sly smile. The boldest I'd ever seen him, his white teeth flashing and making my body quake.

I smile right back. Just grinning. Stalling. *A date. A date.* Had I really thought this day would never come? There he was, John. Staring down at me waiting for me to agree to his invitation *again*. But I knew the truth. I'd agreed to go with him months ago.

"Yeah, it's a date."

Of course, two folks who spent most of our time in his dorm making music, arrived early. I spotted the makeshift bar in the back of the room, a long white table covered in red cups and vodka. I looked up at him,

"Want one?"

We grabbed two red cups and the student in charge of drinks poured us vodka and cran, heavy on the vodka. We said thank you and found a nice spacious spot to stand and stare at bolder partygoers on the dance floor.

Sip. Sip. Sip. Stare. Sip. *What did I just agree to?*

"You good?" He asked me.

"Yeah!" I lied. Shaking from my core and hoping he didn't see. Bopping to a Rihanna tune to keep from falling. I wore a loose-fitting crop top and high waist jeans that made my butt look good. I wanted him to look. I wanted him to stare. And I felt out of my mind for it. Then he grabbed my hand. Tingles down my spine. It hit me that we didn't touch each other much.

"You wanna dance?" He asked. I nodded.

We both threw away half drunken drinks before heading to the dance floor, right in time for Mannie Fresh's "Shake That Ass." It blared out surround sound speakers and the south in my veins took over.

"Ayyy!" I yipped jumping up and down.

I threw my ass back and enjoyed myself until I remembered he was right there. I smiled shyly, thankful for the forgiving nature of party lighting. He did a little two step and grinned and I got wrapped in his warmth. I moved my body the way it wanted to, didn't hear the little voice telling me I was doing too much. I was free. I didn't care that we were two of the four people moving our bodies with intention in the middle of the room. Even though usually this would be totally out of the question for me. I backed my ass up and grinded on him like my life depended on it and he held me close. I didn't notice the song change. And change again. Everything became one. I focused on the feeling of our bodies together. His breath on my back. His musky scent enveloping me. His sweat becoming mine. I turned around and we took a break in each other's eyes. Bodies swaying somehow still on beat. He leaned down, and I was ready. Ready for a kiss.

"Do you need water?"

His question knocked me out of our trance. I shook my head yes as fast as I would have kissed him.

"Let's go to my dorm." I said. Or my body said, because I don't remember my mind telling it to.

He nodded, confusion and eagerness and wanting in his eyes. Barely a full drink between us but I felt high. John leaned into me playfully, knocking my shoulder with his nudges like he couldn't help it, and it sent a tingle up from my toes to my nose. I grabbed his hand, I squeezed it. He pulled me in. Our lips touched. And that is, indeed, when the world stopped. Time escaped us, sound didn't exist.

We barely made it to my room before we went in again, adopting each other's breath as our own for those sweet, sweet moments. I forced myself to pull away only to open the door.

I led him to the bottom bunk that I furnished despite having no roommate. I preferred the top. He ducked down to meet me, removing his jacket on the way. His eyes were gentle, longing,

"I've never done any of this..." He whispered.

And I froze, the weight of his words like a tidal wave. I knew he hadn't had sex. Assumed he probably hadn't even made out before, but hearing him say it, that was heavy. I felt a responsibility to treat him with the most tender care.

"I want to..." He continued. He got on top of me, his body like a weighted blanket. I felt safe.

I helped him get his shirt off, our skin slippery with sweat. I rubbed my hand down his chest, following the trail I made with my lips.

"Can I?" He asked, grabbing my shirt of which we both knew had nothing underneath. I found myself freezing, wanting but seeming I didn't. Unsure how to respond. Finally...

"Yes." Kissing him more to get lost again.

I tried to ignore the prickling, wrong sensation of my chest under his gaze. His kisses traveled down my body. I flinched. He asked me why without speaking. I shook my head. *I want more.* I did want more, even when the more began to scratch at my

172

wanting. He gave me more. More kisses, more caresses, and I unzipped his pants. We broke our bond for just a moment so he could take them off, put on a condom from my bag beside the bed, and return to me. He kissed my chest again. I backed away. I didn't mean to, returning to him quickly because I couldn't let the nagging whispers fighting against me win.

He touched me there, right over boy shorts. I shook my head. I don't know what made me shake my head. He stopped.

"It's okay, I want this." I told him the truth. Our eyes locked. He waited.

"I want this." I said again. I meant every word.

He believed me that time. My body longed for this so much it ached, but the quiet alarm distracted me, kept growing along with my wanting. I tried to stay there with him, but my mind floated away. My first time with a man flashed in my head. I'd grabbed a guy I never met at a frat party, told him to leave with me, and he obeyed. I buzzed with excitement on our walk to my dorm, beaming at this stranger, so ready to try the thing I'd heard so much about. To see if it would do for me what I'd heard it done for so many. But the moment our naked bodies touched, I felt wrong. I did not want to leave our moment with questions and so we tried everything I knew to try. Every position, every inclination of a potentially good time—we welcomed it. And we took our time. I came prepared, had studied up on this moment like the most important test and yet, and still, I felt wrong. Or at best, away, to thoughts of my current crush, a woman in my creative writing class, or to the lingering thought of how strange it felt that I was not topping this man instead.

I never told John the full extent of my experience. I preferred he believed me to be a skilled sex goddess capable of all sorts of splendid sexual tricks. I didn't tell him that the only other time I'd been this intimate with a man was like an argument with my body. I hoped it be different with him. That the other guy before was just some random, meaningless no one. That I was the type of babe that needed cuties to stimulate my *mind* first. If only it were that simple. The alarm in my head grew louder by the minute. More with every kiss. A fiery delicious pain to which I almost didn't mind the burns. But they did burn. The buzz of my desire spun off its axis into oblivion when he tried to go inside.

"Did I hurt you?" He asked me. I felt embarrassment in his voice. Or it was my own projection. I could barely look at him.

"No!" I felt horrible. For myself, for him.

I continued, "It's not you..." I kissed him on the lips. So sweet. If only all of our together was so sweet.

He kissed me back and tried again. Stopped to take a break in my eyes, which had worked every time before this, but not this time. He tried again. I jerked away from him. I couldn't help myself.

"Are you okay?" He pulled back.

"No. Yes! No, I mean, no it's not your fault! I'm so sorry."

"You don't have to apologize to me." He promised.

His eyes grew sadder by the second. I wanted to hold him. Unsure if he felt like being held. How could I explain to him that the pain I felt had nothing to do with how much I wanted him. Nothing to do with that fire between us, the fire that was still there even then.

"I'm sorry, this is my first time and I just...I'm sorry." He apologized. Again, and again, and each time my heart dropped a little further into my stomach.

"It's not you. I promise it's not you." It was my body. My body refused to invite him in, refused to feel goodness that my heart begged to share with it. I got angry, confused by it. I sat up then with my arms around my knees. Hiding my chest that felt wrong in his wanting gaze.

"It's me. It's my fault." I hesitated. "This...happens to me sometimes." I wasn't sure how else to put it.

I hoped that was enough. He nodded.

"I want you." I told him the truth.

"I want *you*." He said to me sadly. He hugged me then.

A hug that would be our last and longest, carrying us through the night and into morning. We let two days pass without speaking. It felt like weeks because every day since we met, we'd smiled at each other at least once. On the second day he texted me. He asked me how I was doing. I told him I was alright. And we left it there until he reached out to me again, a phone call this time,

"Hey. Can we meet up tomorrow morning?"

I said yes.

That elephant in the room we'd avoided for so long was unavoidable now. So, when I sat down at the bench in front of the Commons, facing him, he didn't pretend with me anymore,

"What are we doing?" He asked. A hint of frustration wrapped in confusion in his voice.

I answered honestly, "I don't know."

"What do *you* want?" He asked me. Straight. No chaser.

No space to run, I stared him in his dark brown eyes.

"I want you..." A common refrain in my mind these days.

His eyes lit up. It was the truth, but not all of it. He didn't know that I hadn't finished speaking. I wanted to stop him—to tell him I wasn't finished but I smiled back because I knew this would be the happiest moment we could ever share. Even if it could only live in our memories from now on.

"I want to be with you. I really do. But I don't think I can." I said finally.

His once bright eyes dimmed. It's like he looked through me now. I'd never seen someone deflate like that, in broad spring daylight, outside like we were happy to be there.

"What does that even mean?" Pure frustration now.

I hesitated. The next thing I said would be heavy. I paused to unpack any unnecessary pieces of my truth before delivering it to him.

My body

My body won't

My body won't let me

My body won't let me be

My Body Won't Let Me Be With You.

My mouth refused to fix itself into the shape of that truth. Not out loud, not yet.

I wrangled for the closest paraphrase, "I don't think I can be with *anyone* right now."

A softer blow to my psyche, perhaps no softer to his.

"I don't understand." He was so sad it was turning into anger.

Tears welled up behind my eyelids.

I said more, "I haven't wanted anybody this much in my entire life. But if I can't handle being with you the way I want to, something's wrong."

He shook his head. The force of his disappointment was like a boulder. Tears fell down his face like rain. How do you explain to the man you love that his loving you, his *seeing* you, without knowing your body's full story, is the most painful dissonance to your existence? Let alone the fact you don't even quite understand it yourself. I only knew then that his eyes on my chest, his hands on my sex, reminded me how much those parts of myself never quite made sense, not in the ways he treated them as they should. I couldn't be with him. I couldn't be with myself. I couldn't be with anyone until I figured out why my body felt so wrong in love. It's a noisy resistance I'd tried to ignore for too long and now it could not be dismissed any longer. He'd unlocked a boldness that resisted complacency, if only it weren't so painful to move through.

"I love you..." He told me like an invitation, reaching.

"John. I'm so sorry..." I said, allowing my hand to reach where my heart could not.

It was his turn to reject an invitation now, gently pulling his hand from mine, hiding it under the table. The love bubble we'd enveloped ourselves in burst. I remembered we were in public. Birds chirped around us. The sun shone bright through thick, labeled trees in our gorgeous Arboretum. So unassuming, while I squeezed my eyes to hold back tears.

"I'm gonna head out." He said, standing faster than I could grasp the gravity of his exit.

I nodded, again reaching for him with my gaze. There's nothing I could say to stop him. No words that could make him warm in the ways he needed.

Not even that I loved him, too.

a self-read

yes, you sound Black on the phone

now

say it with your chest

Sometimes Something Is Better than Nothing

Brooklyn and Manhattan, Mid 2015

"Mhmm." I nodded furiously at Pam's notes.

Crossing out and highlighting the tenth page of my printed novel. She'd recommended I edit on paper. A notification from her popped up on my email, and I opened it.

Nodding more, *yes, yes.* Everything she said rang true.

This reads like your first novel.

Oh Pam, it is! Of course, it does, I thought.

More nodding. I had no objections or questions really, because she was so clear. However, this note had been the very first to tilt my head. I'd mentioned very clearly in my Kickstarter that this novel was indeed my first, that I expected several rounds of edits, which is why I longed, publicly, for a skilled editor's help. I found it strange that she said *This reads like your first novel* as if it wasn't, as if I had some hidden book collection somewhere and this was slated to be my best piece, yet. *Who did she think she was working with?*

But then I smiled to myself, because Pam was that skilled an editor. She was commenting on my work the way any skilled editor would. And how would I know, because I didn't even have a Creative Writing degree, nor had I been in any number of writing programs where I would have experienced a real developmental editor like this before. I told myself to relax, to trust the process. Pam knew best, and I knew just a notch above nothing. I'd never been that smart, or savvy or even good at writing like her and I was lucky, nay, *privileged* that she even gave me the time of day. I closed my laptop and got ready for work. I'd been spending every bit of free time on *Juniper Leaves* edits. Including an hour before I hopped on the train or my bike for *Take Off*. It felt only right that I spent the majority of my free time, eyes to laptop, avoiding most weekend gatherings, and all weekday parties and dates working on my book. I even ignored pangs of loneliness at the occasional OkCupid message from gorgeous New York queers reminding me sweet love was just a wild night away. What mattered most is that this book became a real thing I could share with the world. Plus, I was beginning to lose faith in my potential to be with anyone long-term anyway. This helped me focus on writing. These days, outside of my book, all other energy went into my varying streams of work for extra money or experience, so much of my life was work and that helped me focus my energy. I'd craft pitches often to AfroPunk, who I freelanced with, and to the small news site my friend ran, and for smart *Take Off* blog posts, of which many went viral thanks to hours' worth of research of hot-NYC topics over the weekends. I had no time for nonsense, for fun, or extracurricular silliness. Yet, nonsense found me, even within work walls.

It was summertime. And yes, it is often summertime and too close to the memory of Pride, that straights tap into the inevitable need to vomit straight allyship-esque nothings into the ears of the formerly unbothered: Me. I, yes, the one Black queer, only trans, sole gender-non-confirming staff member in our daily editorial pitch meeting. I'd just pitched a post about the best trails in and around the city to polite nods and agreeable rumbles, followed by a light scribble on the board beside my name, to say that I would start working on it after this very meeting.

"Ugh, the outdoors," Our very British EoC droned, pausing for the required laughter that followed, "Do people *really* like hiking? Anyway! Moving on. Features. Ideas?" She rocked her signature beehive, a bright red cropped jacket and a tweed black and white mini skirt with sky high black boots and spotted green and pink nails. I wasn't the biggest fan of Kerri's humor or even her personality for that matter, but the woman could *dress*. And now there was a lull. A lull, meaning everyone wanted to be the first to say something genius, but they were afraid to be first and worst, so the kept their pretty little mouths closed. Any minute now someone eager and desperate for a treasured, *Love it!* from Kerri was about to say something, anything, way too confidently. This time, that desperate writer in waiting was our dear Theater editor, Tom. A tall, lanky 50-something Lower

Manhattan native with an obnoxious sing-songy tenor New York accent.

"How bout we lean into the whole gender fluid craze. Thinkin' Miley Cyrus," he said like it was nothing.

Miley just told *Time* she's gender fluid, a term the queer folks knew but that was entirely new to about 99% of the straight population. Which means this white, skinny rich celeb would be the face of it, as she would be for nonbinary as well, a few months later.

His co-editor then, the Tweedle Dee to his Dumb said, "It's like all of a sudden everybody's fluid these days."

Then our dear EiC, straight as a pole said, "I *love* it. We get ahead of it, talk about the Mileys of the world. Always fashionable, too!"

I was sitting *right there*. The resident they/them office token with my purple nails and septum piercing and dykey little haircut, slowly trying to transfer all my humiliation into one tight fist. No one noticed. They kept talking. Pumped now with the excitement of an editorial team with a good idea, only this idea was not good. At all. They had no idea how obtuse they sounded. How calling gender fluidity a craze ignored entire swaths of truth within our world. The truths we'll never know. The ones we very much do: The Hawaiian Māhū, who've existed in Native Hawaiian and Tahitian cultures as a third gender since their cultures began. The Hijra people in South

Asia, intersex and transgender and gender fluid folks who've been a part of Indian and South Asian culture since forever. Two-Spirit folk of many indigenous and Native American cultures. The many pre-colonized West African tribes like the Dagaaba of Ghana who did not define gender based on body parts. All of the people like the elder queer I'd met at one of the TAKE OFF events I wrote about, a 60-something Black person who'd never been able to ID as anything other than a gay Black man because of the rules we'd been given. They would tell me they admired what I called myself, and that, they too, never subscribed to gender rules. I wondered how many elders like them would find more truths about their being later in life. How many elders and folks before me, my ancestors, my people, yours, never had the chance? Ariel folded her arms beside me. She seemed vaguely disturbed but not enough to speak, apparently. She grunted once, when the young fashion editor, who you'd think would know better, chimed in with,

"I'm almost positive we could get a few like really cute genderfluid folks from IG to come in for a shoot."

I think I'm the only one who noticed this grunt, which could very easily pass as a simple clearing of the throat if not followed by clarifying information. Ariel offered none at all.

"Maybe we could feature gender neutral clothing brands?" The non-fashion having assistant fashion editor added.

Not a bad idea for general representation but in this context made me cringe even further into oblivion. The meeting ended shortly thereafter, with a definitive *Yes*, to this horrid idea, and no counter to it, not even from me. And I brewed, oh, I stewed. I marched to my desk and wrote a furious email that became a text that I ended up sending to Heart, venting furiously about what just happened.

Nobody said anything?!

I texted back. **No!!!**

A yell exemplified through several warranted exclamation marks.

You shouldn't have to be the one to do it, that's so awkward.

I agreed with her. Began working on my blog post but couldn't focus. Opened Google Docs and begin to write furiously, a sort of Tumblr-grade shit post I never planned to share.

"Hey, Jaz, can you look into this real quick, see if we wanna add it to our blurbs?" Ariel asked.

She handed me a cute flyer advertising some art fest in Bushwick. No email shared, only a phone number, so I called it. Didn't hear a word of what the person on the other line told me but luckily, I scribbled notes based on the phonetic sounds coming out of her mouth. Hung up. Then the Film editor pinged me via Google Hangouts...

Hey what's up!

My heart couldn't take it. It nearly leapt out of me. My mind raced to all the assumed thoughtful though actually horrible things this obtuse man could say to me if he'd actually realized what happened in our meeting. I wrote back.

Hey!

The anticipation was killing me. Write back already. It took him too long, and then finally he said...

Would you mind setting a meeting for me and a couple old pals coming in town? In the main conference room?

Okay. Now I was mad. Big mad. I wanted to say...

Look you little bitch, I'm not the dog on office manager anymore so for you to fix your little grubby fingers to type out this request when my Black ass sat across from you this morning in that foul ass pitch meeting is beyond me!

...

I must have been shaking. I had to have been shaking, because the room was spinning and my temples throbbed and I felt the ground beneath me might give out. I fought the urge to press send like a storm fighting entry into a sturdy house. The house being a lifetime of training that told me I never dare speak the truth like that in public, and I collapsed inside when it won, saying instead,

I'm not the Office Manager anymore.

It may not have felt like a ton of bricks hitting my feet had I not already been weighed down. But now I was heavy and lightheaded at the same time. Too frozen to scream, too alive with palpable fury to calm my nerves. I was my own little quiet storm, sitting still in my office chair, and I only grew fiercer knowing no one noticed. I returned to my shit post. Wrote and wrote more and more, fixed it up and punctuated it. Took a deep breath at my desk that came out like a gasp. I'd meant to stay quiet. A bit tough whilst having a panic attack, that you don't know is a panic attack because you did not know this is a thing someone like you can have, as if you haven't had them all your life.

"You okay?" Ariel asked.

I realized then I didn't want to be noticed. I wanted to go unseen, to be a silent storm that stayed in dusty fields away from towns and cities. I felt tight. I always felt tight at work, but right then it was extra, and my bandwidth for the weight of other people's willful ignorance was waning. Working at *Take Off* was like clocking in each day for voluntary paper cuts. Just a stream of them, at random intervals throughout my shift. But when you are already weighed down by your own body, your own inner thoughts that rival your worst enemy's, the little cuts start to feel like knives after a while. I couldn't ignore the steady patter of my heart anymore,

"No... Actually no."

I asked her if I could call it for the day. Work from home because I felt sick, and I did.

"Yeah! Yeah, oh my god, of course. I'll cover today. If you feel like starting some research for your blog post, fine, but seriously, no pressure."

I thanked her. Thanked her again. Threw on my backpack, stomped without meaning to stomp right on out the office. Somehow made it to the subway despite unbelievably short breaths and through anxious spirals of thought, found that angry message again in my drafts. Edited it again, removed all my emotion, focused on the huge PR fail it would be after remembering these folks didn't care about me. Pressed send to Jen in HR.

Hi Jen,

I'm reaching out because of a less than savory end to our pitch meeting this morning. After some discussion, the staff landed on a theme idea for next week's publication that I think may cause some backlash: Gender Craze. As we live in a fairly liberal city, I foresee a fair amount of upset over a controversial topic like gender identity. Also, as a gender nonconforming person, I was personally affected by the flippancy at which many of the editors spoke of my identity. I'd love to chat with you about possible options and alternatives to correct this issue.

Thanks!

At least I said something, maybe not in person, but I said something. And I felt lighter then, as soon as I pressed send. I stepped off the train and out into the busy underground into Brooklyn. Power walked a few blocks to Brooklyn Bridge Park, kept walking, felt good. I could breathe again. I pulled out *The Fire Next Time* from my backpack. Read more until my mind slipped away into frustration. I shook it off. It returned, so I put my book away. Walked, more and more and more until I'd reached my street, Lafayette Ave, then my apartment, up my apartment steps, and into my bedroom, and into my shower, and into my bed. I slept for 5 hours.

I woke up to rain, and three alerts. First, a text from Heart.

Dinner tonight?

I'd say yes. She told me she had good news. I needed good news.

Then a text from Jess,

Ma wants to talk about this thing with Andrew's school later

Now was later, so I planned to call in 5, but only for a short while. I didn't have the energy or time for our usual two-hour exchanges.

And an email from Pam. I perked up, because I always perked up when I noticed an email from Pam Plemons, even though her past few emails as of late were full of red ink and editor's notes. It all felt like progress, and I liked progress. I didn't mind growing pains or corrections because it meant we were closer to my dream. That's what I told myself. We'd come so far. Months and months of edits and backs and forths and though we'd surpassed our original deadline by many months, due to other timely projects she told me she'd be prioritizing, I still felt optimistic, or delusional, but it was a comforting delusion that I held onto because she held on to her belief in me. But I couldn't ignore the pang in my side at her message this time. It didn't even wink at my optimism, didn't nod to my forgone delusion like the others at all.

As you know, this needed huge amounts of reformatting and line editing, which took an incredible amount of time and energy (in future, send your manuscript to a publisher or editor only when it's in the best possible shape; the story suffers when it's so full of formatting mistakes, spelling errors, etc. that it can barely be read. Most publishers will reject it after a few pages at most). Now that those things have been fixed, it's all developmental from here.

On one hand, this seemed an inevitable metaphorical finger wag. I knew that since Pam didn't read my book before signing on with me, there was a clear possibility she'd be woefully disappointed. But something about her message felt so final, though she'd said nothing definitive. It's like she'd finally seen my insides, and they made her sick. I felt shame about it, heavy ugly shame. She went on.

Now for the developmental editing, which basically means improving the story itself. The attached edits, questions and suggestions are all aimed at doing that. A lot of what is needed is consistency and clarity. There are also pacing issues, where it's either moving too quickly to ground the reader, or too slowly to hold the reader's interest.

I felt that she'd said, without saying, that this was my last and final chance. I had no more space to disappoint her, and, embarrassedly, I felt I needed that space.

"It's not *too*, too bad!" Heart smiled sweetly over her California roll.

The rain stopped so we'd both rode our bikes to a new sushi spot in Williamsburg. My chopsticks fumbled over sashimi. Finally, I picked up a plump piece of salmon. Delicious. I almost felt okay. Almost.

"I mean, she sounds like she's almost over me, you know?" I shrugged as a caught my breath.

"She wouldn't have reached out to you if she didn't believe in your work. You're such a good writer Jaz. Like seriously, give yourself a little credit."

I wanted to believe her. I don't think she knew that I never felt that way. She might have assumed, like most people, that my constant doing, writing, submitting, posting, meant confidence. For me, it was simply fuel to keep me going. If I wasn't moving, I was still. And if I was still, I was dying. All of my worth lived in the things I did. It had nothing to do with confidence for me at all. We ended our night without dessert. I road home in the rain, wet and teary and entered my bedroom alone. Not even in the mood enough to see someone off one of the apps. No space to put on for anyone, not even myself. I scrolled through my phone, reluctantly clicking into my office emails, in search for something to do because I was becoming too still. *There.* Jen had responded to my email. A short two sentences that felt like anchors to my now floating away body.

Hi Jaz,

I've talked to Kerri. This story will no longer be in our next issue. Thanks for your email,

Jen

I dropped my phone down the corner of my bed. The smack of it on wood was like a button releasing tension to my too-full spirit. Tears that'd been stuck inside me rolled down like little rivers on either side of my face. The sort of tears that burn like cayenne and salt. I wanted to scream from the pain. I sobbed instead. But I wanted this. It was something, and something was better than nothing.

It feels real good

when you see my

poetry

and I don't have

to say

a word

LOVE INTEREST # 3: CAMELIA

OKCUPID, Fall 2014

My Self Summary:

Hey hey. I'm Jasper aka Jaz. Not that anyone could be reduced to, say, like two personas buuuuut...imagine Max Goof and Prince as one person and that's legit what I be like. Of course, along with other human complexities and nuance and etc, etc.

Something people don't know about me:

I'm a trans masculine person. If you met me years ago this would be a major point of discussion but these days, I'm pretty comfortable with being me in spite of how confusing people seem to find my gender.

What I'm doing with my life:

Creating, creatively. Writing. Figuring things out. Being confused. And, I was never that big on scrabble till this year and I swear I'm hooked on Words With Friends. I don't know how this happened.

Favorite books, movies, shows, music food:

Bojack Horseman is my shit. Just got into it. Also did any of y'all ever watch that UK show Misfits? If so, let's discuss how underrated and fantastic season 1-2 of that series were???

Mykki Blanco has my heart. I also love Frank Ocean but like...duh. Paramore, The Internet, System of a Down, Freddie Hubbard, Thelonious Monk (hence the namesake), Many more...

Just read *The Fire Next Time* by James Baldwin. Shook.

What I'm looking for:

I'm really attracted to femininity but that's not limited to any gender. I love a power bottom. Also, I have a few kinks I'm into exploring more.

I thought it all the way through; Thelonious Punk, as in Thelonious Monk, the jazz musician, and because my name is Jaz(z) and my father is a *jazz* musician, and I'm a punk (in both the gay and the punk rock meaning of the term), and I love jazz. And my dating profile wasn't just a profile for me. It was a piece of my reality I hoped people felt welcomed into. Because queer dating as far as I knew was as much online as off. If you did not meet your people at the party, at the function, you met on Tumblr, on Twitter, on OkCupid. Outside of those options you were left to face-to-face assumptions and though many of us claim gaydar perfection, none of us are truly the experts we claim to be. So, there was simply no hierarchy in the many ways you might connect. Furthermore, your online persona better be just as dope or weird or plain as your face-to-face vibes. No catfishing, and that includes your words. No wonder I edited my OKC profile no less than thrice a week. That is, whenever I felt something about me had changed (which was arguably more than three times a week but a grrl only has so much time).

I wanted to represent myself well, you see. I wanted for the many people who would meet me via this app or that to feel when they met me, that they were meeting this person who wrote this profile, not some weirdo who tried to seem some type of way on the internet and was totally different offline. You know, a catfish. And us very online girlies knew a little something about how it's all real: on and offline. So much. Maybe too much, that I answered a whopping four hundred intrusive questions about my sex life, philosophical views, and random, controversial opinions for OKC's expressly accurate algorithm to really get my matches right.

The profile edit above is quite special because it would be my last. Well, my last for the next nearly 4 years following, because I'd soon meet my soul mate: Camelia Laffite. A 98% match. Of which I called basically 100% considering algorithmic margins of error and how utterly, intensely attracted to her profile I was at first glance. That had to be a magnetic, spiritual, soulmate-tie attraction right there. Dare I say digital love at first sight. Yes, I knew the second I clicked into her profile; Camelia would be my partner. My one and only partner because that is what we, the truly in love, do. We have one. We, the truly in love, who, cannot possibly love anyone else. Anything else. Despite my current non-monogamous interludes as a queer person of New York City. I'd been many another's partner, but never anyone's primary. And I hailed this non-monogamy. Freedom in love, because queerness is freedom. A beautiful concept, until you are faced with your own fears of abandon, and you must then decide if freedom in love is worth your own sanity, because your sanity is in jeopardy, you fear, if you are to welcome said freedom with your soul mate. No. Camelia would be mine and mine alone.

Camelia was an AzMarie Livingston look alike. Gorgeous. But not too masculine that it would challenge my masculinity, because stud for stud and masc for masc were absolutely out of the question, you see. Despite my attraction to masculine folks. Despite the fact I'd been with masculine folks. Loved on, hooked up with. My official partner, the one I actively chose in that loud and out way, could not be *too masc* because despite my extreme queerness, my Black masculinity, leaning towards the more insidious and unhealthy, would not allow me to actively choose to break the rules of engagement that my people, Black colonized people, had already told me to follow. Because don't we all love rules. Don't we all love guidelines. Guidelines you'd think queerness should resist, but no. But I digress. Back to my hard femme (very stemmy) soulmate...

Camelia's profile left much to the imagination. She was a quite mysterious, dark-eyed soul. I wanted to ask her everything, learn everything, know everything about her. One day. But in the moment, I could only grasp on to minor clues about this person. Like, I quickly learned she had an adorable, 2-year -old golden retriever-mix named Bear. I, of course, ignored the immediate impulse to suspect any sort of prejudice like I was wont to do when someone flaunted that particular narc of a dog. I am a dog-lover but growing up in Memphis you must know that golden retrievers were the white people of dogs. But Camelia was not white, and the simple fact that she deemed Bear worthy of adoration was enough for me to love him, too. No, Camelia wasn't white at all, which was exactly what I'd planned. Since my whole night with Fatima, I'd changed a lot of things about my dating life. One of which was seeking mainly Black partners. Though I preferred dating Black folks now, my OKC profile kept the filter open to brown folks and mixed raced people, of which Camelia fit the bill. I told myself she fit it perfectly. Camelia wasn't necessarily Black, at all, but was clearly nobody's white. Never white. Though her features pointed to all sorts of ancestry. Full lips that felt Black to me, straight and strong nose and light brown skin like from the Middle East. And her shaved head led to even more mystery. Even in pictures where she'd grown it out a bit, her wavy thick pattern led to no new conclusions. In fact, her background was clearly a point of confusion for more than just me. She dedicated a whole entire section on OKC to this very inquiry.

The first thing people notice about me:

My race/ethnicity. Don't worry, no one guesses correctly. Short answer: I'm Black, Palestinian and white.

Black! That's all I needed to see. *Just what I'm looking for*, I thought. I told myself I wouldn't be like her other suitors, fetishizing Camelia's appearance. I would welcome all of her identities. I'd champion her Blackness over everything, a la the one drop rule. Because she was also Black. Just like I always dreamed. Camelia was my dream person. That's what I told myself. And my dream came true in a quick response to my initial message asking if she'd go out with me.

I'd love to. I just moved here two weeks ago from North Carolina by the way. Sorry in advance if I'm late from getting lost.

Direct, sweet, thoughtful. *Perfect.* We set a date for Saturday evening, a rainy day in September. Felt sunny and gay. I strolled down 5ᵗʰ Avenue, stopped at a bench across from The Guggenheim. Sat and waited under droplets of rain. Camelia texted.

I'm so close. I'm sorry!

I wasn't upset. I was excited. Figured what's a few extra minutes to years and years together. And she had a great excuse. Camelia lived in Harlem, with, I later learned, a strange woman named Giget who had a vicious tongue and hankering for drama. She'd stopped to check on Bear in the Bronx before meeting me, because though her apartment allowed dogs, Giget refused to house any animals. And the 2 train to me was delayed.

"He's staying with a really sweet couple. They let me visit him whenever I have time."

She was a jewelry maker, a model, a painter on occasion.

"You can call me Cam by the way."

Cam. Cam and Jaz. Jaz and Cam. It flowed brilliantly. Cam found a job as a server within her first few days. Hoped to live off her jewelry someday soon. We were both artists, yet another sign of our fate. I was floating.

She found me sitting. A dimple on her right cheek peeked through when she spoke, "Hey!"

The light rain stopped.

"Hey! You look great." I said, hooked. Already.

"You look pretty hot yourself." She smirked. Settled into that Mona Lisa smile I fell in love with, playing with my mind.

We crossed to The Guggenheim. I relaxed my shoulders at first site of the "free Saturday" sign plastered on the entrance. Sweet relief. We entered without a hitch. Cam smelled like peppercorn and Jasmine. She smoked, a thing I'd say was a dealbreaker except the way Cam did it made it chic. Fine. Added to her shimmering allure. Stench, where?

"I feel like a kid in a candy store." She beamed, looking across at the museum.

She went to art school in Charlotte for a while before leaving early. She couldn't afford to stay,

"But I'll always love it, you know? And I still learned a lot."

She led me through the Guggenheim as if she were a tour guide. Describing paintings as if she were in the room when they were created, noticing tiny details my uneducated eyes soon missed. I was mesmerized. We stopped at a Monet.

"I think he's one of my favorites. It seems so simple, you know? But he's also so nuanced, complicated, it's like...disorientating and comforting at the same time, depending on how you look at it. I love that."

"Wow. Yes." I said, nodding.

An hour disguised as twenty minutes passed us by, then another just like it.

"Good evening, the Guggenheim will be closing in thirty minutes. The museum will close in thirty minutes. Thank you."

"Oh no! There's so much more, oh my god." She shook her head, disappointed.

"We have to come back." I said. Implying a second or third date. We'd only made it through three of six floors.

"We do." She said, and our hands clasped. So naturally, as if we'd been here before. Maybe in another life...

"You wanna walk for a bit?" I asked her. I didn't want this night to end.

It was night now, dark and more quiet in this big city than usual. Or I was too focused on us to notice the noise.

"Yeah, let's do it." She agreed.

The rain scattered down once more like sprinklers in a greenhouse. We, the plants. I felt refreshed. Cam towered over me by about six good inches, so it made more sense for her to carry the umbrella. I told myself I liked her height. That it didn't challenge my aforementioned masculinity at all. Height probably from the Dutch part of her lineage on her dad's side.

"I can't really speak Dutch anymore, just a few phrases. But I understand it." She told me.

She could speak some German, on account of her mother being half German and half Afro-Surinamese. She moved to the states with her mom and little brother when she was five, along with her mom's German mother. I told her I didn't know much about Suriname. That I'd love to learn more about it. About her. We walked and walked, through Central Park all the way to the west side.

"Are you hungry?" I asked her.

"Yeah, you?" She said.

We found a Thai restaurant on the West Side. She had red curry. I had my go-to, basil fried rice. We shared sticky rice with ice cream for dessert. Left. Passed by a fragrant bakery and I, the chronic sweet tooth, would have usually found my body forcing me inside, only exiting with at least one magic cookie bar. But today was sweet enough. We kept walking. Finally landing in a quiet, dark corner of Central Park, leaning against a gentle giant of a tree. The rain decided to leave us for the moment.

"Thank goodness." Was the shape of her words, but I heard no sound.

I leaned into her, she into me. Crashing against the electricity between us, causing sparks. Only balanced with a kiss. A long, warm, besotted exchange of our breaths.

"I don't want this night to end." She told me while we were flying.

There was no going back now. Only forward.

PART II

They said a water sign might

drown you

in your own tears

Issa Dyke U-Haul Party

New York, Winter 2014

I woke up to an email from *Take Off's* HR team.

Our CMS is down.

Something about a full file transfer gone wrong. It was a Monday, and this news couldn't have come at a better time. I'd been craving a break, even just a day's worth of rest from what just months ago I'd deemed my dream job. Now I didn't have to call out sick, again. A thing I'd done two-too many times over the past couple weeks due to random panic attacks. But exactly fifteen minutes from the time of that email, and seconds after I put on my second shoe to take a morning stroll to Dough, my favorite donut shop, down my street, Cam called. Frantic. Out of breath and moving quickly on the other side of my cell. Giget, her roommate who I quickly learned was the bane of Cam's existence, who loved to throw the fact that she welcomed Cam into her space at such short notice, had never once used Cam's rent money on rent.

"We're literally being kicked out as I speak." Cam said through shallow breaths, her stressed voice bouncing off the building's stairway walls.

She explained she only had time to grab a few of her things.

"They won't let me back in. I literally can't even grab my coat by the door. This is fucking ridiculous."

Cam had noticed the apartment was emptier than usual when she woke up. But Giget was nowhere to be found. She wouldn't answer her calls. Only texts, sans apology, as if everything was normal. As if there was any coming back from an eviction. I felt the fury in Cam's voice and it fired me up. I had to do something. I decided I would not be hitting up Dough. I had to go to Harlem and help Cam bring the few items she could keep with her back to my apartment. I knew it without a second thought.

"Come here." I said.

"Babe. No, this is wild, I'm gonna call my coworker."

I persisted, "I have a full-size bed. My room is big. My roommates are chill."

Finally, she agreed, via text, not knowing I was already halfway there. Apparently, Giget arrived on my travels. Realized she couldn't gather her things and stormed off. Not without promising Cam that if it wasn't for the shady landlord, whom she's had a steamy affair that ended just a week ago, they wouldn't be in this mess.

"She says 'he's mad she's seeing someone else.' Like, what the actual fuck." Cam explained.

A mess. We hugged and kissed and plucked up her belongings, a couple suitcases full of whatever she grabbed in those short 15 minutes. And we left, off to my bedroom in my 4-bedroom apartment. This was all a mess. And I felt horrible for Cam. But I cannot pretend that a not-so-small part of me didn't want to jump around my room excited for our new reality as live-in partners. Sure, it was sudden. Circumstantial, too. But alas, live-in partners, nonetheless. It's a dream younger me had given up on, but here we were. And I didn't care about the quickness of it. As far as I was concerned, six weeks was no record U-Haul in dyke terms. Though surely peak sapphic behavior. So here she came and thankfully my roommates agreed after the fact. Just a week later, she quit her job.

"I'm tired of dealing with creepy bosses." She told me one night to my surprise.

But it wasn't all that surprising when I learned how her bosses at the Harlem restaurant had been treating her. Bosses warning her to wear more revealing clothes for 'better tips.' Those same bosses' hands grazing inappropriate areas 'accidentally.' She'd been there a month and maybe that was even too long. Plus, I wouldn't wish that Brooklyn to Harlem commute on anyone. So, I told her, no problem. I'd take care of us. And I ignored the ugly twinge of patriarchy at the sound of my pride, that I was able to do this now. As the so-called more masculine of the two of us, though wildly loose-wristed still. Still. I wanted to be the provider for us. I wanted her to know she could count on me while she found work, preferably in the Fort Greene/Clinton Hill area. I didn't tell her how excited I was to cover us both. Didn't tell her that this seemed almost a dream of mine I'd never known was a dream. I'd just started a new job, Video Content Programmer at AOL that paid 60k, more money than I'd ever made in my entire life. Nearly twice as much as I'd made as Assistant Editor at Take Off. I could handle it. How good it felt to know that.

"I know you'd do the same for me." I bellowed in heart-eyed earnestness.

I believed that to be true. And on a too-quiet night in November, while Cam was out walking the neighborhood, dropping off her resume to worthy restaurant managers, I couldn't keep quiet anymore. Well, neither could Bear, who had to stay with us for just a night since his usual sitters were out of town. He burst out of my room and towards the front door where my other roommate, the film editor, was attempting to gather his pizza.

"I'm so sorry," I said, miserably embarrassed.

I told Jess and Ma on the phone to hold, but I don't remember muting while apologizing for "my dog." They knew nothing of Bear. More importantly, they knew nothing of Cam.

Not because I was ashamed, or that I meant to keep this part of me private but because I'd waited all my life to move to New York City so that I could disclose only things I wanted to disclose. I loved that about being an adult. No one outside of NYC new who was dating at any given time, and I liked it that way. I liked that no one knew I wore a binder, or I'd been taking testosterone for months, or I'd legally changed my name, or I'd just scheduled top surgery for next year. But today, I felt bold. I felt inspired. Cam and I were going to be together for a very long time, after all, so why not clue my mom and sister in on our love story. Especially since Thanksgiving was coming up. She could join us! New family with old. So, I told them.

"Bear is Cam's dog. Cam is my girlfriend. We live together."

At this point I was on a roll, so I even told them the truth about how long we were together, even though I knew these dear, straight women would not understand 6 weeks in dyke time. This is the first time anyone but Leesie knew about any of the queer loves in my life, let alone my new live-in partner. I would have liked a bit more positive reception.

"She doesn't know anyone else?" My mom asked after I filled her in on the Giget problem.

"Is she at least paying part of the rent?" Jess asked me.

"Um..." I hadn't mentally prepared for backlash.

I'd have called it homophobia were the questions not so...reasonable. And I answered them, as reasonably as I could, because I needed this not to be a point of contention for us. Now that they knew about Cam, I needed them to grow to love her as much as I did. It was so much easier for them not to know. Because now, the thought of my family rejecting Cam for any reason became a new fear. Cam did not share this sort of fear. She hadn't spoken to her mom in months. I'd never witnessed any of her family calls. Part of that was because her grandmother and aunts, with whom she was closest, lived in the Netherlands and calls are expensive. But her mom lived in North Carolina.

I asked her about her mom. She didn't like to talk about her.

"I mean there's not really much to say. She's mega Christian. Hates gays. Once when I was like thirteen, she told me she never actually wanted kids. So yeah, she's...herself."

When she was fifteen, her mom and stepdad found her diary where she'd gushed about an ex-girlfriend. They punished her by reading her entries out loud, laughing at the sweetest parts, critiquing the entire book like it'd been sold in stores. I felt for her. I understood her aloof disposition. How difficult it was to pry a personal fact out of her. She hadn't been given the sort of love growing up that showed her sharing was okay. Usually, if I asked too many questions, Cam had this habit of changing the subject to whatever event was coming up the soonest. Dancing and drinking were her favorite mollifiers. When I asked her how she was feeling the day she got kicked out, she shrugged. Her eyes brightened and she said,

"Actually, the fact that we're going to Brooklyn is low-key perfect. I have this friend I met at work who's throwing a party like right around your place. We should go!"

We'd go. We'd always go. Her, to let loose, and me to be close to her. Just like she needed a drink, I needed her attention, and I could not get that at home alone. Even though I was starting to grow tired of nightlife. I hated that there were so few ways for queers to meet outside of a dance floor. A friend of one of my Dyke March pals, a Black trans guy named AJ, and I, along with their Asian nonbinary partner, Riley, had started a group to counter that problem called POCLuck. It was all about bringing Black and brown queer folks together in sober settings to draw, or do karaoke, or be outside. But ever since I'd met Cam, I'd been a poor excuse for a committee member. Instead of meeting early Saturday mornings, I slept in late beside Cam who I'd been out with until the sun came up.

Even if I wanted to, my body wouldn't let me stay home alone. It'd jerk and flinch and cry, curled in fetal position on my side of the bed on the one night I'd decline. My mind would join in with shouts of defeat, yelling at me to call her and make sure she still loved me, that she was even alive and well enough for that to be true. I could never just *be* at home alone knowing Cam was out. And if she did not text me back immediately, the world was surely ending. So, 9 times out of 10 I went out when she did.

"Another shot?" Cam nudged me.

Yes, yes, always yes. Warm, clear sensation flowed down my throat and belly and spine, reminding me we were having fun, together. Our first shots together were my favorite. Second, less so. Our third was like a second wind, and the fourth, a liquid torture devise. By the fifth, I'd have to admit defeat.

"Lightweight!" She'd yell, downing hers.

We'd always be the last to leave. Got real close to the local bartenders.

"What you think, wanna get outta here?" I'd always have to ask twice.

And we'd leave together, arms linked, smiling drunken smiles. Hopefully, I had no plans the next morning. I'd surely miss them. And then we'd rinse and repeat, until Jalisa's favorite bar, walking distance from our apartment, hired Cam. I should have been excited for her. But instead, I was worried about us. About our time together, and how much use I'd be to her now that she had her own money. I wanted to not feel useless. To be so vulnerable to her losing interest. I waited up for her any night we weren't together, anticipating a text that rarely came. Then, early in the new year, Cam caught me on my way to work. She was up so early I thought something sweet might happen like a kiss or hug. But, before I caught my train of thought, she said,

"I'm gonna start looking for a place."

My heart stopped.

"I love you. But I want to be with you longer than six months before we officially live together." She continued.

"Eight." I said. We'd been together 8 months.

I shouldn't have been surprised. I'd heard her say this could happen in the beginning and let myself forget it. I didn't believe it. I assumed we'd live together forever now, but no, this had only ever meant to be a temporary solution.

"I'm literally about to move out of this place, why don't you just wait?"

She said she was tired of not being there for Bear. That she'd always wanted to live alone and this was the first and maybe only time she could try it. I took that to mean that she saw us together forever, too. But I was still sad. Still reaching for something that had pulled away from me. An alternate image of us.

i am not done yet

as possible as yeast

as imminent as bread

a collection of safe habits

a collection of cares

less certain than i seem

more certain than i was

a changed changer

i continue to continue

what i have been

most of my lives is

where i'm going

Lucille Clifton

THE JOKE OF ME

Memphis, Peabody Hotel, Summer 2012

"What's your name, pretty lady?" Asks the white-haired white man with an easy smile, a couple younger men on either side of him.

I tell him with a big ole' sweet grin, 'cause Marcy, who's been working here the longest, says a little flirting gets the biggest tips.

"Well, ain't that something. Beautiful name for a beautiful girl."

I ignore the damp hand swipe across my pantyhose-covered thigh when I swoop down to point out our tapas for the evening, as if I hadn't just recited them off the dome. But I need the extra finesse, because I have only been serving here for three weeks and my tips ain't been hitting, and I still need at least two more months before I have enough to move to New York City this January. Pops got me the job. He's been the pianist here for nearly 25 years and Ma told me as soon as I graduated, I needed to ask him to pull a few strings. And I hugged him, actually hugged him, when he told me,

218

"I've got you a meeting with our human resources manager."

I was genuinely happy. Told myself I didn't care that this was a cocktail server job with an all women staff, or that we had to wear makeup, or that the skirt and blouse required in our uniform made me very uncomfortable.

"A job is a job is a job." Pops told me on the way to my interview.

I think he could sense my discomfort. And I nodded, fluffed up my big frow and checked my dark red lipstick in the visor mirror of his Mercedes, rounding out this full femme drag. We'd been getting closer since I graduated because I think, secretly, he didn't think I'd finish (because I kept saying I didn't want to finish) and he was proud. Prouder than he'd maybe ever been of me. I liked this feeling of impressing Pops, a man I'd never connected with very deeply because I didn't feel he saw me. Talking to my dad was like talking to a wall sometimes. He was so hard to read, and you'd always question if he could read you, either. But now, things were better, and I didn't want to fail him this time, not again, like I felt I had so many times.

So, even though seeing my dolled-up reflection made my stomach turn, and wearing those heels felt like gently stabbing my echelles with a blunt knife, I sucked it up. I'd suck up the Ms's and Mam's and *lady-woman-girls*. This job was my ticket into New York and without it, I could be stuck in Memphis for who knows how long. I'd waited long enough; I didn't have time to be picky. I could exhale when I landed in LaGuardia.

But I didn't know it would be like this. I didn't know that silent looks from hungry men would remind me of the dissonance of my being. I'll admit, I wasn't prepared. Not even a little bit for how disgusting all of this felt. Not that it was any less disgusting for the cis women I worked with, who told me with sad smiles and chuckles that it, "Just comes with the territory."

"Anything else I can get you?" I asked the slimy man with the too-dark toupee.

He wriggled a finger at me, as if to say, "Come here."

I hesitated, stalled with a smile and giggle but he kept on, so I did as he asked. Before I knew it, I was trapped in his grasp. His oddly long arm around my waist, he said to his old, nasty friends,

"She's got that Jungle Fever hair, uh? Just beautiful."

My knees buckled beneath me, and my breath left me, and I told him, "Thank you."

I didn't know what else to do. I could not disappoint myself by saying too much and losing this job that I needed. Couldn't disappoint my dad by making a scene at his beloved Peabody Hotel. I wanted to disappear. But there was Pops right at the piano, playing it and grinning, oblivious when I looked his way.

I remember thinking, *This cannot be my life,* but it was very much my life and all I did after it happened was continue to serve that man and many more like him. At least until I had the money I needed.

After that Peabody Hotel gig, I told myself that if I felt that feeling again and I had a choice to go, I would. Cue, 2015, *Take Off's* little pizza party, thrown for one of the London higher-ups who decided to grace us with his presence for the entire week. Not only could my lactose intolerant ass not partake in this cheesy opus, I also had just endured yet another highly uncomfortable pitch meeting, in which our new photo editor recommended we have a "slang funeral" for all the played-out words like, you know, *bae, thirsty, on fleek*—Black words. The forthcoming Incident happened around the water cooler, because what better place to commit such an antiquated office-place faux pas. The offender was old-school white, aka British, with dull, colorless, stringy hair. She and my editor, Ariel, and one of the salesmen from upstairs were talking about summertime in the city, because the weather is all we really had in common, I suppose.

"I feel like it's not as bad here cause, like, there's so much shade?" Ariel said.

"Yeah, all those tall buildings?" I said with a smile, because I rarely spoke without one at this job, despite my actual mood. And as I closed my lips at the end of my sentence I spotted, out the corner of my left eye, the grubby, crusty hands of that British executive, reaching, child. Reaching, slowly, for the top of my high-top where my curls lived, usually in peace. The world stopped. I heard the words "May I" at the very moment her index and thumb pinched one too many strands,

"That's really something!" She smiled, still touching.

I was frozen. Didn't even know Kerri, our EiC, was right there behind me. Only found out because of that still bizarre cosign,

"Isn't it?"

Isn't it? Like this woman had been somehow eyeing me with such a predatory gaze this whole time, without me knowing. Like she'd ever had the privilege of touching any part of me.

"Oh my god," said Ariel, the only one in this equation beyond me to respond in a way I found remotely acceptable.

The salesman, a Black man, said nothing. Though our eyes did meet, and I know in my heart he felt my discomfort. And as my palms grew sweaty and my throat closed, I said to myself, *that's the last fucking straw.* As if I didn't have so many moments just that week that should have been it for me. As if I couldn't have sued the whole damn company the week before, when Kerri insisted I write a "lighthearted" blog post about "cool things" folks in the city who "don't want to protest" can do amid Freddie Grey's murder. I'd had to take that day off. I was reeling. Angry. Feeling like I could slap that lady with a slice of pizza. But I never spoke out. Not really. And when I did speak, I used my white voice, and when I laughed, my white laugh. As if any of that made me less Black. As if any of that would prompt Kerri to give me that raise I'd been asking for, as if I hadn't proven to be an asset and rung in the top blog posts for three months straight. As if all this was worth $35,000 a year. It was a joke, all of it. I'd had enough.

"Don't you think you should wait till you find something else?" Asked Jess on our three-way call that day.

I'd texted her and Ma and Leese that I was quitting. My mind was made up. I'd just been approved for a credit card limit increase, almost exactly enough to cover me for one month. I told myself that was fine enough. I ignored how flippantly I'd used credit cards in times of pressure, or pleasure. For my Kickstarter, for impromptu tickets to New Orleans and Europe. One of which I'd forgotten I'd even bought till the trip came around a year later. It's an impulsivity I'd learn later was an obvious sign of mental illness.

"I've got enough savings for a month." I said, a small white lie for my family's comfort.

I printed my resignation letter the next day. And the day after that? Sheer panic. Dropped eight hundred on my increased rent off my credit card to avoid future worry about covering it later. But then serendipity blessed me in the shape of a gamer twink called Matt,

"I'm leaving, too," He said all low in the printing room, leaning in so no one could hear, "I'm so fucking over this place."

We laughed. Matt was one of two computer technicians. He told me he was headed off to AOL—which was also Huffington Post, and more largely Verizon Media—to be a Video Programmer.

"Actually, you have a film studies degree, right?" He asked.

I nodded, even though I hadn't done anything film-related other than go see a lot of movies since I got to NYC. But in the beginning of our friendship, Matt and I bonded over being cinephiles. It's mostly all we talked about, because cinephiles can only avoid obnoxiousness when discussing films with each other. Matt knew my background very well, and that I, indeed, missed doing so much of what I'd learned about film.

"Awesome, I'll tell Sven you're interested, if you want."

Oh, *I want*. I gave him my personal email address and just a few days later I had an interview. A few days after that, a job offer. And I'd be making twenty thousand more a year, without even a lull of unemployment. I could work from home, only four days a week. The only catch? I, the ever-morning person, would have to work from eleven at night into four in the morning. But alas, this daunting fact barely swayed me in and of itself. I felt too free and liberated to worry about keeping my eyes peeled in the late hours of the night. No, what made my palms itch was the spine-tingling realization that we, Cam and

I, would not spend her favorite hours together for at least four nights a week. At least not until I'd be promoted into a few months later, so that I'd work a comfy Monday through Friday of 8-4pm. But I knew nothing about this future. I was scared and already mourning.

"Are you still gonna go out after work?" I asked Cam.

I'll admit, I expected an easy "no," but I quickly learned Cam is not one to placate feelers.

"I mean...Yeah? If I feel like it, maybe," She noticed the slump in my shoulders, "Would that bother you?"

"Nah, I mean, do you," A lie I lied. then asked, "What if I work on the patio?"

It felt like a lightbulb moment.

"I mean...It's not really that kinda bar, but if you want to..."

And, so I did. The first night I worked I brought my laptop to the outdoor patio and I ordered chicken wings and fries and I tried, with all my might, to focus. But my ears lingered into the table beside me, where a couple contemplated their end, and the table beside them, where a few grad students cheers'd to a future South Africa trip, and my eyes floated onto the sidewalk, where a tall Eastern European man parked his bike, and a woman asked Cam if she could bring her dog onto the patio beside me,

"Yeah, that's fine!" Cam said. She was so good with customers.

She was her most outgoing, friendly self with them. So personable, loveable. I wanted to kiss her. I wanted to close my laptop and commit to five more hours of this, watching and enjoying Cam in action. I couldn't stay here. I hated it, but there's no way I could stay. We kissed and I threw on my backpack and road my bike back to our apartment. Plopped on my bed and plunged my face into my pillow and screamed. I tried to focus on my work. But I couldn't break free from under that blanket of loneliness and despair. It did not help that when she slipped through our open bedroom door at 5am, a drunken grin occupied both corners of her mouth. She'd touch me then, a sweet, sweet, sour attempt to embrace the iciness of what was left of me after hours talking myself out of her love. She had been having fun without me. Smiling, drinking, *flirting*, without me. And that smell. I grew so disgusted by the scent of whiskey sours.

"Kiss me." She'd say, a thing hours ago I begged for her to say, but at 5am I was the vampiric remnant of myself.

I was too angry at this smiling face with all that joy I didn't know the origin to... It didn't help that she could not tell me about her joyful nights. She never remembered.

"Why didn't you answer my text? Or my call?"

"You're always breathing down my neck!"

"Where even is your phone?"

"Fucking relax!"

We'd go on like this, until she'd speak incoherent words and pull off her clothes and stumble into the shower, and I'd know, she would forget all this, too. I'd get quiet then and follow her into the bathroom to make sure she did not fall or drown in her ritual morning bath before an hours-long rest where she'd wake and remember absolutely nothing again. It was an ugly cycle we entertained, until my promotion, which was like a reset to our love that I told myself would wash away all resentment of the past few months. It felt good, and I never thought it would, to be away in an office most of the day, instead of in that room with my love, counting down the hours till her next shift and our next argument. Especially since this office, at the AOL and Huffington Post headquarters, was a refreshing reprieve from anything I'd ever known and office to be. Plus, I'd be making even more than ever before, 62 thousand a year. *With* benefits, a first for me.

My new supervisor, Sven, was queer themselves. They made sure to get an update on my pronouns the moment I walked in. I asked theirs. It felt like a normal thing to do there, because everyone did it. They got me and Matt lunch at a Middle Eastern spot near our East Village office as a welcome onto the full-time team. Said just because we were full time now, didn't mean they expected us to dedicate our whole lives to working.

"I know you both have a life, we all do. No job should distract from that." Said Sven.

They had Harry Potter glasses, a signature undercut-mullet hybrid, and a brilliant bowtie collection that put mine to shame. I liked them, and them me. And I liked Matt, and the other folks I met on our team who spent the day writing and analyzing headlines. I told myself things were good. That even though Cam and I still had tension, we were good. That it was a great idea for Cam to quit the bar and work on her jewelry design full time because we were good. We had enough money with my new job. And the thought of me providing for the both of us felt good, felt right, in the way I think men are told to feel. In 2017, 71 percent of adults felt it was "the man's" job to provide for a household. Queer folks aren't insulated from silly societal rules like those. They seep into us the same way, are just as toxic. It takes our own purges to relive ourselves from deeply rooted nonsense, but I hadn't purged yet. So, I told myself Cam quitting meant she loved me more, because she trusted me to provide for her, and everything was, so, so good. Money made us better. I was even able to cover off a credit card payment for our Europe trip that was coming up very soon. After just a few months and a bonus for the year, I had enough to move into a bigger room in Bushwick. And with my side job as a features writer for Pride, I could even save money, just for the sake of saving. I'd never been able to do that, and it was all such a grand feeling. Good enough for new tattoos, and to dye my shaved head every color under the sun in the span of a few weeks. Good enough for me to take up stand-up comedy on the weekends, hitting up various open mics on usually Saturdays. Telling jokes about my queerness and my sadness and my ex-relationship with God because I was feeling good enough to share.

"I've been trans now for...25 years. Ironically, I've been alive for 25 years, so that's been interesting." I'd say to a crowd of strangers.

Cam and I were so good again she agreed to move in with me and my new five roommates into our two-story apartment, in the large upstairs bedroom where we had our very own bathroom and access to a lovely rooftop garden we shared with just one other person. We were happy, I was happy. Happier than I'd ever been, perhaps. And on top of everything, I had ample time and energy to work on my edits from Pam now, of which were becoming quite distressing. Also though, her notes were dwindling. I was hearing from her less, because of projects she expressed were far more pressing than mine. And I accepted that, because I already knew my book was nowhere near as well written or as promising financially as anything else she might have been working on separately. As I waited for her responses, I bought other books and audiobooks to read and listen to. I read and reread the edits I'd already done and rewrote the parts I felt needed improvements. Months passed, I read more, I learned more. I heard nothing, still, from Pam. I was excited just thinking about telling Pam all I'd learned, but then, three months had become 12.

Pam had made thoughtful suggestions, like switching one of my supporting characters from white to Black. "It will add a sort of complexity you need here." A great and necessary point. She urged me to cut an odd dialect I'd chosen for some of my fantastical characters.

"It reads as confusing." She said.

I agreed. She dragged some of the tone of my book, that it read as if I were writing for a white audience, a thing she felt I need not do. I agreed.

She referenced Toni Morrison, "What I'm interested in is writing from outside the white gaze."

And from her mention, I read Morrison's *Bluest Eye* for the first time even though it'd been assigned to me in high school. I was moved. But her growing silence reverberated. No emails, not a one. Just my growing impatience, constantly refreshing of my emails became a pastime. Fully in anticipation for her, hopefully, final edits. I didn't care that I felt a heavy layer of frustration in her last email to me. That she said, out right, that her other projects were more pressing, more important. But I begin to wonder if I'd made a mistake accepting her offer to be my publisher. Not because of her frustrations with my work. That's a thing I'd expected in our journey together. Her frustration, my confusion, a learning curve between us. But because I'd signed up for something entirely different than what Pam had ever meant to offer. I'd signed up for a mentorship. I'd signed up to work with my literary idol, a Black queer woman I admired more than any other person in my industry.

But Pam was not my Black queer writing godmother. She did not have familial patience for me, nor did she ever tell me she did. Pam was a businesswoman. A queer Black capitalist. A person with expressed skill whose main goal was to build an empire because of it. Not to edify up-and-coming writers with unfinished books. Didn't matter that they were also Black and queer, that they came from the same community. Pam had found a way to break barriers in an industry that so often pushed people like us out. She'd become an exception. But I'd misinterpreted the reality of this truth. Just because someone is of your community don't mean they are your people. Don't mean they share your goals or your dreams. Pam was not my mentor. She wanted to work with me because my queer little book, if all went well, would make her and her people good money. But my book was not the cash cow she'd thought it'd be. So, we'd both failed each other. Neither of us delivered our end of this unspoken agreement. I wasn't even mad at her. I was angry with myself, for failing to be the skilled author she hoped to find. For handing her a book I knew damn well wasn't great, because I'd assumed the only road to its greatness included someone else that was not me. Still, a soft and open wound on my spirit did drum at the thought of her lack of tenderness, her immediate annoyance with my imperfections. I know she didn't owe me tenderness. I know she didn't owe me any level of care beyond what was allotted within our contract, but still. I wanted it. I wanted not to feel ashamed for wanting it. I wanted to believe all of the tenderness of her essays on BLS to be true. All her community-first musings. Essays that spoke of anticolonialism and damning the patriarchy. Shamed those interested in exploitation. Constantly uplifting of people like me, who had potential but needed a bit more guidance, who'd been lost or broken around the time they were meant to grasp fundamentals. She'd never lied to me, though. We'd only misunderstood each other.

Hi Jaz,

I have to be really honest and tell you that I don't have high hopes for this coming together at this point. Writing a book requires a huge amount of attention to detail, and I'm just not seeing the needed attention to detail here. I don't think we have the capacity needed to bring this to where we need it to be. I know that you were originally crowdfunding to publish this book yourself and that we stepped in and got you on this track instead. I want to be mindful of that while also being really real about the situation at this point...

I saw it coming. Still, my heart was at my feet. She was right. I didn't know what to do. It was an issue I'd had my whole life that if I knew how to fix, I would have. She said she would keep the money. I decided that was only fair. And I wasn't angry with her, I was angry with myself. I tried not to feel defeated, but it all felt like the clearest example of failure. Long after a successful

Kickstarter, long after the schedule to release that I'd shared with its supporters, I wasn't nearly ready to share this work. My embarrassment was almost comical, if not so debilitating. The writer I looked up to most felt my work unworthy to support. Unworthy of her cosign. What a joke I must have been to her. The most unfunny joke. Even the joke of me failed.

You live through that little piece if time that's yours, but that piece of time is not only your own life. It is the summing-up of all the other lives that are simultaneous with yours. It is, in other words, History, and what you are is an expression of History.

Robert Penn Warren

THIS IS THE BRIDGE

Sometimes my pain isn't mine. Not that it doesn't belong to me, it does. It lives here, in my body and who else could claim it if not myself? But it ain't *mine*. I'm anxious more times than not. I get mood swings. I feel sad out of nowhere and I couldn't tell you why. Sometimes, a wave of despair hovers over me like a blanket for days, weeks, until it retreats for a while. I don't know where it comes from or where it goes when it leaves me. But I do know that I am always carrying something just at least bit too heavy, and it don't always belong to me. Even though my family's fridge was always more than full. And I shared my bedroom with just one sibling and not six. And The Joyners went on summer vacations around the US, and I live in this country, where they say you can be anything. Both my parents went to college. I got to know I could before I ever did. Still, I am weighed down by the sum of my ancestor's truths, living deep within the depths of my dark skinned, Black American body.

The day I was born in Memphis, TN, I came in very much alive. So alive that sometimes I breathe more than I need to, offering shallow breaths to the world like some Navy Seal in-training. Ma jokes that I haven't relaxed since my very first breath at Methodist South. Because while I was busy on my way out, on the outside my mom was literally trying to stay alive. She and Pops had been trying to reach Dr. Davis, the Black woman who was supposed to deliver me, but she was in Mississippi with her sick mother, not expecting me for weeks. And so, some white man, who'd already removed his gloves for a swift exit, threw on some new ones to rush me into the world via C-section and get on with his afternoon. And amid all his nonchalance he and his nurses injected some, *something* into my mother's veins that she said had her, "drifting away." She would know, because my mother had died before.

When she was five, all it took were three watermelon Jolly Ranchers and a mischievous child left alone for two seconds. My mom still doesn't remember that epic fall that followed, thrusting her small body to her mother's hardwood floor, or the rustling sprint of her auntie and Grandma Palm racing into the living room to see what they'd just heard. But she does remember looking up at angels telling her,

"Not yet, Jo Young. You've got much to do."

And so my Momi has held her head quite high ever since. She used her unique connection to the afterlife to totally debunk traditional religion by the time she was 7 years old. And she used it to frame even the most dismal turn of events with a rose-colored optimism, even when her single mother was raising ten children all by her lonesome, when all they had were beans and a bit of cornbread to eat. Because the angels had her back. Sadness was not sadness; pain was not pain. Constantly reframing every hard story in her life into something saccharine sweet, because the angels had spoken, *We got you.*

"I am the architect of my life." Ma'd tell us during one of our homeschooled lessons.

Confident as they come because the angels, darling. Slowly trying to sculpt excellence into our little minds because she'd never been given any other reason to think otherwise. And rarely would her words recall the pain that lived within her that'd show in panic attacks. She would not tell her children about them, but they would lead her into several late-night hospital visits with Pops. Crying heart attack. Stroke. Her mind, attacking her. And in the daytime, her body would ache with constant stomach aches and headaches and high, high blood pressure. She didn't speak on them things. Only remedied them with herbs and supplements to the high heavens. And prayer, passed down from her mother, from her mother's mother. And she wouldn't know that all she carried, as would I.

My pain ain't my own sometimes. Maybe some of it came from Pops. THEE Memphis legend, Philip Drew Joyner, Jr.. Trained his eyes out of glasses at 30 years old. No armed forces yet learned how to fly a plane, for kicks. Jumped out of a plane for fun on one birthday just to one up himself. One time some cops pulled him over and he asked, "Do you know who I am?", and it worked!

Memphis did know who he was. A beloved musician, a walking encyclopedia of musical knowledge and a local celebrity, well-known internationally among folks steeped in true jazz. Pops could play over a thousand songs off the top of his head on just about any instrument, but mainly his specialties were trumpet and piano. He made money from music gigs around Memphis and beyond, also teaching high school band then orchestra. He was Peabody Hotel's piano man for nearly 30 years, till he passed in 2019. Never quit a thing he started. And in public, he was never not smiling. You couldn't run into Phil anywhere without a joyous, "Hello!"

But my daddy had pain. He never talked about it, never motioned to it on purpose, but I know because he showed us in his demand for perfection. Beat good notes into us when we'd play the wrong ones. Crafted his own quartet out of his first four children to show the world we were the right kind of children, that he was the right kind of Black man. Used to call himself the healthiest man in the world. He moved so fast you couldn't see the hurt. The illness, the pain. None of us knew he'd been diagnosed with cancer. That he battled it for likely over twelve years. None of us knew he carried the pain and pressure of keeping his family afloat even after he passed, a thing I know now he must have thought about all the time. And he carried the heavy weight of a secret in need of protecting. Worked as hard as he did to stay Black Memphis upper middle class. Not to be confused with white American middle class. Maybe he could have slowed down then. But he could not stop, and so he did not stop. He literally never stopped. Never retired. Till the very end. Oh, the pain he carried, that he never spoke about, not even to my mother. Yet, here I am, flailing under the pressure of providing. Wondering why not making enough money, not doing enough *things*, brings me into mental overdrive. My daddy knew the pain of necessary perfection. He knew what it meant to have to be the best when there's no exaggeration of the term. It's literal, and its life or death.

I wonder what my grandparents were like when they were younger. How did they carry their pain. What kind of pain, and where in their bodies did they carry it. None of my grandparents are alive anymore. I got to know some of them, only the joyful parts, and I'm grateful. But I wish I knew more. What did my great, great, great somebody's give my other greats. And I feel strange about this sometimes. A lot of the time, really. That I exist in a much better reality than my ancestors. I breathe in and out, knowing my breath is my own.

There's this show, *We're Here*, a gay ass show on HBO that's kind of like if *Too Wong Foo* (1995) were a (far more progressive) docuseries. In one of the episodes, Bob the Drag Queen, Eureka O'Hara and Shangela met with freedom fighters who marched in 'Bloody Sunday,' from Selma to Montgomery. One of the women, activist Lynda Blackmon, recalled falling unconscious after being violently beaten by cops on the Edmund Pettus Bridge. She was only a teenager. And as she told her story, Bob the Drag Queen, a dark skinned Black American queer from the south, began to sob. Sob, uncontrollably.

He said, "I think in the Black community we have not been taught to deal with our collective trauma. And then we end up with what feels like survivor's remorse."

Bob the Drag Queen is the direct descendant of enslaved people. Just like him, my grandma's grandma was enslaved. And she survived, so her children's children could survive, so that I can be here writing a book about my cushy life. Cushy compared to many of my people. I know this. And so, I carry her truths with me like my own because they are. In *Redefining Realness*, Janet Mock speaks of a different kind of survivor's guilt. She said, "I have been held up consistently as a token, as the "right" kind of trans woman (educated, able-bodied, attractive, articulate, heteronormative). It promotes the delusion that because I "made it," that level of success is easily accessible to all young trans women. Let's be clear: It is not."

We have both survived so many of our trans ancestors. Some who will never live past my current age, or even half of it. Who were too dark, or too Black, or too fat, or too big, or too poor, or too femme, who did not go to college, who did not pass, who, for these reasons, were not afforded the right to life. The right to thrive. We need no more exceptions. We have enough "exceptions." We need more survivors. And us thriving folk can't forget about the rest of us, still living. Still here, against all odds. Whose stories are just as important, lives just as precious. To thrive as a Black trans person is to breath in luscious breaths that feel like they might be stolen. And so, I hold the truths of these ancestors in my heart, and I do not forget who's child I am. I am only here because we have always been. Still, and always.

About three nights a month, or less, or more, I will take myself to bed and fall asleep, only to wake up some time between 2-4am. My body won't let me sleep. No pill, no Xanax, melatonin, weed, edible, stops it. No matter what I do before that night, if my body wants to lie awake, it does. I thought this was a me-thing. I thought I was the only one. But I told my mom about it, in passing, not meaning to make a big fuss, only that, "I'm tired today, didn't get back to sleep until after 3:15am."

Only to find that she too woke up at 3:15am. On the dot. And that three nights a month, or more, or less, she wakes up at odd hours of the night and cannot fall back to bed either. And so did her mother, and her mother's mother. She said,

"Momma always told me it's just your body resetting itself. Getting the demons out."

Now. You can't tell me there's no magic thread connecting you and your people. And with all the pain, in weaved is also their hope, their joy. I carry on the legacy of laughter steeped in my transcestors stories; the ones not often told. I can have so much fun I forget time exists. I can laugh so hard and loud you'll think there's something wrong. I carry my great grandfather's love to cook. I didn't know he was a chef until I invited my Aunt Treacy and some of my family over to try a feast I'd made from scratch. Crab cakes with crispy potatoes and salad, old school velvet cake with the boiled icing for dessert, adding the spices whispered to me from somewhere outside or inside myself. Just like he might have made it. My auntie's mouth fell open and she said,

"You didn't know your great grandfather [Claudie Ricks Joyner] was a head chef on the Memphis Riverboat downtown, did you?"

I would not be a writer without Joanne Joyner, who wrote her first book before I was ever born, who fought to self-publish it before going her own way. And though she never spoke of this, at least not till I was grown, I somehow knew to write my stories as soon as I could hold a pen. Music would not be the salve that sooths my bones, the foundation to the rhythms of my poetry had it not been for my father. That rhythm is in my being. It's in the blood of my ancestors. In the spirit of so many of my people. So, no wonder I came in hot onto this earth breathing quick, shallow breath like I was tired. Like I'd been here before. Like I knew something about what's to come. Because the pieces of my people that live in me guide me, carry me and I carry them, and we are a team. And I hope that now, because they have made me, and I am surviving, I can live long enough to heal some of our collective pain.

san·ko·fa

baby, before you leave

go back

in the family room

your folks left a case

full of memories

why don't you go on in there

see what you can find

THANKSGIVING WITH THE FAMILY

Right outside of D.C. - Fall 2014

"What's your mom's name again?" Cam asks while rolling up her third pair of black pants for our trip.

"Joanne...Oh! Also, maybe call her Ms. Joanne at first? Not that she'll be weird about it or anything just...respectfully..." I fade out.

Opt out, really, because I know I sound nitpicky, and I've quickly learned Cam don't like nitpicky. But I also want to be clear that my mother is a southern Black momma and that means a few different things, and I worry that maybe there's not enough time between now and our afternoon train ride to D.C. to really break that down. And there's something about introducing your girlfriend who, after six weeks together, moved in with you after emphatic side-eye and warning from that very same mother that really puts you in a bit of a bind.

Anyway, Cam didn't respond to the last thing, "And we're sleeping where...?"

I tell her we'll sleep on a surprisingly comfortable blowup mattress in the large nook of Jessica's one bedroom apartment. It's almost like a bedroom, I tell her. That's a pretty sweet set up, I tell her, compared to Leesie who'll sleep on the couch. Everyone else will stay in the 2-bedroom temp apartment for visitors in the same complex that my mom's rented. It's a new thing we're trying, Thanksgiving in D.C. Usually all the Joyner kids fly into Memphis from wherever we've spent the rest of the year. But things are changing, so to fight the inevitable, Ma made the executive decision to have Thanksgiving in D.C. which is basically the middle ground between all of us.

Did you know it takes exactly three minutes to get to Centreville, VA from the Time Square Amtrak stop when you are as distracted as I was? Amazing. Absolutely no time to slow the heart palpitations heating up my chest like a stew. I take Cam's hand, remembering she is the odd one out here, not me.

"Remember if you want us to go at any point, we can go," I say. Admittedly hoping this conversation never happens. Not so much that I don't want to leave but because the thought of the backlash of a decision like that gives me chills.

"I appreciate you saying that," she says.

We kiss. I breath for the first time in hours. Joanne Joyner exits Jess' Volvo and sashays towards us in a deep blue flowing jumpsuit. We'd caught her during her scarf phase and so she rocks a floor-grazing floral muffler which is especially dramatic on her 5'10 frame (5'7 and a half without heels but I assure you,

you'll never find her without them). My breath is short but calmer because I haven't seen my mother in months, and it feels nice, until I remember who is right beside me. She hugs me first, a long squeeze worthy of our time apart, and then,

"Camelia! It's so great to finally see you in person!"

Southern charm oozing off her deep red lips. I have not warned her that Cam is not a hugger. Cam leans back as if to avoid it but my mother disregards this very clear gesture, leaning in closer. Cam concedes.

"It's great to meet you too, Joanne." She says.

Dammit. Ms. Joanne, Ms.

My mom doesn't miss a beat, smiles steady as before and says,

"Well, you can call me Ms. Joanne."

And she turns back to Jess' car. We follow. I'm mortified.

I shoot Cam a wordless *I-told-you-so*. She rolls her eyes. I am not at all excited about this trip. Meeting my siblings goes fine enough. Thankfully Jess isn't a hugger either, and the boys simply waved from the other side of the living room when we entered. Leesie wouldn't arrive till the next day, but she and Cam already met. Only one left is Pops.

"Your father's having a look at the gym." Ma told us, "But you can help me start with this sweet potato pie in the meantime."

I followed her gaze to a bowl of unpeeled sweet potatoes on the island. Cam didn't. No, she went to sit in the living room beside the boys who were watching *Boondocks*.

"I love this show." She said, all friendly.

These lil' negros said nothing in response. I glared from the kitchen, and they couldn't care less.

"Camelia?" My mom said from the kitchen.

"Yeah?" Cam says, though a full 'Yes' would have been far more acceptable.

"You wanna help out with the pecan pies?"

Cam seems confused. She stands but she doesn't move and I want to fill her in. I have to fill her in. I didn't even think to explain this unspoken rule. I assumed everyone knew you can't just be sitting in somebody's home while they slave away and not ask how you can help. I'd never known a soul to not know this, but I also had only really invited other southern folk into my home up until this point. I'm sweating like a bad joke, peeling potatoes and hoping the power goes out so we can cancel this whole thing. I admire Cam's poker face hiding definite annoyance when she walks over to me and says,

"What part of it do you need help with?"

My mom calls me by my birth name when she explains to Cam that I know what to do. Cam wants to say something. I know it, I feel it. She doesn't. This talk, we've already had.

"My family still uses my deadname, old pronouns, all that. I know it's gonna annoy you but it's for real not a big deal to me." I said to Cam days earlier. A mostly true statement in hopes of defusing any future, let's say, tiffs.

"*It is* a big deal to you." She says.

Dammit. Cam sees right through me. It's why I love her. Also, why I shuttered at the thought of what might come next. But really though, it's not a big deal in that I don't see these people 80 percent of the time and when I do, they see me. I know they *see* me. Sure, they don't have my updated IDs but they see me. They didn't know why I have stubble now, or why I dress this way, or why I look just like my daddy and not in the daddy-daughter kind of way, but they *see* me. I couldn't explain then that I knew they knew this "me" that I am is who I've always been. All the pomp and circumstance around my identities, my aesthetic, was not relevant in their company. At least all but my father's who perhaps could never claim he knew me. But "coming out" was not a narrative I needed, or even valued beyond the mild annoyance and more seriously, possible danger of calling me something old in public.

Anyway, Cam said, "I won't say anything. But if shit gets disrespectful, I might go off. You know me."

"My family's not disrespectful like that." I tell her.

We left it there. And so you can imagine my relief when, after my mom both deadnames me and misgenders me in the same sentence, Cam simply rolls her eyes. Sweet relief, for now. But it doesn't last. The front door opens. I think it might be Jess. She'd left real quick for some last-minute ingredients at the Wegmans around the corner. But no. It's Pops.

"Hello!" He bellows like an NBA announcer, a thing everyone but Cam is used to because it's the same way he's entered since the beginning of time.

I nudge Cam, "We should go say hello."

I've learned over the years that the best way to deal with Philip Drew Joyner, Jr. is head on. Be assertive, meet him where he's at. The more you cower, the worse it'll be. So, she wipes her freshly washed hands with a paper towel and leads us both into the entry way of the apartment where my Pop is taking off his running shoes. The last I saw him was last Christmas. And we hadn't spoken much at all since, except for the few passing hellos when my mom had me on speakerphone. So, I wasn't just nervous for Cam, I was nervous for me. Because last Christmas, I didn't have a mustache or a high-top fade. I didn't wear sweaters and chinos from the men's section of Topshop. I was in my stylish boi era and my dad had absolutely no reason to know this about me. And no, no one had seen this version of me before other than Jalisa. And no, I didn't tell anyone that I might look, or sound different thanks to months of pure testosterone running through my veins. But I wasn't worried about anyone else's reactions but his. They'd at least had glimpses of the octave change, inklings from my Dyke March updates on social media. And I'd never once brought home a boyfriend, and I never once pretended not to be the weird queer nigga I am, and I always dressed like some variation of an extra from a sapphic 70s film so, who could really be surprised? Other than my dad. I don't know, something about Pops seeing me like this felt especially exposing. Extra revealing.

I'll never forget the look on his face when he raised his head from his Rebooks. It was a dripping sort of disgust that turned him into someone I didn't know. And I already didn't know this man very well. And then he opened his mouth, slowly, his eyes fixed on me, up then down then to Cam. Cam, famously known to avoid hugs, reaches out to him. I'm shocked that even she feels the need to placate this man. He simply had that effect on people. But he raises a hand to her like a screen.

"Don't think I don't see you." He said glaring through Cam into the wall behind her. He continued, "You are controlling my daughter and you don't belong here. Know that."

Whoa. And I mean, *whoa*, because what the fuck and why and how and when did my father decide my partner was my personal demon. I have no words worthy of speaking out loud. I am stunned to attention, frozen and so is Cam.

"What are you even talking about?" Cam asks him. Her voice sharp like radar.

He just stands there, staring at our dumb faces and I want to run tattle on him to my mom who I know at least doesn't hate Cam. Doesn't love her, but at this point I'll take any old crumbs under the carpet. I gulp down a familiar intensity in my throat. My arms itch and my heart feels like it might burst, and I'm thrust into the past of the two of us, this very same never-ending discordance between us. Him, glaring down at me, so unsatisfied with what or whom I've just presented to him. I wish my siblings had witnessed this so that I'd know it was real. I wish Drew hadn't just turned up a Stevie Wonder mix that drowned out this entire event. I wished to think up a joke to tell or a word to say that could diffuse this affair as if in adult life this gimmick still works in the same ways. As if it's worked in years. But no, this familiar feeling, the one that begs for mercy in a merciless place, lingers.

I fix up my mouth to speak, I'm shaking more than I want to, I dust off nonchalant inflections I once used with him so much and say, "You're doing entirely too much."

"This ain't you." He says to me in response.

I'm stunned. Shook by his slang because my father, *this* father, *never*, ever used it. I wonder how much he had to hate me to step outside his respectable words.

"C'mon, he can act like this if he wants, it's really whatever." I pull Cam into the kitchen.

Jess comes in then, seconds too late. Pops goes and sits in the living room, pulls out his trumpet mouthpiece and buzzes along as he's wont to do when he has any bit of free time, which for him is rare. I don't know what I was expecting. I already knew from what Ma and Jess said on the phone when I admitted that Cam moved in that the reception wouldn't be grand but...I didn't expect this. And maybe it's because I rarely even thought of my father because thinking of him made me resentful and frustrated, and likely to spiral. I'd warned Cam of my dad. Told her,

"He's weird as hell and rude, don't expect him to be nice."

But even then, I didn't anticipate this. My father was a man's man. Full of masculine vigor and brass and he never had any space for niceness. Too soft. But he was also always an honest man, I never knew him to lie. Every word he ever said, though harsh, was real. And so, I couldn't help the part of me that felt crushed under his perception of me now. This weak, dimwitted fool not even strong enough to look how I wanted to look. Controlled by some evil, mysterious devil woman. I knew he meant every single word. I hated that I still cared.

And like I thought, no one noticed a thing. Not a damned thing, and even when I quickly recapped the whole debacle to my mom, quietly of course, and the music was a nice camouflage, she downplayed it as she usually did,

"You know your father has no filter, he'll get over it. Don't let it get to you too much."

The night was heavy. I carried shame and disappointment, and Cam's annoyances, that grew as the night went on and on and we continued to pretend everything was fine while watching *The Princess Bride* as a family.

"I really don't get why you just won't make them use your pronouns. It's weird." Cam rolled over on her side of our air mattress at 1am that night to say.

I for one had the energy of a sloth in daylight. Definitely not enough to entertain this mammoth of a conversation. But as a dyke whose New York life was now 100 percent steeped in my queerness I could not ignore the glaring gap that was this part of my puzzle. It wasn't lost on me that my family was the only group left out of this very significant truth of my existence. Fine. But this was a privilege I cherished. I'd spent years under their roof, unable to bloom and now they had no power over me. I could yell dyke out loud and friends would cheer. And I never saw them anyway. And when I did it was for seconds and in those seconds, even if stressful or upsetting I could still turn around and leave fairly soon. And why should I subject myself to another moment like ours with my dad. Even the clash with my dad, I could leave that. I was lucky. I knew I was lucky. Why not embrace that luck and stay the fuck quiet? Even when we went out to a movie that night and Pop's went out of his way to buy tickets for his "three daughters and two sons!" Or when Ma said my deadname loud as hell across the theater hall and bystanders nearly broke their necks trying to figure out what lovely lady she might be speaking to. Even when I knew, *knew,* interactions like this were not sustainable. Not safe, even. Still.

"I'm not saying anything." I mumbled, two hands propping up my head up on that flat pillow Jess found at the bottom of her closet.

That was the end of it. For two minutes. Then,

"Do you seriously feel like your mom would have a problem?"

Dammit. Time to sit up.

"Bae."

She said nothing, gave me time to think. No idea. When I was thirteen, I told my mom I was never having children,

"You have 4 other kids so you'll definitely have *at least*, like, 2 grandchildren."

I was adamant. She was so very understanding. And when I was 19 and depressed and Jess and Leesie had boyfriends, and she asked if I was dating anyone, I told her,

"I'm not really into boys like that..."

Not so much a "coming out." More like a soft preview into my not-so-distant future just months later when I'd go sneaking off during college breaks to the local LGBT center or going on quiet dates with the queer cuties from the now defunct Memphis College of the Arts. And I never had any plans to say more to her. For what? The only plan I had was to get away, far away, to a place I knew didn't care how the hell I showed up in the world. Or at least according to its lore, and all I really knew then was the lore of New York City. Plus, Ma didn't even flinch when she saw my peach fuzz. I'd always had a bit of a moustache and sharp features too, just like a younger version of my dad. But I looked just like him now in a possibly jarring way to someone who didn't know about hormone replacement therapy, or trans folks, or trans masc this or that. And I hadn't even learned to accept the little Pops staring back at me in the mirror myself. It'd be the catalyst to me pausing testosterone for many months before getting back on. And going off it again. And back on. But this wasn't just me living my queer ass life. This was actively telling my mom that I was not the kid she thought I was, that the pronouns she used for me were not my pronouns, that my old name, that she'd given me, was not my name?! That I'd actually had a court mandated name change. I couldn't fathom it.

Cam sat up with me, grazed my arm in that way she did that warmed me from the inside. We kissed, sweetly, just a short one that reminded me of our love and she said,

"I see how you look when they use your deadname. I just want you to be able to feel like yourself."

I let her love on me even though I did not agree with her. But I did agree with her point, that the deadnaming in public was unsafe. Was not something I could keep dealing with, not when I was out here looking like somebody's whole son.

"Just tell them to not say she. Start there." She said.

She made points. The next morning, we planned to walk around the complex with Jess and my mom before picking up Leesie from the train station. It was a lovely complex, with a lake in the middle and a walkway paved with gorgeous bushes and flowers that charmed the last of the autumn butterflies. Cam was right. If there was ever a perfect time to say something, it was right this moment.

"Your dad won't be around." She urged, which was important because the thought of saying anything else to my dad on this trip, let alone this news, was out of the question.

Bright and early, aka 10 am because we all slept in past our initial 8am roll call, Jess, Ma, Cam and shivering-with-nerves-me gathered beside the complex's gym to begin our walk (and talk, that they knew nothing about).

"It's really cute over here." I said, as sort of a diversion. They had no idea what mess I was 'bout to drop on them.

"Right?" Jess grinned, "And they always have fresh cookies in the welcome room too, we could get some after our walk."

Oblivious. Oblivious, I tell you. Shit, I could change my mind if I wanted with how oblivious they were. I could bail on this whole thing. Why not? We're doing just fine? Why ruin a perfectly fine thing?

"...Did you show your dad that last article you wrote? The one that went viral?" My mom asks, so innocently, so proud, not knowing the frown forming on Cam's face had everything to do with the first few letters of her question. My birthname.

This was supposed to be the beginning of our conversation. I was supposed to say something like, "Actually, I go by Jasper now..."

And from there would be a whole thing, but I couldn't. Or wouldn't, because I no longer wanted to shake shit up at 10am on family vacation. But, Cam did. Oh, she was ready.

"Actually, it's Jasper." She nudged me adamantly in the side like, "follow the plan!"

And I shake my head but it's too late. There's no turning back now. So, like a fuzzy muppet off of *Sesame Street* I grunt, "Yeah, like the gemstone." I laugh. I try to treat it like a joke when it's anything but.

Silence.

"Joanne, do you know any transgender people?" Cam asks in that bold way I both love and was growing to hate about her.

"Transgender?" My mother parroted, head cocked to the side walking beside us.

Jess, the ever-helpful supporter chimed in then with a reasonable example, "Like Laverne Cox?"

Sure. There were only a couple, if even that, well-known trans folks out there and Laverne was great, so why not. At least it wasn't after April 2015 and she mentioned Caitlyn Jenner instead, forcing me to both agree then denounce the woman all at once. Too confusing. This was better. Maybe even not bad.

"Yeah, like Laverne Cox, only I'm not a trans woman. I am trans, though. "I say," finally.

Tumbleweeds. Crickets. Nothing but dead silence from a black hole. We're walking so slow we might as well stand still when Ma echos my words,

"Trans?" She said.

"Transgender." Jess confirmed, because neither of them know that "trans" is absolutely fine to say. They know nothing about it really, and this reality hits me like a stack of bricks. In 2014, the number of people in the U.S. who knew or worked with someone trans had doubled, from 8% in 2008 to 16%. Still, I'll bet the majority of people who knew of someone lived in the country's biggest cities, because us trans folk know we're safest in higher numbers, not that we're ever fully safe at all. The trans masc ones aren't safe from erasure, a thing that likes to kill us from the inside out. The trans femmes aren't safe from hyper visibility, a thing that boldly kills them from the outside in. Cam and I speed up a bit. Dialed it back about when we noticed we'd almost passed them. Finally, Ma says,

"Are you saying you're a man?"

The front of my Nikes clamped the back of her Keds.

"Sorry. Can we sit down?" I ask, not because I'm tired but because this has now become a sit-down conversation.

Thankfully everyone agrees and as we're walking to the nearest picnic table I explain the term non-binary, a term I no longer use due to its antithetical nature[1] and as I believe there are as many gender expressions as people on earth, but at the time it made the most sense.

"So, are you saying you don't want to be called a daughter or a sister?" Jess asks, and the confusion in her voice made my heart drop.

I'd always been number two. Jess' day one A one, but never quite "sisterly." whatever that even meant.

And I really worried now. When Jess is especially confused by something I say, there's not much hope for my mother. I try to save us,

---

[1] Jasper Joyner wrote an essay titled 'Nonbinary is not the flex we think it is' in their self-titled newsletter to address their issues with the term.

"I mean, think back, did you ever really think of me as *your sister*? Like, legit, have we ever had a sisterly dynamic?"

I said this confidently, because Jess and my relationship was unique in its ambiguity. We bonded over music and doing art things together, and playing make believe, but even then, I, for all intents and purposes, was not anybody's idea of "a sister."

"I guess I never really thought of you as a girl or a boy..."

I beamed when she said this. I dare say any gender nonconforming or trans person would likely beam at a response like this, because there's no more affirming response than someone saying they always saw you as the someone you are. But then Ma spoke again,

"I mean I don't care what you say about it, you are my daughter."

"Ma." Jess pushed back, but at this point my mother had her arms quite literally folded on the subject.

I tried not to let this cut too deep, but it did cut. She continued,

"This "nonbinary," is that your word?" She sounded like the world's biggest skeptic.

My mother. The woman who taught us that fairies most definitely can exist in our very backyard, now the world's biggest skeptic. Funny, that.

Cam interjected, "It's literally in the dictionary. It means they're not a man. But also, not a woman."

I mean, I would have said this differently. But I remembered, she was doing this for me. I couldn't get too caught up on Cam's signature crass delivery. But I did try to defuse.

"You know Prince?"

Yes. I said this, and once I said it I had to explain, "'I'm not a woman, not a man, I'm something you will never understand...'"

These are in fact Prince's lyrics from "I Would Die 4 U."

I peeled back my already short fingernail. Sunk in my seat, "That's me." Commence weighted eyeroll. I was annoying myself.

"You're so dramatic." Jess laughed, and I had to too cause, yes. Drama. But truth. And I knew she knew what I meant.

I wiped away a smile when I caught a glimpse of my mother's face. It was one I didn't know well, which worried me. This thick veil of suspicion like I was some salesman touting a useless catalog of arbitrary goods.

"So, you're saying you're what?" She blurted out, as if she hadn't heard a thing.

I knew where we were now. We were in the point in the conversation where my mother had decided how she felt already. But I wouldn't stop. Plus, I needed Jess to know all of this, too.

"I call myself a non-binary trans guy. I purposefully don't say "man" because I'm not a man. I'm like a pansy, basically." I said, thinking I was really doing something. Of course, my family knew nothing of the deep history of pansies in queer spaces, of the fact that pansies, the flowers, were actually self-fertile, hermaphrodite. So perfectly encompassing my fluidity. My colorful nature.

"A *pansy*!?" My mom sucked her teeth.

"A pansy. Like effeminate but also masculine. Speaking of, they use 'they/them' pronouns. Like gender neutral pronouns." Cam added.

Whatever frustration I had with Cam was reconciled clearly. We were finishing each other's sentences on purpose now.

"Now, that doesn't make a lick of sense to me." Ma said.

Okay. I could have predicted her saying this. I wasn't sure what else to do or say on my end though. I thought so hard about it I froze.

Cam chimed in,

"Yes, it does. You've probably used it even today. It makes perfect sense and it is grammatically correct. Before you say it's not."

Uh oh. That delivery. My mother wouldn't like that one bit. I interrupted, speaking softer than what would have come out my mouth otherwise.

"You know when you're talking about someone, and you may not know their gender? You automatically say, like, "They went that way," or "They sent this,", "You wouldn't say "he or she went that way.' That's what would be unnatural. Not they/them."

They were thinking, processing. Listening. I stayed quiet, patient, because it wasn't a dismissive silence. It was a pensive one.

"And you have to stop calling them their deadname. It's Jasper now. Or Jaz." Cam said like a hammer over glass.

I prayed to dissipate into a pile of dust in my seat. The only true reprieve from this outrageously awkward moment.

"Jasper?!" My mom shouted as if this name isn't what started the conversation, "You sound like an old man!"

"Why would you pick Jasper?" Jess asked, scrunching up her nose in disgust.

263

This is exactly why I changed my name in private. I ignored the actual question and tried to sandwich in a positive, "I kept my middle name!"

"But *Jasper*?" Ma said my new name like it burned in her mouth.

"Why not James...Joseph?"

"Is the name the issue, or is it the fact that they changed a part of themself that you came up with?" Cam was a roll, and by "roll" I mean digging an even deeper grave for herself and me.

"The name!" My mom spewed back. Let the record show I didn't believe her. Not one bit. There's a reason all of our middle names rhymed. My mother loved that her kids were mini versions of her. But I didn't say this. Didn't see the point of challenging this lie amidst every other thing happening in that moment,

"And this whole them-they nonsense is ridiculous, too." Ma tacked on with a huff.

"I tell people they can use 'he/him' with me, if it's easier. You can do that." I said, keeping my tone light though I wanted to shout it. I knew how I showed up now. It was much safer to he/him me in public than she/her my bearded ass. It was a funny, strange thing because at its base, none of this pronoun nonsense really mattered to me for real. My queer friends used all pronouns for me and I embraced it. In the right company I could be everything, I didn't have to choose. It felt so trivial if not for the many societal ways these distinctions could help or hurt my interactions. I felt silly for making distinctions. The silence returned but this time louder than before. I tapped my foot beneath the table. Cam grabbed my hand, squeezed it. I tried wiping the fearful frown off my face, but it was stuck there.

"We don't have to figure all this out right now." Jess said, logically, reasonably.

But logically speaking I didn't know where we could go from here that wouldn't feel just as heavy as this moment. Still, we did stop speaking. We got up and headed for the Welcome Center and I had a warm chocolate chip cookie that tasted like air, and we went to get Leesie and returned to cook and bake some more. Like I was all there. I wasn't. I was floating off somewhere. I'll admit that not much changed with Ma on the trip. She still used my old name, same old pronouns. Rolled her eyes when Jess wouldn't. At least *she* was on board. Cam and I considered that a success. And it only took my mom two years of Jess and Leese's nagging to get it right. But my dad? Let's just say the angels had to knock some sense into him before he left this earth. But he got there. Thank goodness he got there, just in time.

Poem for the starving artist

Money come

Like my ideas

Money big

Like dreams

Money stay

Like my obsessions

Money long

Like will

My

Money steady

Like drive

Money ready

My Money ready

Money ready

Like me

My money ready

Like me

MONEY ENOUGH TO BUY A CLUE

Brooklyn, NY, 2015

"What the hell are you writing this early?" Cam rolled out of bed, saying.

"It's 2 o'clock." I didn't look up to respond.

She'd technically slept a normal, 7-hour but since she'd been asleep only since six that morning, the afternoon is the earliest she'd rise. I know she heard my response like a judgement call.

She shuffled to the bathroom and groaned, "Did you clean up?"

The question irked me. As if I didn't always clean up the tornado of her drunken entrance after a night of partying. I kept my eyes on the Google doc that I was now attempting to proofread for a Pride.com article.

"Yes." I mumbled back, still reading.

Cam had gone from full time to part time, to — as of one year ago — no job at all. But the partying continued. I'd been silly to think it wouldn't. It was the only time I'd witnessed her fully happy, so of course it continued. Outside of bars and crowded dance floors, a heavy darkness loomed over Cam like an extra awkward shadow. I had a hard time separating that darkness from myself. Discerning which parts of it came from me or from her past or from her present. I took some blame. My obsessive need for her attention had to be draining. It was even draining for me. And then there was my pushing her to build her jewelry career which, the more I pushed, the more she seemed to avoid. But I worried that this only added to her depression. Cam hadn't made one piece of jewelry in months. No updates on her website. Only a couple weeks at a Bushwick craft fair that I'd set up for her. And I hated to admit my frustration with her lack of work ethic, clashing with her overwhelming desire to be out when the sun went down. I told her as much. Told her she lacked balance, as if my panic on account of her absence harkened to any sort of mental balance within myself.

"I shouldn't feel trapped by you. I should be able to go out." She said to me.

I knew she was right. I had no rebuttal to comments like this, and so I'd usually get quiet, apologize. Hope that her anger with me wasn't enough to push her away. There it was again. Pushing, pulling. I told her I needed help, because I did. I didn't know how to *be* without her. I was in therapy. I wanted to figure out a way to be less of a strain on her. I apologized again through bawled up fists full of quiet, growing resentment that I did not feel the love from her I felt I'd been giving.

She asked, "Are you mad at me?"

I was. I didn't know it until she asked, and it hit me from the inside out. I absolutely was. I usually would have said no without thinking, but I said,

"What do you think."

I never spoke to her this way.

I had always prided myself on the gentleness with which my toxicity floated out into our atmosphere. A toxic though tasteless venom that'd appear in my passive aggressive text messages and accusations of her cheating. In promises that I could not exist without her, though said with a smile because oh, how romantic a thought. But now my words stunk in a particular sort of stench reserved for old, molding things.

"Don't do that." She advised.

"Yes, I'm fucking mad." I said. But I think I was more sad than mad.

"Why are you mad?" She asked me.

So direct. There was no space to run from our reality. It had been nearly three years of us, one trip to Europe, one secret elopement in the wake of Trump (who I knew would win) with Cam's lack of U.S. citizenship while looking far more Middle Eastern than any white supremacist cared for, plus our one move into an apartment together that was simply ours. I couldn't tell you why none of this felt good. It felt like a mess of a thing I could not explain, yet I wanted nothing more than our mess. The blurry version of our mess I could get lost in, though. Not this clear and unambiguous mess that made my stomach churn.

"Jaz," She commanded my attention.

I had nothing good to say. I didn't want to speak with nothing good to say. Or, I didn't want to acknowledge our reality out loud. So, I didn't answer. I asked, instead, "Do you still want to be with me?"

You don't just ask this question. You think it, like an intrusive thought always whispered in the back of your mind and you quiet it, when it allows, but you do not ask this question. Not when you know full well that you require something of your love your lover cannot give...Not unless you are ready to break free of it, of which I was nowhere near feeling,

"I don't know." She told me.

This is why I never asked. It did hurt as much as I knew it would. Still, the hopeless romantic I embraced of the thorny bouquet of roses she'd just handed me. I basked in the fact of the hopefulness of us, because she did not yet say, "No." I could not handle, "No."

Cam would never ask me such a question. No point. My answer would always be, "Yes." One thousand times, "Yes." No matter what happened. *Yes.* Until the end of time itself, because our love affair could not end. I couldn't take the repercussions of that reality. There was too much at stake, including parts of me I'm not sure I could retrieve after the fact.

"I'm not happy." She said then, a thing I knew she felt but I never wanted to hear.

"I know." I told her.

"I really want to be, though. I really want this to work." She said.

I took her hand. This admittance was enough for me. I could have floated to the ceiling with this boost of hope. She wanted us to work. As long as she did, so did I. We talked and talked about us, until she pointed out the circle we'd traveled. We landed on couple's therapy. My insurance would cover it, I said, and I could afford the co-pay with my new side job. She asked that I find the therapist, since I already had one. I was good at things like this, she said. I did not have the tools to understand why this felt unfair. That constant push and pull of us, that imbalanced fight and flight in our relationship.

"I love you." I said. A desperate plea for reassurance.

"I love you." She told me, and I noticed how the words rested strangely on my ears.

Oh darling

didn't you know?

You were already drowning

just fine

on your own

THAT MOMENT

Brooklyn, NY, 2016

INT. CAMELIA AND JAZ BEDROOM. MORNING

JAZ awakens in the dewy sun, beside a thick comforter just inches from their body, fully covering their partner CAMELIA.

JAZ

What the hell?

CAMELIA

You're hogging the covers again.

Cam shifts her body in the opposite direction.

JAZ

Well now I don't have any.

Camelia scrunched up the cover into a ball and shoves it to Jaz.

CAM

Here.

Jaz settles into it. The two are quiet for a moment. Then, a jerk of the covers in Camellia's favor.

273

JAZ

Cam!

Camelia jumps out of bed. Leaves the bedroom stomping.

CAM

I'm sleeping in the living room.

Jaz's eyes dart. They jump up and follow with quick, nervous steps.

JAZ

Bae. You don't have to sleep out here, I'm sorry.

Cam found lying under a throw on a grey couch.

CAM

I don't want to be around you right now.

Jaz throws up their hands.

JAZ

Over some cover?!

Cam faces the opposite direction.

CAM

No, Jaz, over all this bullshit. I'm tired of it.

JAZ

We've been good, where is this even coming from?

CAM

I'm tired of you hovering over me every fucking second of every fucking day. I'm tired of telling you I want space and you cry about it. I'm tired of you trying to push me back into this relationship when I want out. You can't even let me be for a few hours to sleep.

Jaz hesitates before speaking.

JAZ

You really think I... push you to be with me?

Camelia doesn't hesitate at all.

CAM

Yes.

JAZ

Bae...what are you saying?

Jaz's eyes water. Cam wraps herself more tightly in the throw. Jaz gestures towards the bedroom.

JAZ

Look. You can be in there, alone. I'll leave you alone, okay?

Cam slowly stands, confusion covering her face. Jaz backs away to make space for her return to the bedroom.

JAZ

Can I ask you one thing before I go?

Beat

CAM

What.

Jaz stutters.

JAZ

Do you...do you think you still want to be with me?

CAM

You have got to be kidding me.

Jaz tries to hide a tear.

JAZ

Cam —

CAM

Right now? No. I don't want to be with you.

Cam enters the bedroom. Mumbles.

CAM

Just leave me the fuck alone. I'll let you know when I want to talk.

Jaz's hands shake. They sweat, and cry, heavy and laboriously. They start to enter the bedroom, stop. They power towards the door, slam it as hard as they can, then scream.

Are you sure, sweetheart, that you want to be well?

Just so's you're sure, sweetheart, and ready to be healed, cause wholeness is no trifling matter. A lot of weight when you're well.

Toni Cade Bambara, *The Salt Eaters*

NOTE: *This next chapter is heavy.*

Skip it if you need to. Return to it if you can.

TransLife Hotline: 877-565-8860

EDIT SOBER

Brooklyn Methodist Hospital, Fall 2016

"Just enter through those doors. Someone will be able to help you in just a moment," Said the kind nurse with the soft brown eyes and scratched up glasses.

"Thank you." I said, following her gaze to the grey double doors past the waiting room.

I liked that she looked me in my face but not directly in my crying eyes. I hated that I couldn't stop crying. I cried when I filed the paperwork, cried when they asked me why I was there: *Suicidal ideation.* I knew the term because I'd just spoken to my therapist, Andrea (a young Latina woman because since I could not find someone Black, I at least wanted someone brown) who told me that she did not feel comfortable trying to help me in this state. That I needed to admit myself to the nearest hospital, and that she would be available all day, whenever and if ever I needed to call. I didn't have a therapist my first year of college, when I planned to leave this place for good before. I'd have thoughts like it all the time but never so strong that I made a plan. Even when I'd find myself this close to leaving, it's as if my body did the thinking for me. But this time was different. I didn't think I'd get back to this place. I hated that I was back to this place, but at least this time I was at a hospital.

I didn't like the shock in Andrea's voice when I told her what happened. I didn't like that she told me to breathe through panicked breath as if I had the tools for such a request. I didn't like that I'd not told her everything in the year that we'd been meeting. Only the stuff I felt made me seem sane, and so she didn't know that any time Cam showed signs of distance, I contemplated leaving this earth. I'll admit, this was all news to her. And I'll admit, I hoped her therapeutic skill included reading minds. But it was too late to stay angry at her, all that anger now lived inside my chest, tight and twisted. It was all mine now. My only reprieve was the veil of numbness like balm to all the feelings blaring like jazz in my body. Yet, still, I'd been an endless river of tears flowing since I left my apartment, all the way here. And it was a twenty-minute cab ride. I said nothing when the driver asked me if I was cold, because I was shivering. I couldn't stop shivering. I wasn't cold at all. So, I kept my arms folded, praying I didn't bring attention to myself with the other seven folks sitting in the waiting room with me. And if they did notice, I hoped they thought my distress stemmed from some unseen physical injury. I felt embarrassed. Foolish. Because less than an hour ago I wanted to jump from my apartment window more than I'd wanted anything in the world and now I was standing in front of a nurse at Brooklyn Methodist Hospital, crying. Still very much alive. Feeling, too much. I kept my head down when I walked through those doors. Kept it down when I sat between two other teary someone's in the other room, that felt heavier than the front room somehow.

"Jasper?" Said another woman, a Black woman not much older than my 26 years.

She had me hand over my phone and the backpack I brought with me, and follow her to a large, dark room with barren walls, no window and a small uncomfortable cot. My heartbeat too fast and my fingers came back to life with a painful prickle.

"How are you feeling now?" She asked me.

Ha! I could laugh at the simplicity of her question. I shrugged. I wasn't one to shrug when asked a question but all my 26 years of home training were lost somewhere. She kept talking and I know I responded somehow but I don't remember even half of what she said. Some series of questions I'm sure she'd asked hundreds of people like me before. I'd float back into myself every now and then, feeling the jolt of her words like a splash of water on my face.

"Are you still having suicidal thoughts?"

"No."

"Can you walk me through what happened before you got here?"

The prickly feeling in my fingers traveled up my arms and into my hurting chest. What was cold turned warm, or warmer.

It's like I was arriving. Then the embarrassment, I was overwhelmed by it. To admit to her that a tiny little argument led me here...it took me ages to open my mouth. Each word was like an upchuck and my mouth felt dirty afterwards.

"Is it alright if we contact the woman you wrote down as your mental health provider?"

"Yes."

Before she left, the nurse pat me on the shoulder and said,

"We're going to have a doctor come in in just a moment to ask you a few questions. In the meantime, just wait here and give me a shout if you need anything."

There was a button on the wall she showed me before she left, that I had no intentions of pressing. I didn't want to be bothered, yet I didn't want to be left alone. There was nothing to do when she left but twiddle my tingling fingers. My thoughts were jumbled words, my breath a fluttering joke for breathing, yet I was still alive. I'm sure that's what this doctor would want to talk to me about. Being alive, and how I felt about that living. I'd barely said a full sentence since I arrived. But now I knew for sure, mental health doctors cannot read minds. I did not care to keep wasting my own time living like this. Lying. I told myself I'd tell as much truth as my mouth and mind would let me. I don't know how long I waited there in that dark, grey room. Ten minutes. One hour. But finally, when my breathing felt steadier, I heard a gentle knock on my door. In walked a tall older white male who, after gesturing to me that it was okay, sat on the solitary seat beside the cot I'd seeped into. He reminded me of a biology professor I had at Vandy who spoke like Colonel Sanders, only when he spoke, he sounded more like a New Yorker. I didn't like that professor.

"How are you doing, Jasper?"

I breathed deep and hoped for the best.

"Fine," I told him, not bothering to look him in the eye.

He asked me another series of questions that felt familiar to me and I answered them the same as I did for the nurse, but then he said something new,

"What do you think is the matter?"

I wanted to say, *What do you think? The fuck?*

Instead, I stared at him like he was a whole fool, something I never would have done any other day but I just didn't have the energy to play pretend. He said,

"I understand this is a difficult question," and rested his hands on his lap, all patient.

"I really couldn't tell you." I told him.

"Well, I spoke with your current therapist — with your permission, of course — and she let me know that up until recently she thought you might be doing fine."

I grunted. *Of course, she did.* My whole MO with my old therapist was to seem okay, not get better.

He noticed my hesitation, then continued, gently,

"But you mentioned to her you think you're dealing with," He paused to check his notes, "Borderline Personality Disorder?"

I grunted again, a sort of half-laugh, curious what their conversation was like. Andrea shocked out of her mind, this doctor probably agreeing before he even met me that none of my actions today made real sense based on what she knew about me. I'd been raised to always be on my best behavior. I'd never planned for that to seep into my therapy sessions. Shit, I never planned to need therapy. I'm not sure what I planned for. Much of my time was spent following the right rules so that I could, one day, feel free enough to just exist. I assumed I'd stumble into that okay feeling one day like some people stumble into a lottery win. Or I wouldn't, and I would die before it happened. That was my assumption. Doing what I was told so that I'd get through to the next thing I was told, so that one day I could have done enough following orders to be free. It seemed the natural progression of my life. I lived as if there was no other option, and so when I decide to go to therapy, because something felt wrong in my body, but I didn't know what, there was no turning off that obedient child who made it *this far* being good. And yes, once I started searching on my own for what was wrong, I found a thing that spoke to my mood swings, and obsessive, scary thoughts and sometimes delusions, my constant anxiety, my incessant need to hyper-focus on one person for all my love, and that person never being myself. I knew my almost violent longing to feel whole and loved was not a normal thing, so yes, Borderline Personality Disorder seemed right. It felt like an answer, and right then, I needed answers.

"Yes, "I told him.

"Hmm. The reason your therapist may have hesitated there is usually when interacting with someone with BPD, there are a few clear signs in behavior, a lot of which it seems you don't have. Not saying that this isn't your experience, but just want to bring that to your attention, does that makes sense?"

I said nothing. He'd parroted exactly what Andrea said. I didn't fit the description of this kind of hurting. And if not this, then what? Because it was a fact, I was hurting. I didn't expect him to understand. I knew now I was almost too good at seeming good, at looking "okay." Or perhaps I was too dark for anyone to see my scars. Or too brown to seem blue, or too well-behaved to seem broken. Whatever it was, I was tired of it. I wanted it, in me, to die, if nothing else died within me.

"Let me ask you Jasper, in your childhood, or growing up, did you ever feel like your life was in danger?"

His question gave me shivers. Like he'd just opened a forbidden door in the basement of my mind. I resisted the urge to close it. If there was any time to explore, this was it. I looked the doctor in his eyes for the first time since he entered. He had furry eyebrows that hung over almost comical sweet grey eyes. Months before, I'd been in the hospital for top surgery. It is a thing I'd hoped for since growing boobs in middle school, a thing I'd prayed for before knowing how wrong they felt on my body. Only back then I didn't know it was a thing so I morbidly prayed for breast cancer so I could get surgery to remove them. And once I got top surgery, it felt right. I breathed better going out into the world knowing it'd help people see me as who I knew myself to be. But I never quite breathed full breaths. So shallow. Because under my surface there was always a layer of hate I could not shake, not even after a surgery I knew I needed to survive.

"I... I never thought of it that way..." I said, shoving stubborn words out of my mouth.

Flashes from my youth. All the times I'd hidden in my childhood bathroom, reciting fantastical stories out loud through cloudy eyes for whomever might listen when my mother wasn't home, just trying to avoid my father's bubbling anger amid a quartet practice gone wrong. Afraid his hand would swing on me too hard, or that he'd shove me like he did with Jess that time, that drove her body down the stairs. How, in high school I dreamed of dying to escape my body. Only because it was my body and from what I'd been told, and what I knew in my heart, it seemed something had gone wrong, and the dissonance hurt too much to stay here. I remembered when

I stopped believing in God in college and I lost trust in everything, and I feared every interaction.

"I don't even feel safe in my own body..." I remember hearing myself say.

I hadn't meant to say it. It was the sort of honesty I reserved for just myself. Not even a thing I felt safe writing down. My body isn't a thing I cared to talk about. I lived in it and with it, but it was not something I'd call home, not something I even called mine. I was always fussing with it. I'd tried to shrink it into non-existence. Starve it to death. Mold it into a shape more familiar to me when I looked in the mirror. Testosterone helped it. So did top surgery, and so did dressing it in clothes I'd dreamed of wearing but never could without judgement from my mom, sisters, old friends who didn't know me like I wanted to be known. But all this time I'd searched for spaces inside of being unscathed by whatever life's fires hadn't burned. I found none. Where is solace if not within the corners of your own mind, within the curves of your own body? Where do you get away other than to die?

He asked me to elaborate, and I did, because all of my filters had flown out the door.

"I've always felt wrong in my body. I leave it all the time, just disappear so I don't have to think about it," I said.

He called it dissociation. I told him that since I can remember, I'd somehow just disappear. The last time I did it was days ago, walking up to the one-bedroom apartment I shared with Cam, I inserted my key and struggled, furiously trying to open a door that was not mine. I was two stories above my own place. An angry man answered it, I apologized. Understood why he looked at me like I was trying to rob him. But I didn't even remember how I got in the building. This was not the first time something like this happened. It would not be the last. We talked and talked until, like a brick hitting pavement, I realized I'd never felt safe in my entire life. I'd been afraid for as long as I could remember. I'd simply mastered the art of pretending. The essence of me lived somewhere, deep in the ruins of a life I'd created out of fear, and Camelia had been a sort of shield from it all. Before her, it was my mother. And I loved Camelia. I loved her so much, but she could have been anyone. She could have been any number of one-night stands or flings before her had any of them given me the time of day, because, until I loved myself, I was not picky about how I shielded myself from myself. We spoke some more.

Finally, he said,

"So, from the looks of it, you may be dealing with bipolar disorder, or, also with a sort of complex PTSD, possibly triggered first by many of your experiences in childhood. Seems you also deal with intrusive thoughts. Anxiety, compulsive behaviors. Of course, I'd need more time with you to be able to say for sure... "

I had nothing to say, or too much, so I sat still. Blinked away disbelief. *Bipolar disorder...* He was still talking. Something about Dialectical Behavior Therapy. *Bipolar disorder...*I'd never considered it. Borderline Personality Disorder was a thing I'd never heard of until I looked it up, but bipolar disorder. I'd heard maybe too much about it. I knew of so many movies where the person with it came through like a tornado in their loved one's lives. I didn't want to be like that.

I tuned in again,

"DBT focuses on changing behavior patterns with deliberate practices, with worksheets, even group meetings with like-minded people. It's been proven to work with a number of mental illnesses, alcoholism, eating disorders, PTSD, definitely bipolar disorder...."

He had me wait while he grabbed some brochures from the front desk, all DBT-related programs in the city. Told me, often, these programs were booked up to three and four months out. Told me maybe I'd get lucky. He actually used the term "lucky."

"Now, there are some therapists who specialize in DBT, it's not too common but they're out there. They're usually psychologists. I recommend you try and find one of them as well, who can work with you while you go through the program."

He told me since I said I was okay now, and that I seemed stable, I was welcome to go rather than stay for the 72-hour hold. I'd been there all day. I walked out of the hospital feeling odd. Surprised it was that easy to go, as if I'd dropped by for a routine checkup. But I could breathe. And as light-headed as I still felt, it's as if I'd been given an anchor. I would not float away. Because for the first time ever someone had believed me when I said I was not okay, and they told me some ways I could get better. I could do something about it now. I noticed Andrea emailed me, asking if I wanted to meet with her. I agreed, not telling her it would be our last meeting. Not because she wasn't good, but because I felt I'd already tainted our relationship. I didn't see how I could truly be honest with her in the ways I needed to be honest. Plus, I wanted a therapist who understood DBT. Whether I had cPTSD or bipolar disorder or not, it sounded like something that could really help me. And I wanted to start fresh.

Cam didn't come home that night. I couldn't blame her. I still don't know where she slept, but she did text me around midnight to say that she'd be out. I did not panic like I usually did. I told her, "okay," and called Heart to see if she could come over. She was there in thirty minutes even though she'd just moved to Queens.

"Do you think it's over?" Heart asked, cuddling Bear on the couch beside me.

Usually that question would make my heart stop, but I breathed in the way Andrea told me to. Responded, slow.

"I don't know. But I don't want it to feel like it's the end of my world if it is, you know?"

In that moment, it did still feel that way. I didn't know how to make it so, but I knew there had to be some way to be okay enough with myself that what other people did around me didn't lead me to where I went that day. There had to be. Heart nodded. I don't know if she understood how literal my words were, that I meant that I would end my life over a relationship. I knew what it sounded like. I knew it sounded ridiculous and I knew that even then, it was something I hadn't quite overcome. But the difference was I wanted to. For Cam, but also for me.

"What if you stayed with your sister for a bit? You could maybe work from home...?" She asked me.

This question did shake me. Jess was in Alexandria, Virginia, a short, cheap train ride, but the thought of being that far from Cam made me cold. I was embarrassed by it but in one of my last lies surrounding all of this I said,

"I think that's a good idea," It was a half lie, because I did believe it was a good idea, in theory. Just not something I planned to do any time soon.

I found Dr. Patel like a needle in a haystack of overcrowded DBT-group programs. Hours of Google searches and Reddit forums led me to his website. He was a DBT-focused psychologist with the space to meet with me. The hospital doctor was right, I had to be lucky to find him. I must have been lucky. His office had minty blue walls and a couple paintings of the ocean. And his secretary had a smile that warmed the room. I felt safe.

"Jasper?" Called a small, dark skinned Indian man about my height, with a voice just primed for ASMR.

He had the kindest eyes and choppy short hair like a 5th grade class president. I immediately felt relaxed with him, because he reminded me of the big brother I always wanted. Or more like a version of myself I wanted to become. He had me settle into a plush green chair beside a bright, big window overlooking Central Park.

"When you feel comfortable, I'm going to ask you to close your eyes," He said.

"Okay," I said. Nervous, but open. More open than I'd ever been for someone to help me.

I wriggled around in my seat a bit, looked around until it seemed strange that I was still looking around, and then I closed my eyes. He asked me,

"Tell me what's going in your mind. Am I reading correctly that you feel a bit uncomfortable?"

Oh. There it was, that mind reading I'd been searching for that now felt so exposing. I laughed a nervous laugh. Told him yes, I was uncomfortable. That I'd tried to meditate before, that I even grew up on it, but it never worked. I was way too squirrely. I couldn't focus, not even for a second. And he asked me, calmly, to try. Just, try. I closed my eyes again. Took a deep breath with him.

"Now focus on your breath," he said, "Tell me, what do you hear around you."

I stayed quiet. Listened, closer. Outside cars honked their horns. My focus lingered on the ticking clock behind me facing Dr. Patel. I heard his breath and my own. I told him all of this. He asked me how my breathing felt. I told him, somehow, it was calmer. He told me to try and keep my eyes closed as he read a simple quote, a poem of sorts.

"In the now is a good place to be. Here in the now, we can breathe, we can exist. We are safe."

I felt my heartbeat slowing and speeding up again, working for and against itself. I kept trying.

"Now, that wasn't so bad, was it?" He asked all of a sudden.

We laughed together this time.

"No, it wasn't." I told the truth.

He told me we'd try this a bit before every session. He asked me what brought me to him, and I told him, even though I know he spoke to Andrea. He knew almost everything. Almost. He nodded through my ramble, which I never intended to be a ramble but this new thing of being honest led me down winding roads. So many caveats to my reality. I was insecure, I felt empty and sometimes too full, I had no confidence, I hated my voice, I wanted love, I didn't love myself. Cam and I got in a fight and it ended in my wish to leave this earth. I stopped speaking before I was finished. He didn't write anything down, only nodded and listened, sometimes interrupting me, gently, for clarity.

"Do you still believe you need to end your life if your relationship ends?"

I struggled to answer him, not because I didn't know what to say but because I was ashamed, and I couldn't say no because it wouldn't be the truth. But he heard what I didn't say in my expression, and he didn't press for words. He'd just said,

"This is something we'll continue to discuss. Not everything will be addressed in this session, but I want you to know that this, suicidal ideation, will be an ongoing topic. Is that alright?"

I nodded. We agreed to meet weekly. Each week I'd update him on my life, on work, on me and Cam. Each week, something I said would prompt an assignment out of the DBT Workbook in his desk drawer. He always made me a copy: Emotional Regulation Skills, Mindfulness practice, Distress tolerance. We skipped around the book depending on my need.

Finally, one week I admitted it, I was absolutely ready to die if Cam left me. Yes, I still felt that way. I didn't read any shock or judgement in his gaze, only curiosity and compassion, when he asked,

"And how would you do it?"

His question shocked me. I stuttered into my explanation, and he listened as I told him. About the oxy pills from my top surgery, the knife I kept sharp just in case that I'd use to slit my wrists. That, for some reason, I always envisioned myself jumping off of a balcony from dozens of feet above, if I happened to be at work when I was ready to go.

He didn't say anything for a moment. He nodded, and we breathed together until he asked,

"What do you think life without Cam might look like?"

"Um..." I grumbled, fully unprepared to answer this. It had never, ever crossed my mind.

It was always; Cam leaves, I die, in that order. His inquiry sparked an internal journey that would lead to my resolve. Eventually. But on that day, a question like that swallowed me whole. He noticed me suffocating and said,

"We'll return to this, but I hope you'll give that some thought. Life after Camelia."

We moved on. Talked about Pam Plemmons, who, I'll admit, I still wanted to avoid. Of all the heavy things I carried each day, this is the one I tried to hide the most from myself. But I'd already told him I was editing a book, in passing, weeks ago, and the attentive listener he was, he asked me how it was going.

"It's not. Not really." I told him everything.

I wanted to cry but the level of testosterone I'd been taking lately seemed to block tears, so I sat with fists furiously tight in my seat instead. And he pulled out that damned workbook. Pointed to "black and white thinking" when I told him my book was bad, assigned me the task of beginning to debunk that belief.

"You have already proven that you are not a bad writer." He told me.

I'd told him all the publications my work had been featured in. That several editors had already complimented my skill. He noted none of their opinions mattered more than my own, of myself.

"Of course, a lot of this can be subjective, but to reduce your work to "bad" because one editor did not approve of it, that's what we call black and white thinking, do you understand?"

I did. I went home and I dusted off my printed book draft after months of pretending it didn't exist. I begin to read it with fresh eyes. Told him what I did, and he said,

"I'm very proud to hear that, Jasper."

I felt like I'd just won a difficult race. I finished reading it the next week, a week focused on spending quality time being present and positive with Cam. We went on a date to a vegan spot in the Lower East Side.

"I saw you reading your book. I think that's awesome. You know, if you want help editing it, I'm so down. You know I'm a perfectionist," she said, dipping fried cauliflower into nondairy ranch sauce.

I beamed. We held hands under the table. We didn't argue at all that night. And the next night when she went out, I didn't want to scream.

"What is your hope for *Juniper Leaves*?" Dr. Patel asked me the next week, taking a sip of chamomile tea he always offered me before sessions.

"I want it published, and I want it to be publish-ready. I want to share a quality piece of work." I told him.

He asked me steps I might take to make that happen and saying everything out loud made it all feel a bit less daunting. Cam already offered to help edit, and so did Jess. Leesie was a skilled graphic designer because of architecture, and she was happy to update the design. And he was right, I had as much time as I needed now to make it happen.

"I can't wait to read it," He said.

After weeks of avid no's, I took his advice to visit a psychiatrist.

"I understand the apprehension. And nothing may come of it. But medication can sometimes be a very useful tool to recovery." He said.

I'd been raised to handle it. To avoid all doctors and to first look in my pantry or prayer for my own healing. I honored that legacy, of Black healing, of (good) Black magic, and I kept it for other things. But now felt different. I wanted to move differently than I ever had because, I had to finally admit to myself, what I'd been doing was not working.

One of my favorite books, *Heavy*, is a memoir by Southern Black author Kiese Laymon. The book wouldn't come out for a couple more years, but I think of it often when I consider this time in my life. Laymon spoke of his Black southern upbringing with a mother who so valued education. In the book he relayed his mother's lesson, "The most important part of writing, and really life," you said, "is revision." It's like Sankofa, a word from the Ghana Twi language that means "to retrieve," literally to "go back and get." The Sankofa bird is a common symbol in traditional Black and African diasporic art. It's a symbol of how important it is to learn from the past, communally, and personally, so that you and your people may have a fruitful and fulfilling future. I'd been living with my head in the sand for so long, reliving the same sorts of hurt over and over again, ignoring all the ways I might find a better path. But perhaps I could use those memories for something else. Perhaps I could revisit my pain again this time with purpose, and start, finally, to learn from it. So, I began editing. I begin reworking, and rethinking, and editing everything in my life. And I begin to feel less heavy.

Let home be

baby wanna go home

mama say stay

a lil longer

it's some people I want you to meet

she say

some errands I want you to run

food I want you to try

and beautiful places and things

you must see

on your own now

I'll be here my sweet baby

when you return

I'll be here

but for now

let home be in your heart

let home be in your spirit

let home be and I'll stay

right here

right here

right here

just watch

Happy and Gay

Europe, Spring 2017

We landed in Amsterdam, pennies pinched, grins plastered on our happy little faces and hands intertwined like a couple of fools in love.

"We made it." We said in insufferable unison, giggling at the adorable coincidence as we stepped off an airport shuttle onto the dark damp grounds outside Amsterdam Central Station.

It was 7pm and despite our 7-hour, transatlantic flight, we had every intention of exploring till our feet gave out. But first, we needed to drop off our luggage at Cam's aunt Mila's place in the heart of Amsterdam, a quaint townhouse but a stone's throw from the station, and right across from the cutest little antique shop. Or at least that's what it looked like in Google Street view. But I'd never been outside the United States, let alone anywhere near any place in Europe. I hadn't anticipated narrow streets so thin, the few cars riding down them seemed out of place. You were more likely to find bikes of every variety, tandem, electric and even uni, more than you would any other vehicle; except the white and blue cabs that would roll by slow as a still river every now and again. Trams glided on railways over cobblestone and brick streets but rarely asphalt like in New York. Each stout little building stood no more than a few stories high. These were vintage structures, no younger than a few hundred years, but inside them were modern cafes and clothing stores, and your choice of all sorts of cannabis. Weed bars, weed cafes, weed restaurants, often rocking Jamaican flags and tiny little mary jane leaves beside on-the-nose signs like Greenhouse and Mellow Yellow, always English for some reason. Yet, I saw no one smoking in the street, and none of these shops were necessarily packed, no more than the Forever 21s and tiny grocers beside them. It was interesting, this strange land where weed reigned supreme, but there were barely any bloodshot eyes around us. Instead, there were hundreds, nay, thousands of stilt-legged white humans with casual strolls and clothes, as if heading to, or leaving Pilates class. There was a relaxed air to the place, one I'd only seen before after accidentally entering smoky study rooms on a late evening in college. And I also noticed the lack of smell in the air, so crisp and clean it didn't feel right in my nose after years in New York. The ground was spotless. Spotless! Almost shining. I was really feeling Amsterdam. Even more when I noticed several visibly queer couples pass us on the street, exchanging knowing glances.

Cam's aunt urged us to take the scenic route to her place without her, promising the view would be worth it. She wasn't wrong. I'd expected a rather aloof woman to answer the door. Cam described her family as cold. Not the friendliest of folk, and as I'd grown to know Cam's own resting bitch face, I had every reason to believe it ran in the family. So, I couldn't believe the jolly, boxy-figured woman with hair like tattered yellow wheat and a blue knit sweater stepping out to greet us.

"Happy birthday!" She grinned, squeezing us both between her long, warm, blue knit-covered arms.

It was March 11th. A day before Cam's 28th birthday. This was only the third of her birthdays her aunt had shared with her, so this was a momentous occasion. I could see in both their faces the gravity of that fact. Mila let go of us and looked at me, deep behind my eyes and into my soul and said with the faintest Dutch accent,

"You, my dear, are absolutely beautiful." I grinned like my father.

Still in shock of her kindness I exclaimed, "It's so great to finally meet you!"

She opened her townhome door a bit wider for us and stepped aside, revealing old hardwood floors and rustic decor only she could pull off. Let's just say her sweater wasn't the only Mila original on display. In front of us was a large wooden table like in *Game of Thrones*, and behind it, a small orange couch and orange chair. The multicolored knit rug beneath her furniture had been through some things, and it all made more sense when her giant fuzzy cat strolled in from the back doggy door.

"This is Franklin! Happy to see you both!"

Out back was a small garden with a wooden bench she told us her ex-husband built.

"Now it's just me. Your cousin lives in Berlin now, you know." She waved one hand in the air like dismissing it then rose from the bench and guided us back inside. I could tell she missed her son. The kitchen reminded me of the one from a favorite childhood film of mine, *The Borrowers* (1997), with an old-fashioned stove and oven and all those ancient appliances.

"Around there is my bedroom, and right up these stairs," She pointed right beside us where one flight of stairs led to a lofted space, "That's where you two can stay, as long as you like."

She offered traditional, leftover Draadjesvlees, a slow-braised beef stew about five times before finally hearing that I didn't eat red meat.

"We ate on the plane." Cam assured her.

Her aunt's eyes twinkled when we reminded her of our plan for the next day.

"Do you still want to go to the farmer's market in the morning?"

"Of course!"

We'd agreed to spend the next day with Mila, starting at the market near her house and then just around her neighborhood. Mila lived in Amsterdam for thirty years and hadn't left since.

She knew her own few blocks better than the coordinates of her own full, square face. She was the older sister to Cam's dad, and like the rest of her dad's family, hadn't seen him in years. She wouldn't say much about him, even when prompted, but the bite in her delivery said enough.

"He abandoned us, you know. He once told me he didn't even want white friends anymore, not even white friends. Isn't that something?"

It was something. Something I understood quite well and didn't have the energy to explain to this middle-aged European white lady. I wished for his side of the story. He was the only brown person in a sea of white; White mom, three white sisters, and afro-Palestinian father he never met. And by the sound of her resentment, they didn't even begin to try to understand that about him.

"All I know is he's living with a woman in, I think, Berlin. Or no, perhaps they're still here, and they have a daughter about your age, Camelia."

Cam wouldn't react much to this sort of information, just a polite nod, never pressing for more info. I knew she was curious, but I could only imagine how difficult it was to discuss a dad she barely knew with an aunt she hadn't seen for a decade.

"I'm gonna ask Vel." Cam told me that night after we returned from a short walk around Mila's block before bed.

Vel, her grandmother, was so far the only one she trusted to discuss family with. A lot was riding on our trip up north in the Netherland countryside to stay with her. We'd even fought about how long we decided we'd stay. I thought a few days would be fine. I wanted more time in Amsterdam which I knew I'd love, and even if Vel was cooler than the other side of a pillow, there wasn't shit to do in the country parts of Holland. Plus, we only had so much time on this Europe trip after all, and since Leesie had been to Paris and sung its praises on almost a daily basis, I couldn't wait to see for myself. But after a week's long argument we landed one week at Vel's, a couple days in Amsterdam, a few in Paris and Rome. A little over two weeks, total.

And ever since Cam saw me, bloody-handed and suicidal in our kitchen, fully ready to exit stage left on life, I felt this unabating need to placate her in situations I'd usually play victim in. In my mind, this was an argument she had to win, because I was the one who manipulated her in the worst way possible. I hung death over her head, and somehow, she'd forgiven me. So, if Cam wanted to spend one measly week with her 80-year-old grandmother, so be it. I couldn't stand the thought of inadvertently pushing her away for what surely would be the last time. I may have been learning to not feel this way, but I wasn't there yet. So, I hushed. Hushed anger, hushed resentment, hushed unpopular opinion.

Tried staying present as her giant Dutch family trickled into Mila's home. Giant in size, not quantity, as the average height in the space was about six feet tall. It was us, Mila and her older aunt Maud, the quieter aunt Esmee and Mila's son (whom she clearly hadn't seen in forever). All of which could drink Cam under the table, easily. I was quite outnumbered.

"Happy fucking birthday!" Her gangly 20-year-old cousin Willem roared over "Suspicious Minds."

This crew were obsessed with my city ties to the so-called "musical legend" Elvis. Opted to play an entire Spotify mix of his greatest hits on my behalf. *Fuuuuuun.*

"It boggles my mind you lived so close to his mansion and *never* visited." Her gregarious Aunt Maud bopped around to the almost-beat, a colossal mug of ale in one hand. She only spilled it a couple times.

"I mean, you'd be surprised by how few locals have seen it." I said.

An understatement because Black Memphis locals couldn't give two fucks about Elvis.

She and her sisters' mouths fell open with shock.

"That's amazing."

"I cannot believe it."

I let their fanatic murmurs fade out without objection, vastly outnumbered here, as Cam also enjoyed Elvis. What a relief it was when Maud switched the playlist to BB King Radio, a choice solely based on an intense need to flaunt her "extensive knowledge on the origin of blues."

"Did you know he lived in Memphis for some time?" Maud raised her bulbous head to the heavens as if this information came from God. She almost choked on beer and pride when I responded,

"Yeah, actually my dad's played with his band before."

Gasps all around. I, Jaz the resident Black from Memphis, was a hit. A Black exception once again. I wasn't sure how I felt about this. But enough about me, this was Cam's birthday celebration. Me feeling commodified around a bunch of white Dutch folk was the B story at best. I focused on Cam, who was smiling. Ignored Maud who was standing now. Actually, somewhat hovering over me nearly popping my personal bubble as she ranted on and on about her run-in with Miles Davis shortly before his death. Then Mila groaned. Right in the middle of her rant, she groaned so loud I couldn't help but giggle.

"Oh my goodness Maud, can you even help sucking up the air in the room, how tiring," She rolled her eyes to the back of her head.

The quieter of the sisters, Esmee touched Mila's arm, "Mila."

Mila noticeably calmed but her face was stuck in a wince of sorts.

"What's tiring is how you can't be bothered to drink at a party!" Maud was full out dancing now or moving to a melody in a way I think some might call a dance.

White-lady-wylin.

"Now, let's not make a scene in front of Camelia and Jasper." Esmee said sweetly, quietly, "After this song how bout we turn it down a bit, talk some?"

It was clear this was the first time everyone had gotten together in a while.

Didn't even need Esmee to mention it later in the evening, "What's it been, eight years? All of us together?"

"And even longer without Mum." Mila added.

Everyone grew silent.

Maud broke it, "Damn, lunatic, she is."

"Maud!" Esmee cried.

"What! She's a sociopath if I ever met one. Don't matter she's our mother," Mila groaned.

"Stop it. She did her best. We're all doing our best." Esmee barked.

The silence returned. It lingered. I sipped cold beer to drown it out and wondered how Cam was feeling. We came to party, to enjoy her family but we hadn't considered the realities of that. How her family was not close. How there was a quiet distain for the matriarch on her father's side, except with Esmee who'd clearly taken the role as family mediator. I suppose we'd let ourselves embrace the fantasy of this trip. The reality of it felt too stark to focus on.

"Anyway!" Mila interjected, "All thanks to you Camelia for bringing us together!"

Maud whooped.

The rest of us clapped awkwardly and then sincerely. Cam seemed uncomfortable but tried to hide it.

"Oh!" Mila said with a smile bigger than her face.

She scooched out of her chair. Darted over to the kitchen and we all looked at each other while she made kitchen noises. Finally returning with an adorable small yellow cake with one white candle.

Instead of "Happy Birthday" they all begin to sing "She's a Jolly Good Fellow." Tears welled up in Cam's eyes. I'd never seen her show so much emotion in public. The tension melted like ice. We laughed and talked over music until we were warm and dry, and the night was ready to end.

"Please, visit us before you leave, would you?" Esmee requested.

We promised we'd do our best. Maud hugged Cam and whispered loudly with one foot out the door, "Don't give Vel too much of your time. She'll drain you."

An ominous word of advice that would linger with Cam and me on our train ride north to the middle of nowhere.

Beside me in our lofted bed, Cam sliced through the awkward air between us, "I feel like Vel's very, like, "tell-it-like-it-is. No offense to my aunts but I'm not surprised they can't take it, you know?"

Famous last words. We arrived in Biddinghuizen at the end of the morning. Called Vel immediately after the train's announcement that we'd arrived, no answer. We expected to see Vel parked up front in her light blue hatchback as we discussed the day before. But we left the train stop, tracked the lot and sidewalk, luggage in tow. No Vel.

"I'll call again." Cam said, dialing up on the cheap pre-paid Nokia we bought to save on international calls.

She puts the phone on speaker.

"How can you expect me to be there on time if you do not in fact call me an hour in advance?" Vel barked.

Cam fixed her mouth to speak but there was no time.

Vel continued, "No bother, I will leave now. Expect me in an hour."

Click. We stared at each other like we'd both witnessed Lucifer himself drive by in an ice cream truck.

"What. the hell." Cam shook her head. I shrugged.

I would not say that this was foreshadowing. Not out loud. But it felt that way. On the bright side we got to explore the homely Dutch village we'd landed in. It's like we'd stepped back in time to an alternate reality where Hobbit aesthetics thrived. Canals were as common as subway stops in New York, little bridges decorated either side of the road. We passed by at least three taverns before settling in the window seats of a delightful mom and pop bakery on the quaint strip across from the train stop. After exactly one hour and twenty minutes, Val honked her hatchback horn alerting us of her arrival. Shouting loud enough for us to hear with the bakery door closed, far jollier than before, "Welcome to Biddinghuizen!"

Her cropped-haired head peeped out her car window and a fierce smile covered her dry, weathered face. Cam shared her thick eyebrows and nose. Her eyes were grey and sullen, somehow clashing with this oddly happy expression. Such a jarring figure. I moved with caution. Cam reached her first, and I was glad about it. I inched towards the trunk, strategically placing both our suitcases among piles of art supplies. Vel hobbled out of the car draped in various muted, flowing fabrics in the tune of scarves, tunics, and ballooning linen pants. She grinned wider, her dull eyes brightening at a closer glance of Cam.

"I decided to park and have a look at you," Vel spoke with a thick German accent, squeezing her granddaughter's cheeks between her fingers.

I finished packing the car sooner than I hoped. Felt awkward so I teetered towards her. Her energy perplexed me.

"And you, *you...*" She smiled that rugged smile at me revealing a charming gap between greyish teeth, "Lovely, just lovely."

I would have smiled back if her next remark wasn't,

"You know, you're smaller than I expected," She chuckled, "Darker, too."

There are so many things I could have said. Clever, cunty things. But instead, I laughed, awkwardly. My eyes traveled slowly towards Cam, who was busy doing the same.

Vel raised a proud finger to her nose, grinning back at our grins, "*I know* I'm quite amusing! Others disagree!"

We both sat in the back seat because Vel only allowed her dear dog son Rover, a Herculean-sized, dreadlocked Puli, to sit in the front. He wasn't even there. This would have been a strike three had I not preferred it this way. The closer we were the more my face itched. And this way Cam and I were a united front, able to share questioning glances when Vel would say things like,

"You know, Jaz, Camelia's grandfather, my *ex*-husband, was colored as well? Black as night."

Cam and I would squeeze each other's hands like some sort of morse code. I'd smirk as more performance than actual feeling because inside felt much more like disgust. But Cam seemed genuinely amused, and I refused to be the reason this trip went poorly. But when she kept going...

"You know Camelia, your grandfather, my *ex*-husband? He claimed Egyptian. Ha! Can you believe it?" Vel threw back her head in long-winded laughter, "He was a negro Palestinian. Not as distinguished a background, you see. He was quite ashamed of it, too! He'd lash out, you know. So ashamed. I'm sure you're not ashamed like he was. I can tell."

I had to say something. I had to— "Don't." said Cam's squeeze of my hand, like a stern whisper.

I wouldn't.

For most of the ride she thankfully only explained almost every single art item in her car from the back to front. She assumed this was of interest to us. Boring, but harmless enough. But we'd barely parked in the muddy wooded lot of her beautiful countryside cottage before she'd vomited out yet another rancid point.

"Jaz, you've heard of Zwarte Piet, yes?"

Oh no. I had. In Dutch tradition, Zwarte Piet is the black-faced companion to Saint Nicholas known for his gaudy gold earrings, literal black skin and exaggerated lips. Cam's aunts already shared their two cents, denouncing its existence and making sure to stare me right in my Black face when they did it. But not Vel.

"I am." I said with caution as the car made a full stop. Then I opened my door and hopped out, straight to the trunk. Wishing to run. But she appeared beside me somehow in the span of a millisecond. Hand clasped over my shoulder, forcing my eyes into hers,

"I know many colored folk. You know what they tell me?" She squeezed my shoulder again, "You know what they tell me? They tell me, 'It's fine! I love it!'"

My irked eyes darted directly to Cam. She looked sorry but said no words.

"Pretty sure colored is an outdated term." I said to anyone in particular, hoping at least vocalizing it would ease the tension in my temples.

If I'd entered Vel's space without knowing it was hers, I'd have assumed it belonged to an artist, and it did. As soon as she opened her front door we were met with a stack of dirt-smudged, blank canvases beside a coat hanger and shoe rack. Paint splatters the dark wood floor leading to her art studio beside the bathroom. She was a sculpture, a painter. All sorts of paintings by her and by others, buried the walls. Her living room and kitchen were bright and open, massive windows wrapping most walls revealing her lush vegetable garden and fenced in backyard. And a clear bowl of what looked like salad sat on her white, tiled island. Right, smackdab beside it was a tiny grey sculpture from, I'm sure, *somewhere* in Africa, of a naked Black woman.

She pointed to it, a twinkle in her eye, "A gift from a dear friend of mine during an Africa trip. I call her Mother Africa. Look at her full bottom. Lovely, yes?!"

"Um..." I hated the curveballs that were her every comment, leaving no time in between for me to process so I was left with round bruises all over my body.

"Sit, sit!" She demanded.

One day passed and felt like ten. I couldn't take much more, I had to at least try to get us out.

"Cam..." I started the moment we had a sometime alone that night, in the guest dwellings beside Vel's she had us stay in.

"I know what you're going to say." She held my hand and squeezed it. Her expression soft and ardent, her voice a balmy cloak of sweetness, "*Please* give it more time."

How long did she really feel it took to know the only good thing about this woman was her dogs? But I paused. I assessed my next words. This was her oma, after all.

"Bae, I hear you. But you and I know this woman is heavily racist. I'm sorry."

I hadn't meant to say "racist." But I also hadn't lied. I wanted to be gentle and honest, but there is nothing gentle about the word "racist," and sometimes it is the only word that fits. I braced myself.

"That's not fair. "Cam said to me, patting her face with a towel and turning off the sink.

I'd offended her. I didn't expect the spasm in my own gut at her response. *Not fair?* What did fair have to do with it? How could she not hear me fully just because I'd used that term to describe her grandmother and not some random person? It was true all the same. Not even being shady.

"I feel like it is." I had to say it.

"I don't want to talk about this right now." Cam looked at me through the bathroom mirror. Her eyes said more than her words. I didn't want this conversation to become an argument. I didn't want to anger her in a way we couldn't come back from. We'd been there. We couldn't afford another, *there.* So, I hushed. We slept. Or, she slept.

Another day passed without either of us saying much. Vel spoke enough for the both of us. But on the third day Vel invited us to an early dinner with one of her close neighborhood friends, a white Dutch man who had lived in the states for some time as a youngster, and who felt his opinions on the United

States were valuable because of it. The moment we entered his eerily plantation-style mansion, most likely custom designed to capture the essence of the average patriotic slave master of the antebellum south, he yelped,

"How about that election?!" Mimicking the popular phrase, "How 'bout them Cowboys?"

Vel's brand of racism, and it is racism, wasn't pro-Trump. She donned the liberal, heroic, white savior for the poor Negro-type racism, quick to declare disapproval in front of the right crowd, but always with a wink and a nod to any antagonists. That's how, after over forty years, she and this blond and blue Trump lover were still the best of friends despite so-called opposing views.

"Daan Bakker loves Trump. Loves him. Bleh." She mimed a spitting motion and shooed him away. Smile big as the sun.

"Now I wouldn't say "love." Admire, respect, of course! Would I have a beer with the man? Sure!" Daan led us through a spotless, rustic kitchen with shining new appliances, then into a dining room best described to look how any number of plantations fully running in the antebellum south likely felt. A pure cotton tablecloth covered mahogany wood, except for its long, fantastically carved legs. I could picture a white family seated all comfy at each haunted, wooden sculpture of a chair, waiting with noses up and eyes shady while Black servants hovered behind them awaiting their next command. It gave me the creeps. I wanted *out!*

"Really beautiful." Cam smiled as we left that space I'd just had ancestral flashbacks in. I winced without meaning to. I felt strange beside her. I ignored my feelings.

Finally, we made it to the well-lit living room, giant windows reaching the ceilings from down to the floor, with two large Victorian-style couches and an ugly, grey velvet loveseat. In the middle of the room were biscuits and crackers. I would not touch this man's food.

Cam quickly grabbed a cookie and took a dainty bite.

"Help yourselves." A feminine voice announced from their echoing hallway. It was Daan's wife, a petite woman with bright blue eyes and pearls. *Pearls.* This was starting to feel too ridiculous to be real.

Her voice was altered by lips plumped with filler, cheekbones tight with Botox. Her blue-floral sundress, fitted around her bust, poofed out around her waist down to right below her knees. On her feet she wore creme colored espadrilles. I wondered if she'd dressed up for the company or always pranced around her home giving Kentucky derby fashion show.

"So let me guess, you're one of those Bernie-bros?" Daan's eyes sparkled with the same fire igniting devil's advocates everywhere. I refused to give him the satisfaction,

"I'm a anti-capitalist 'bro.'" I said in a mocking tone I hope he noticed.

He let out the sound, "Ha!" No real laugh followed and he wagged his finger, "That's good. Very good." I shrugged.

Cam squinted in that way she did when she had an interesting question, then said to Daan,

"Why? Why Trump?" A genuine, innocent curiosity painted her face.

I resented her innocent curiosity. It's a question I expected from a talking head interviewing white supremacist leaders, ready and willing for some reasonable explanation. Not from Cam, who I'd assumed understood that trying to level with a man who said people were being too sensitive about all of Trump's harmful rhetoric was quite unreasonable. I was confused, until I remembered myself not long ago. How I welcomed whiteness into my periphery in hopes it would accept me back. As if to be accepted in white spaces meant some sort of protection against the ways of the world. Myself then, and Cam now were not all that different. We made space for whiteness in ways we didn't need to. Are we not all conditioned that way in white supremacist capitalist patriarchy, as bell hooks and other Black philosophers have taught us? But it takes introspection to break free of that. A sort of introspection it seems the closer you are to whiteness, the more you tend to miss.

Nothing surprised me about Daan's response to Cam's question. Of course, he loved how "bold" Trump was. Of course he loved that this man won. And how the man said whatever he wanted, no matter how racist or harmful. But I hated the way Cam tipped her head to the side like she'd just absorbed some transfixing information. A sort of gentle understanding I'd hoped she'd reserve for more gentle views. It felt jarring. Eye opening. Now in this man's scary home, I'd been cornered into a truth I cared to avoid for as long as I could. No longer. Cam leaned into her ambiguity in a way that sometimes welcomed the conditioning of whiteness. Despite all that projecting I'd done, claiming Cam's Blackness above all else, she valued the white parts of herself just as much as the Black and brown. And it is not wrong to love your Dutchness or your Germanness, but to ignore the whiteness of it all...That's a different thing. This racist white woman was her family and she loved her. But did she love her enough to challenge those parts of her that caused harm? To love her in a way that is uncomfortable, that so many close to whiteness have the privilege to avoid?

Angela Davis said, in *Freedom is a Constant Struggle*, that "...if we don't take seriously the ways in which racism is embedded in structures of institutions, if we assume that there must be an identifiable racist who is the perpetrator, then we won't ever succeed in eradicating racism."

It's as if the more space Cam had for Vel the less she had to think critically about the ways in which whiteness can be insidious, as if you cannot love your white grandmother and hate whiteness, the construct, at the same time. I'd made the mistake of thinking we felt the same about this.

I left Daan's drained and hungry, back to Vel's, but not before enduring a car ride full of Vel's analysis of the visit.

"Daan had some fair points, indeed he did. But I couldn't possibly stand by a man who's wig's so poorly glued onto his giant orange head." Of course, she found her own joke hilarious.

I didn't think she had space to joke if she thought Daan had any fair points at all.

"He did have points! But he was also *so* wrong about so, so much!" Cam laughed.

I couldn't tell if she wanted to seem agreeable with her grandmother, or if she actually believed what she was saying. Then I remembered, Cam didn't just say things to say them. And then, I reckoned with the twisting of my gut, that pang that told me the cost of her compromising words. That clash that was a shock to the system of us. We went to our cottage to wash up before dinner. I said things to her I wanted to hold in.

"Do you actually think he had good points?" I asked her after closing our bedroom door.

"I just feel like we talk all the time about how we all live in our little bubbles and at least he's willing to talk to people that don't agree with him."

On the surface, I agreed with this sentiment. I believe that we should have reasonable discussions with empathetic people whose views are not our own. We need those conversations to grow and change as a society. But some debates are shrouded in apathy. Some debates, like those that question what rights should belong to Black people, queer people, indigenous people, ask us to denounce parts of our own identities before we can even participate. I am not interested in joining those discussions. I am not interested in complimenting supporters of those discussions.

"How do you feel about the fact that Vel agreed with so much of what he said? Other than literally not liking Trump's personality, I'm not actually seeing how she's that different..." I poked. Prodded. I'd thrown chill out the window.

And I'd hit a nerve. Cam backed away, like she couldn't be physically close to me.

"Vel is so liberal, though. Especially at her age."

Girl, what? I'd had it.

"Liberal doesn't *mean* anything! That's my point, it's all the same shit. Why do you think they're still friends after 40 years?"

She nodded, but confusion enveloped her like a cloud. I wasn't mad that Cam and I didn't see the world in the same way. No. It was the thin line separating us, feeling more like an opaque wall between us, that I couldn't ignore. Not anymore.

We did end up leaving Vel's place early. The last straw was her infamous breakfast rant. An epic last hurrah in which Vel somehow found a way to call Cam's mother a talentless whore who didn't deserve to join her family in the first place. At that same breakfast, she blamed her children and grandchildren for her loneliness, Cam's father's selfishness for any and all of his own experiences with racism, and dozens of other ex-friends and foes for every other aspect of her sad, pathetic life.

"We've decided to head back to Amsterdam." Camelia told her after our whispered agreement in Vel's backyard while she was in the bathroom.

Mila promised we could hang out at her place until our train ride to Paris. We claimed we were leaving to see more of the city. Cam's request, so as to not hurt Vel's feelings. But it was another tear in our relationship's foundation, because I very much wanted to cuss this old ass racist out. My stubbornness worked as a shield for us. Her patience, a life raft.

Our train ride to Paris was quiet. I spent my time embracing brilliant French terrain and farmland and trying to read the last of James Baldwin's *Giovanni's Room* to help set the tone. Every now and then Cam or I would point out something too beautiful to keep silent about,

"Look at the water!"

"Oh my god, those mountains!"

Beyond those little outbursts, we kept to ourselves.

One of Jalisa's friends who'd fell in love with Paris enough to stay after their trip, Cher, welcomed us at Canal Saint-Martin with booze and pastries, and an eclectic group of expats she'd met since her move. Cher, who had just come out as bisexual had very strong and positive opinions on Cam and my relationship.

"Ya'll are literally my favorite couple, like seriously. I stan. Please, like give me some advice because it's hard out here!"

Usually flattered by Cher's blind adoration, I had no space in this context to feel truly worthy of it. I felt like one half of a divorcing couple to their dear, oblivious child. Both Cam and I tried to guide her back to earth. Me first,

"We're literally both in therapy now. We argue. Like a lot."

"We are nowhere near "ideal," I promise." Cam added.

She threw back her head in unadulterated laughter at our honesty. But did she believe us?

"See that's why I love you two, you *work* on your relationship. It takes so much to, like, look at your problems and be like, 'Let's work on ourselves. Let's be better for each other.' It's seriously so romantic!"

Oh, girl. She thought we were being modest. No point in trying to convince her anymore. We glanced at each other across the growing wall of emotions between us. It was getting harder and harder to see Cam through it all. The rest of the night was a hazy fever dream of fanciful Parisian stories and potent wine and edibles.

"Wanna meet up tomorrow for brunch?" I asked Cher on our way out. We were the firsts to leave.

We stayed just a couple blocks from the Louvre. Our view was so beautiful it left us speechless. A good speechless, not like the heavy silences we'd grown accustomed to as of late. As Cam prepped for bed, I enjoyed sporadic whiffs from the popular bakery beneath us. There was a pub beside it, and we even shared a laugh at the loud drunk French folk chain smoking and arguing outside. We crawled into bed without saying goodnight. I slept like I had died.

We woke after morning to a cheerful text from Cher,

We're all meeting at Le Valmy at 4pm! Come!

I texted back,

We'll be there!

We stopped at the Eiffel Tower and a crepe place before it. Then headed over, our walk there felt foggy, though we were both sober as bats.

The promise of Paris' beauty is not an over exaggeration. It is like a painting come to life. Even when you are sad, or lonely, or confused. There is nothing confusing about Paris' beauty. I embraced the assuredness of it. It felt good, especially then. Because we did not speak on that walk either. Cher dressed like

Lolita all grown up, which somehow suited a Parisian backdrop. That day she wore knee-high ruffly socks and a pale pink miniskirt with a lacy cropped top.

"Babes!" Cher cheered, running from her outdoor dining seat on to greet us.

Maggie, a scruffy sort of ChapStick lesbian from the Midwest, and her new boo, one of those white-blonde skinny DJ types, who spoke with a thick French accent that somehow sounded fake, waved to us from our table. Maggie flew to Paris with money she'd saved for years just to relieve herself of the bland and boring life she'd left behind. With no plans to return, she hoped to one day marry her DJ girlfriend and live happily ever after. The only problem is her DJ girlfriend had proudly stated no desire to settle any time soon. I empathized with Maggie, who feared the thought of "sharing" her girlfriend's attention with anyone else, as if any one person belongs to anyone else to be hoarded. I understood Maggie because with Cam, I too muffled any thoughts of love for us outside of those touted in traditional fairytale. Though lately, that feeling was waning. I hated that fact, feared it. Hushed it. Tuned in again to our conversation. Beside Maggie was who we came to know as Bee, a gorgeous lifestyle-influencer Cher met on Tinder.

Cher joked, "You look so hot today, oh my god."

And Bee laughed, exaggerated as it was, confused us until they both explained.

"We dated. Like once."

Bee said more, "Like three minutes into the date we were like, 'We should obviously be friends!'

The two women laughed louder.

"This is high key a queer trope." Said Cam.

I nodded in vigorous agreement. It was so familiar. Two Asian women from the American south, it seems Cher and Bee mistook shared histories and culture for attraction, a thing Cam and I promised was queer-folk wright of passage. Again, re-establishing ourselves as the elder queers at the table. We basically invited the question that came next. Especially since it'd been an hour and this oh-so-popular inquiry hadn't been raised. But still, I'd hoped we'd avoid it on this trip.

"How'd you two meet?" This time it was asked by a slightly tipsy Maggie, who at this point was clinging to her girlfriend like a parasite to its host.

I'd usually start us off. *On OkCupid, believe it or not:* My go-to line, and Cam would swoop in with our especially high 98% match rating. But on this sunny afternoon in Paris, our weathered souls just didn't have the juice. So lost in the cloud of this trip, we hesitated. Finally, Cam said,

"Online!"

DJ girlfriend decided this was a good time to speak,

"Amazing. How did you know one of you was not a catfeesh?"

"I mean, we met pretty soon after I messaged her..." I explained.

"Jaz looked exactly how they looked online, cuter actually." Cam's eyes were on me, smiling like she meant it, or wanted to. I looked away.

"We were super into each other from jump. And then, like the gays we are, we moved in together a few weeks later." I adjusted myself in my seat. I would not say more about our move.

"And we've been together ever since." Cam swooped right in, rubbing my back. Finishing my sentence like we were "that couple" Cher thought we were. Three years in, we had the longest relationship anyone at the table had ever had. Cher clasped her hand over her chest like the personification of the heart-eyes emoji. Something in me felt dishonest, wrong. Telling our story as if it had a happy ending, as if we were happy in that moment, or even remotely satisfied. I felt Cam's eyes on me still. I couldn't confirm, I wouldn't. Instead, I ran through all the less-than-sparkling details we hadn't shared, and wouldn't even if asked, because we were both too embarrassed to admit them. I hoped that the numbness I felt was a phase. Maybe I was still reeling from our disastrous visit with Vel. But I knew this "us" was something different than before. Now resembling more of a stubborn commitment than adoring matrimony I'd told myself it was all that time. The spasm in my spine found its way to my stomach. It quaked in a way I couldn't stand. Like a visceral response my mouth twisted into words I didn't expect,

"I wanna stay so bad but I'm feeling a little sick." I told everyone. It was true, perhaps not for the reasons they might think, but true.

I rested a hand on Cam's leg, like an apology.

"Oh no! Go, go go, it's totally okay." Cher, forever gracious, said.

"I'll come with you. Maybe we can order something." Cam said sweetly, softly.

I hadn't considered that maybe she should have stayed. Joined me in our flat. I was getting used to doing things without her, sometimes even preferring it.

We returned with that now familiar silence, until Cam asked,

"Emotional or physical?"

We'd reached a steep inclined of the cobblestone hill leading to our flat. Short breathed and tired, I stalled,

"What?" Looking down to her where she stood a few steps away from me.

Sterner now, she asked, "What kind of "sick"? Emotional or physical?"

She met me where I was.

"Forget it." I told her and kept walking. I should have just told her, "Both."

She grabbed my arm, "Wait, hold up."

"It's always something, isn't it? And I was actually having fun, too." She kept marching, full speed ahead, up, and up and up and around the corner.

I power walked to catch up to her long strides. By the time I reached her she'd made it into the building. I raced up the stairs, knowing I'd made whatever this is worse.

"It really won't bother me if you go back, seriously I won't be mad."

She laughed, a guttural angry laugh.

"You have got to be fucking kidding me. *You* won't be mad. I'm supposed to believe that why? Because you've never gone off on me for going somewhere without you? *Drinking* without you?"

I hushed. There's nothing honest and good I could say in response. She was right to not trust it.

Finally, I said, "I get why you wouldn't believe me. But, the only way to prove myself is if we create some new patterns."

I'd only regurgitated Dr. Patel's words. I felt silly saying them out loud. She didn't say anything back. She threw her purse on the couch and slunk into the bathroom. Shut the door. Stayed there for so long. I slumped on the couch. Pulled out my phone. Scrolled through the week's photos to a smiling image of the two of us in front of the Eiffel Tower. The portrait of two lovers enjoying themselves. Or so it seemed. And I hoped that like a spell it'd become true if I shared it with the world. I tapped away, typing an Instagram post with a caption that read, *Loving this city* instead of *Shortly after this photo Cam and I argued about the nature of our relationship. This may very well be the beginning of the end.*

The beginning of the end is a river flowing fast, faster. You will be tempted to swim against it, like a salmon upstream. But don't unless you care to drown. The only way to survive is
to let it guide you where it's going.

SISTER KNOWS BEST

Centreville, VA - Summer 2017

"Have you seen *The Flash* before?" Jess asked.

"Like the little speedy white boy?" I said back.

I knew what *The Flash* was.

"It's actually really good!"

Of course she thought so. Jessica, the 4th grade special education teacher whose favorite genre was any film or TV show she could comfortably watch with her future children. Followed by nerdy sci-fi shows like *Doctor Who*, and of course, ever-cheesy, soap-opera-esque series with incredibly low production value (basically all of the CW). As far as I knew, *The Flash*, a CW series in fact, fit all my sister's requirements. Typically, I'd drag her taste and recommend something I deemed worthy of an arrogant film studies grad like *Mr. Robot* or *Black Mirror*. But today, just hours after she picked me up from the West Fall Church D.C. Metro stop where I wiped reluctant tears from my eyes before hoping in her car, I had no extra energy for shade.

"You're lucky I'm tired," I said.

The smell of fried chicken and waffle fries from a fast-food Korean spot called Bonchon drifted through her one-bedroom apartment and up my craving nose. I hadn't eaten in 24 hours, unfortunately on purpose, because it was the only thing I really felt I could control lately. But I'd listen to my growling stomach today. I was too tired for depravity, for discipline. Perhaps I'd continue this starved saga when I returned to Brooklyn. Perhaps not. Since, lately, minus this anxiety-induced relapse due to the anticipation of this trip, my eating had been far less disordered than usual. It was tougher these days to starve or binge when I had to be so on top of my being in therapy. It was nothing if not embarrassing to report I'd withheld from eating *again*, only to hear some inevitably wise response from Dr. Patel. Especially since I told myself I had to tell the truth now. The whole truth. So, I gave myself the space to embrace old school toxicity a la starvation for 24 hours. Hoping I'd return to Brooklyn with a different desire. Return to Brooklyn, where Cam still was, who I'd just kissed only hours ago, who told me to stay as long as I wanted, who didn't know how much it stung to hear those words. But it was my idea. To leave. Well. I had to credit Dr. Patel for the inception of such a thought.

"Your assignment this week, start thinking of ways to enjoy your time alone, without Cam. Ways to enjoy your friends without Cam. Be creative, have fun with it." He said this to me months ago.

Since then, I started hitting up bookstores after work, all by myself, to write things I wanted to write or work on my book. I started riding my bike to movies on the weekends again, alone. Started being more consistent with POCLuck, and helping out with bklyn boihood, offering up my PR and writing skills to the Brooklyn-based collective of queer and trans bois of color, which I'd admired for years. I'd even started helping out as one of the media specialists at Hetrick Martin Institute, teaching local Black and brown queer kids about Wordpress and blogging. I would never have signed up to help there before Dr. Patel, with all the anxiety that came with being seen. But he encouraged me to be the mentor I'd hoped to have and so I was trying, trying hard. I reached out to Heart for the first time in weeks and we hung out, alone together, without my love who I'll admit, was always, always on my mind.

"It'll get easier. The more you make a practice of enjoying yourself the less your thoughts will revolve around your relationship to Cam." Dr. Patel assured me, and he was right.

It was getting easier, so when Jess called to check in on me without Ma on the line, a nice reprieve from our usual three-way call, I wasn't entirely turned off by her offer,

"You know you can come to D.C. too if you wanna get away for real. We're like two seconds from each other."

"I might take you up on that." I told her, which I was being honest about but had no real intention of cashing in on any time soon.

Dr. Patel had been right about more than he'd even addressed out loud. Because one day, I didn't see Cam in the morning, or after work or the next morning because she crashed at a friend's after being out till 5am, and we barely spoke until later that evening at dinner. But I did not panic. I did not assume she hated me, or that she was planning her escape, or that she was off, dead, in a river somewhere when she didn't respond to my texts. I even texted her less. When she didn't respond, I didn't craft a story of her being at all. This seemed to me like growth.

But when I did see Cam next, I knew that we were not okay. Because she told me,

"I realized something the past few days. I feel better when...we're a part."

I didn't catastrophize her words like I would have before. Though they hurt me, they stung. Instead of begging her to clarify, to promise she still loved me, I texted Jess.

Cool if I come down next week for like a day or two?

You can stay a week or more if you want, idc

Cam wanted a break. She would not call it a break though,

"I just need...some time. I need some time alone, not long."

Sven, my manager, was cool with me working from home for a week and so I left, alone, for the first time since Cam and I got together.

337

"This is huge, Jaz. Great progress. How does it feel?" Dr. Patel asked me.

I told him to wait and ask me again when I got back.

"Too soon to say." I laughed, nervous laughter.

I did not tell him that I was leaving *for* Cam. I knew he would not appreciate the complexity of that truth because what was good for Cam felt good for me. I knew he'd say something like,

"Separate from doing this for her, how is this choice good for you?"

Actually, I didn't tell anyone I was leaving for Cam. That I was removing myself for the greater good of our relationship, for *us*. I tried to focus on the fact that I would have never felt comfortable leaving Cam's side for any reason just months ago. This also felt like growth to me.

Here I sat in Jessica's living room, a few feet from the air mattress in her nook she'd blown up for me, and I felt...I felt. I pulled out my phone. Tapped into the mood app Dr. Patel recommended I download. Searched through the emotions— tired, stressed, confused, focused, joyful, peaceful, lonely...

"Feelings, emotions, they can be guides. They can be useful tools for mindfulness if you use them in a healthy way." I remember Dr. Patel saying.

Vulnerable. That's how I felt. Vulnerable. But otherwise, okay. Safe. Something about that felt like growth. And Jess had this great skill of distracting me from thinking about Cam even more than I'd gained the skill for. She promised she'd only speak of Cam when I'd bring her up. Which I'd do several times. Like when I said,

"It's not really a break..." Unprompted, right when Jess was about to press play on *The Flash.*

"No?" She asked with a bite full of chicken, still staring at the TV.

Usually Jess didn't pry, but I'd already told her about submitting myself to a hospital for suicide. Might as well be forthcoming about any and everything else.

"I mean, Imma be honest. It kind of sounded like she was...over it? But I ignored it?" I shrugged as if what I just said was not quite serious.

I stuffed my mouth with fries. It felt like a heavy confession. But like a half-truth in my head, which was constantly telling me that all the fears I had about Cam and me were untrue, that we'd never end. *How could we?* Jess raised a piece of chicken to her mouth, placed it back down.

"Did I ever tell you about how me and Isaac ended?"

I stopped chewing, even though I had much more to chew. I grunted because I couldn't laugh, but what she said on its face was funny. Of course, she hadn't told me. Though I was quick to spill the proverbial beans of my life to my sister as of late, that's not something any of us did, really. Especially not Jess. She never once twisted her tongue, not ever, to tell me about her love life. Never. *This* was a first. She'd successfully fostered this air of elder sibling perfection that every one of us other four bought all these years. Though I had to know Jess was no golden child. There was really no such thing. I'd just never pried. I'd assumed not perfection, but another almost equal thing, wholeness. As if we are not all whole, as if we don't all hurt sometimes. As if her wholeness implied, she never needed anyone's help. It's true though. I left ample space for the myth of my sister's perfection. It gave me hope like a beacon of what could be. But as she began talking about her and Isaac, who I'd only ever understood to be a mostly happy couple, who simply grew apart, I couldn't help but feel the embarrassment of my own, unfair assumptions.

Three times. Five years together and three major breakups.

"I love a project!" She laughed, a hint of sadness in her chuckle.

He had bipolar disorder. Like me. Prone to delusions, much more dangerous than my own, but delusions, nonetheless. And in their coupling, Jess would be like his therapist, always around when he needed her, even when he refused his medication or any other treatment.

"He needed me, sure, but like, when do I start setting boundaries for that? Because I matter too." She said.

I leaned back in her couch cushions. Flashes of Cam and my every fight blinked across my mind. I'd demanded so much from her. Constantly, I tried molding us into my greatest dream of love never asking Cam what shape she preferred. The shape of us was ugly now, a thing neither of us wanted, neither of us found comfort in.

"If I hadn't set a boundary for real, honestly? We'd probably still be together."

I understood Isaac. I hated that I understood Isaac. That undying longing to feel loved and cared for, at all costs. It's an unfair state. And it's not enough to blame your shortcomings when you know the truth. Mental illness does not mean freedom to cause others pain.

"Sometimes the best thing you can do is let go. I'm not saying ya'll should, I'm just saying. It's the best decision I've ever made."

We sat in comfortable, uncomfortable silence, as if paying our respects to something that had died. She nodded to her TV, I nodded back, and she started the show. It wasn't half bad. I told her so. And I wasn't bad. Neither was Cam. But is it peace if neither of you sleeps through the night? I stayed at Jessica's four nights. Cam and I didn't speak, didn't text, until the third. I told her that I'd be home Friday evening. She said *okay.* I rode the train like a soldier back from battle. I wouldn't need to tell her all I'd lost. She'd see it in my eyes when we met at our apartment door. Her arms outstretched for me and me, surprised to see them that way. But grateful, so, so grateful. We hugged like we hadn't seen each other in years.

"I'm sorry." I whispered.

"All either of us can do now is just be better." She said.

We were both doing our best, and I suppose that's all you can ask of two hurting people trying to love each other.

How to read poetry

It's always best to speak the truth

out loud

MY FAMILY, MY PEOPLE

Memphis, TN - Fall 2017

I am not saying my little brother Andon marked Cam and my end. You could even argue we were over far before any of this happened. But what I am saying is that Andon-gate was the catalyst to my shifting view on family. It started with a phone call, innocent and trivial as they come. On speakerphone my mom's strong voice bounced off our apartment walls, "So I was talking to Andon and you know he's been talking about maybe moving to New York..."

I did know this. It'd come up in one of many of Jess and Ma and my three-way calls, probably shortly after discussing something complicated going on with either of my brothers. But Cam, who sat beside me on the couch, with Bear in between, hadn't ever heard a thing about this. Confirmed by the sideways glare on her face. She knew what was coming.

I nodded, pretending all was well, "I do."

Ma continued, "Well he's thinking about coming up there in maybe a week —or just a few days! — Before graduation to

344

explore the city...What do you all think of letting him stay with you for that time? Not long..."

Her voice trailed off like an ellipsis. Felt like it echoed as Cam kept glaring at me.

She mouthed "mute it."

And I did. My palms were sweaty. I wished to fast forward through our conversation. I didn't want to hear what she said next because I knew I wouldn't like it. I knew it wouldn't match the thoughts in my own head, that were, *Of course, my little brother can stay!*

Cause if it were up to me, this had been a non-issue. A quick and easy "yes." A way to welcome at least one of my brothers into my arms in the way I'd always hoped I could. But here I sat with my partner, who I loved, who said,

"I'm not comfortable with that at all."

Okay. I expected hesitance. The last time Cam spoke to her own little brother was at least six years ago. She kicked him out her apartment after months of sloppy, inconsiderate roommate antics. They hadn't spoken since. It's a fact she told me early in our relationship, after explaining to me how close they used to be,

"He was my best friend," she'd told me.

I practiced empathy, trying to understand how an argument over dirty floors and counters could have led them both here. I know it was deeper than that. I understand the pain that comes with not feeling the respect you deserve. But after six years, not so much as a text between them? It was difficult to feel more couldn't be done to salvage what she told me they had. I'd learned to respect that for Cam, family did not mean the same thing as it did for me. There were many more conditions.

And sometimes there is no option but to cut someone off for your own peace. I could learn something from Cam about boundaries. Many things, in fact. She even inspired me to stand up to my oldest friend from college, the funny Jewish one named Jenna who was the only of my current friends to know me prior to my name change, prior to much of my evolution out of hating my own Blackness. But even after our fallout, when we did not speak for months, Jenna then apologized, changed. And I lived and learned that perhaps no person is irredeemable if they are willing to do the work. And we were family. She was my people. I found it so difficult to give up on family, chosen or not. I wondered what Cam could learn from my family of forgiveness. Of redemption. It wasn't until this moment that the full picture of our cultural clash revealed itself to me.

"I barely know him. "She ran it all the way home.

But, she had known him. As much as any partner might know their in-laws. We'd been together for years. We spent every holiday since with my family. And I felt a distance to Cam now more stark than I ever had because the unfamiliarity with which she spoke had the most unsavory undertone. She could not explain what she meant when she said she did not feel comfortable having a strange man in her home. She could not explain away the unsettling resemblance of her words to those of harmful folk. The type who wouldn't be caught around young Black men if someone paid them. Who've allowed their own fear to lead them to attacking people like me, or worse. Cam was nobody's white but her words were so devoid of color and compassion that it made my stomach hurt. But she promised this was not what she meant. She did not mean to sound "that way." She simply did not feel comfortable. Period. No deeper meaning, and she needed me to respect that. I told myself I must believe her, because denying my family welcome was already too much for our relationship to carry and survive from. We had to survive. We had to...

"Cam." I said, as if saying her name was all it took to drastically change her heart. To resolve all of the muck that led to discomfort at the thought of my baby brother's presence. It didn't work. Of course not.

But first,

"Hello?" My mom lingered on the other line.

"My bad, one sec." I told her, muting us again.

"It's how I feel." Cam doubled down. Shrugged.

She folded her arms, leaned back. Let Bear snuggle into her side. I wanted to scream at the state of her comfort as she proceeded to demolish the bridge connecting us and my family.

I told her as much, and it meant nothing. I pressed, even when it hit me, I was pushing my partner again. Push and pull, push, pull. Somehow, I lacked the foresight necessary to predict a scenario like this, one where Cam's boundary and my personal need collided so dramatically.

I unmuted the phone and forced out the words,

"I really wish I could say something different, but Andon can't stay here."

I told her I had to go, and technically I did, because I needed to get off the phone to focus on my panic. I just know she called Jess right after, because she texted me.

Is it like a no, no?

I drafted several responses. They all felt like blame. I didn't want to throw Cam under the bus. We were supposed to be a team. Finally, I wrote,

Cam isn't comfortable with him staying here, and I have to respect that.

Then moments later my mom sent a group text to all her kids,

Andon can't stay with Jaz and Cam. We'll have to figure something out.

The nail in my fucking coffin. Her putting me on blast. Everyone had opinions.

That's just ridiculous. (Leese)

Cause 'she don't know him.' (Jess)

They've met several times! (Leese)

Stupid (Drew)

And as if she could convince a stubborn Cam different, my mom asked to speak with her.

She agreed, "As long as she knows I'm not changing my mind."

"I know." I said, and I did.

Cam's phone rang two times before she answered, "Hi, Joanne."

Cold as ice, just like the rest of the conversation, of which I only heard Cam's side. Beginning as it ended, no Andon, not even for one night. "Family" be damned. And months passed. And Cam had no idea of the shift in how my mom and Jess talked about her, the many times this very instance came up and I'd try and change the subject. Looking like a fool trying to smooth drywall over crater-sized cracks in our foundation. Christmas came, and Cam still agreed to come down to Memphis with me. I let myself ignore the distance growing between us, because her coming to Memphis after what happened seemed like the greatest act of love.

Ma was busy prepping sides for our annual Christmas party the day we landed in my hometown. She had Drew come get us instead, and Andon tagged along. It'd be the first time we were all together since last Christmas, and I was not looking forward to it. Not one bit. All eyes were on Cam as they rolled up to American Airlines, windows down, glaring. Popped the trunk, and we threw our bags in. Cam rocked an impressive poker face getting into the back seat but even she couldn't play off the suffocating tension in that Mustang. The windows rolled up and we zoomed away. Through a wall of cannabis clouds, I watched my brothers cackle and coo up front. Cam and I rocked around in the back seats, our shoulders knocking into each other like pins at a bowling rink. Plies permeated the space, seeping into my ears and out through the thumping in my wrists. I breathed, hoped to get lost in it till I could get on out of this car. But then,

"Can you turn that down. My god!" Cam shouted over bass.

I cringed, not wanting to move at all, I still cringed. This would not go well. I felt it in my bones. Then gradual decrescendo of music. Maybe it would be okay. But no, Drew had only lowered the music so Cam could hear his guffaw nice and crisp, *full* of disrespect.

"My god!" Andon mimicked in the same voice he reserved for the mocking of white girls.

Then Drew,

"Can you turn that down?! Fuck outta here with yo' goofy ass."

And more laughter. Laughing, laughing, laughing, and then crescendo of "Rich Nigga Shit" by Plies.

I fix my mouth to speak, already regretting it, "Ya'll are being so wack right now."

Knew I was speaking in vain. The music got quiet again. Damn, I should have known. These were my brothers. I knew once words got flying, they'd keep flying till they cared to land.

"Jaz you just know you don't wanna get in on this, too. Ever since Cam punk ass came up in here you *been* wack." Said Drew.

My heart dropped into the wheels of that black car. Not just because I knew my brothers spoke to me even less once Cam and I got together. Or because I knew Cam had said some genuinely corny shit to them over the years. Or because sometimes Cam did act like a white girl to me, and so it never surprised me that they treated her like one. Or even because I knew I wanted and loved so much about this person that my brother's hated, and I had to reconcile with that feeling.

But because this is the furthest I'd ever been from my brothers, and we'd lived in different world before, so that was saying a lot.

"Your raggedy ass couldn't let him stay for a day? A damn day?" Drew said.

I interjected, "She wasn't comfortable with it, you have to respect that."

"No, *you* do. I ain't gotta respect shit." Drew said.

"And she been trash even before that!" Andon said.

I sat there small and shriveled and frozen as a raisin in ice. Trapped in the complicated, thorny truth of this clash. The one I told myself didn't matter, the one I claimed Cam and I would overcome, because she was Black, *is* Black. Black, a word that means some things, or everything, or nothing, depending on who you ask. I never dared asked what it meant to Cam, or if she even claimed it fully.

My brothers proceeded to drag the shit out of her, and us. Dragging her for the time she admitted not knowing what a durag was. For trying to talk like them and failing. For saying a young Black man made her uncomfortable. A young Black man she knew, a man who was supposed to be her family. For talking about both of my brothers behind their backs, because they somehow knew that sometimes, Cam would join my three-way conversations workshopping solutions to my brothers' various struggles. Two Black men she did not love but had many opinions about.

I'd never heard Andon speak this way. I always saw him as the baby, quiet one. Private and skilled in the art of minding his baby-brother business, but not that day. But this was his business. I'd apologized to Andon via text in October when it all went down. He wouldn't answer the phone. I chalked it up to 8 years and a generation separating us. But his response in that text, "it's fine" definitely meant "it's not fine at all." I knew that. I reckoned with the irony of meeting this version of my brother now, in this way.

"And how you 'gone have something to say about neither one of us, and you don't even fuck with us?! Like the fuck?" Andon said.

"And you be just letting her say shit, too!" Drew said to me.

Another shot, fired. I deserved it. I could count at least a dozen times I held the phone as Cam would cut in to speak, often curt, sometimes flippant, and I'd pushed every urge away to take my phone off speaker. Because she was family, and I told myself she spoke up because she cared. And who was I to deprive her of family participation. But after what happened with Andon that October, I couldn't keep pretending that we thought of care in the same ways, family in the same ways. Cam didn't love my family, she loved me. And in the world she came from, where loving deep looked different, or didn't persist at all, and Black didn't have nothing to do with loving, she had never needed to reckon with the double meaning family had for me or mine.

I grabbed her hand. I needed to feel closer to her than I felt. I needed to feel like us, together, was worth all this. And we sat there like feckless derps, hand in hand, as they kept going, as if practiced. Maybe so. Years-worth of frustration and only a 40-

minute car's ride of our unwavering attention. I had to give it to
them, a perfectly timed read for the ages, and not a lie was told.
If only it weren't at our expense. Like clockwork, when we
turned the corner to my parent's house, Drew said,

"We said our piece. We gone leave it at that. But don't you
ever, ever try some shit like that again."

And with that, he turned the music up once more for the
last three minutes of the car ride. Cam's eyes welled up with
tears but her face was stoic, cold. She got out before me.

"What the fuck." I said to them, knowing exactly what the
fuck.

Still, I couldn't sit back and let my little brothers drag us
from here to next Sunday without at least a little fight.

My mother stopped stirring greens to ask, "What's wrong?"

I know she could see it on all our faces. Cam had already
made it upstairs by then. She would not speak to my brothers
ever again. And since she wasn't drinking, she could spend even
more time alone than usual. And I wouldn't bother her,
wouldn't push her to join us for the family movies downstairs,
or the marshmallows in the backyard. No point in faking the
funk. The annual Christmas party felt like an illusion everyone
bought but me. My brothers and sisters grabbed mixed drinks
in the kitchen and huddled upstairs in what my parent's called
the entertainment room, formerly the room my siblings and I
used to have class. Downstairs Ma facilitated a karaoke night

with my aunties and uncles, my dad's friends, and everyone from the spiritual center my parents attended. And me? I floated somewhere in between, mostly on the balcony where I could play with the family dog, a Peekapoo named Ziggy, who cared as much as I did about who was and wasn't celebrating. I also had easier access to Cam this way, who lay on the bed my mom reserved for us, in what used to be Andon's bedroom. I'd check on her every fifteen minutes or so, see if she wanted any food or drink, non-alcoholic of course. She'd snuck downstairs only once to make herself a plate of my mother's turkey and cornbread, my aunt's mac and cheese. After getting lost in conversation with one of the few white folks there, a sweet but chatty hippy type from the spiritual center, she returned to the room where she'd live the rest of the night.

"I'm just gonna take a nap." She told me finally, after my fourth time checking in.

So, I shuffled my way into the young folks party just a few feet away. Didn't plan to stick around. Stepped right into one of our family friends, also named Jessie, infamous worldly tales, as he was wont to spin ever since Leesie and I met him on the school bus ten years earlier. Now he was pretty much a part of the family, never missing at least the tail end of a good ole gathering like this. He came out as gay not long ago, though he's the type who honestly never needed to on account of being so fully, brightly himself. But ever since, he had new and fresh international antics to share and we all lived for the tales.

"Gurl, when I tell you this hostel was cheap as hell, I'm not playing with youuu," He laughed.

Everyone was warm and tipsy and relaxed, and so I took a sip of my spiked cider and settled in. Covered my mouth when a chortle escaped, because Jamie had a way of cracking me up despite myself. I hadn't planned to stay. I'd meant to show my face and then return to my moping grounds with Ziggy in the hallway. But this was before I noticed, this is the most fun I'd had at a party in a very long time.

"Where's your girl?" One of Jessica's old friends, Deren asked.

A sarcastic, funny fellow, with locs like Rapunzel who never seemed fazed by any point of my evolution, who, when he met Cam, simply gave me a thumbs up and said, "Nice."

"She's...not feeling well." I told him, and now everyone was looking at me right in my eyes.

And I smiled to myself because, before he asked, I hadn't thought of her at all. Not since I'd entered the room. And then I frowned and sipped my drink to hide the shame of that realization. It was the first time since I knew Cam that she didn't live in the largest room in my mind. She was somewhere else now, in a closed in space and I had to search to find her, and that scared me. Dr. Patel said this could happen. I didn't believe him. Now I could only think of what came next.

And when?

I hope that Black Memphis man learned to love

the flow of water

NAWLINS

New Orleans, January 2018

New Year's Eve we rode from Memphis to New Orleans on the love train. Nine doting hours past swamp, forest and bayou glazed terrain, never letting go of each other's hands or hearts, because baby, we didn't need anyone but ourselves. We didn't need my family. And as much as I wanted their love for her, I knew it wasn't realistic, not after all that'd happened. I couldn't let that end us, I wouldn't, couldn't let go of *us*. Not yet.

"Where do you wanna go first?" I asked her eagerly as the train screeched to a stop at the edge of Central Business District, New Orleans.

"No idea," She shrugged, staring plainly out the window.

I squeezed her hand, she pulled away, "We should probably start getting off?"

I agreed. Out the window all you saw were train tracks under great dark shaded structures stretching hundreds of feet ahead. And when I tell you I'd experienced nothing more beautiful. It wasn't the site, but the feeling, when I first stepped foot on Crescent City concrete, that let me know I'd found love. A big ole' goofy smile refused to leave either side of my face as we and the crowd rolled luggage past the shelter and into the afternoon drizzle. It could have been storming and I would have welcomed buckets of rain with a grin.

"I love it here." I said, blinking away a drop that fell on my eyelash.

"Babe, you haven't even seen anything yet." She scoffed, laughing at the end of it.

Our hotel was somewhere in the Garden District, but I'd forgotten my charger.

"Maybe we could stop on Canal Street, hit up a Walgreens or something?" I asked.

A weak excuse to explore. Thankfully, she agreed. Luggage in tow, we hopped in a Lyft for the corner of Roosevelt Way and St. Charles. But our driver was the talkative type, a New Orleans native who could tell from our accents we weren't from around these parts. He missed the stop and instead offered us a driving tour amid the traffic.

"You gone love it here, I already know." His voice was syrupy smooth, bending round and wavy with Nawlins charm.

I was staring out the window like a pup on their way to their forever home. Two to three trolleys passed through at any minute. Young Black boys drummed on buckets on the sidewalk, and across from them an older man played trumpet. These buildings weren't unlike those I'd seen in Paris but were somehow countrified. Down the road I spotted Harrah's Casino, and across from it a majestic Hilton hotel on the same lot as a plaza-styled mall. Folks glided down busy sidewalks with their favorite cocktails in-hand. Seemingly unbothered when they'd inevitably spilled its contents.

"You know, Canal Street was gone be a real canal? Water an everything." Said our driver.

I didn't know. I'd read a lot about the city, as I did any place I was about to visit, but much of what he said was new information for me. I soaked it in. Every bit.

"Well, there go your Walgreens right there." He pointed to a neon sign before an old-style pharmacy on the corner.

"Thank you!" I said, cheeks starting to hurt from grinning so hard.

The sun peaked out behind pink clouds. I forgotten it'd been raining at all.

"We should buy an umbrella." Cam said on our way inside Walgreens.

Along with two umbrellas, we bought a NOLA brand chip called Zapp's in Voodoo flavor, and Rap Snacks with a digital painting of Lil' Romeo, a NOLA-native born rapper, on the front. We also got some pralines, which I'd had a few times in Memphis, my charger, and a couple sparkling waters.

"So, what do you think, you wanna walk around some more or maybe drop our stuff off and come back out? I was thinking we could go to a restaurant in our area cause from what I read it's super nice over th—"

"I just wanna rest." She said.

Her eyes hung low and so did her head, though she tried to lift it every few seconds as if gathering a heavy load. Sleep didn't revive her. She woke two hours later with the same bags under her eyes.

"You wanna grab food?" I asked, fully dressed, fully expecting to leave again in the next hour or so.

"Can we just order in?"

Her words were little needles in my side. Nine hours on a train and three lulling around seemed quite enough recourse for getting acclimated but she said she didn't feel well now. And selfishly I wanted to leave her behind, walk the New Orleans streets on my own, breathing in that familiar air that felt like home. But I didn't. I held tight to that desire like a once-lost baby doll and then I dropped it. Tried forgetting it. We opted for take-out from a Creole spot near our hotel, instead. I had rice and beans that reminded me of my mom's. Cam had crawfish etouffee.

"Honestly? It's whatever." She shrugged when I asked her how she liked it.

"Seriously?!" I could barely believe it with how much I savored mine.

Cam laughed at my surprise, "Relax, it's fine. I'll finish it."

She did. We watched *Spongebob* for hours and I played Words With Friends on my phone and we cuddled until we both felt tired enough to sleep. I imagined where I'd be right now if I were on my own. Maybe French Quarter at a bar meant for queers drunk enough on absinthe to spark conversation without fear of hesitation. Then I shook the thought out of my brain, ashamed I'd ever entertained it. We were here together.

The next morning I'd planned for us to hit up a popular brunch spot called Cafe Fleur De Lis. It was in the heart of the French Quarter, close enough to other spots I'd researched that we could walk around and explore. The sun woke me up bright and early. I'm already an early riser, but my excitement had me going at 6am. I couldn't sit still. So, I kissed Cam sweetly on the cheek and sent her a text that I'd be walking around the neighborhood. I slowed my usual power walk to a calm and happy stroll. Feels odd to rush amidst New Orleans rhythm. A steady 1,2, so Black, so rich, so familiar. Gayer than I remembered the south to be. Casually flaunting so much of what I ran from the south *for* and daring me to hate it. I couldn't. I loved every bit. I stopped at a local donut shop and grabbed a plain and chocolate glaze for myself that the cashier, a Black woman, told me I'd probably like best. Got a raspberry filled donut for Cam. It's the only kind she liked. But when I returned, Cam was still sleeping as if I'd never left. And waking her was blasphemous, I wouldn't dare. Though, after an hour more, and five completed Words With Friends games I was tempted to do the unthinkable and wake her up. Instead, I took out my journal from my suitcase and wrote furiously about wasted time. About dream cities and could-be memories that will only ever be dreams, and my prose became pure ranting on the page, at how sweet this all might be were I here alone. The thought of that felt like cheating and I wanted to wake Cam simply to apologize and then,

"What time is it?"

She was awake. Fifteen minutes till 1pm and she was awake. And I was furious, but my anger felt so, so unfair. I tried masking it.

"Twelve forty-six."

"Don't do that." She said.

Apparently, I hadn't masked a thing. She rolled out of bed, stumbled into the bathroom and said, "I'll be ready in like thirty."

I added our names to Cafe Fleur De Lis' via a wait list app and I started a new game while I sat. She left the bathroom in exactly twenty-two minutes, a layer of dewy makeup covering her tired, drooping face. She pulled a long, green knit dress over her head and said,

"Okay. Just putting on my shoes."

We rode an Uber to the outskirts of the Quarter and with all the traffic, the driver recommended we walk the rest of the way. I didn't mind. I hoped Cam didn't either. I liked seeing the praline shop we said we'd hit up on the way there, and the Sephora Cam assured me she must step foot in before we left. And I didn't even care that we got a little lost along the way, passing by the Market so that I could peak in just so, and spot all those little shops thriving with all those patrons stopping by.

"Ahhh, I love this place." I reached out to hold Cam's hand. She pulled away.

The gesture stopped me in my tracks, leaving me looking silly in the middle of the street. A cab honked and I kept moving.

"You good?" I asked Cam who stood with arms folded on the sidewalk.

Shrimp and grits and dark liquor wafted up my nose, coming out the open-door Creole restaurant at the corner we stood, or at the one across the street because they were everywhere. And I knew the answer to my question. Of course, Cam wasn't "good." She turned her head from me, then back in my direction but not quite at me, then, the worst of her glances, she looked through.

"We should get out of the way." I said, because no other words felt honest or right enough.

So, we crept from St. Ann Street and Chartres to Jackson Square, where a jazz band of four serenaded locals and tourists like it was any other Tuesday. And we sat, because it was the only thing we could do that didn't hurt. In front of us a curious family stared intently at a sign in front of the St. Louis Cathedral. The older man in the family shrugged to the woman and they walked away.

I studied Cam's face. Her eyes were sunken and sleepy. Her mouth a drooping line, revealing nothing more than the weight of this. Of us.

"I feel like somethings wrong with me." She said.

I'm not sure what I was expecting to hear from her. I don't know what would have made more sense that those words, but they felt strange to me. Perhaps because I knew that whatever loomed over us had everything to do with us together, not her alone. Or because I had been selfish, on purpose, to ignore the storm riled up in her own heart, because it was too painful to witness the truth of it without accepting the full truth of us. I wanted to touch her, but I didn't feel I should. My hand said it all, reaching and then pulling away.

"Do you wanna go back?" I asked her, as if that would solve everything. As if we could just cuddle in our hotel room for three more days and return home like it was nothing.

"I don't know...I just," I followed her gaze to the trumpeter basking in a solo, swaying back and forth, and his new fans swaying with him, "I don't feel anything, like... I feel...nothing."

Nothing. *Nothing.* The irony of the word when here we were, pretending this conversation wasn't our everything. I felt it. I clung to it, but I felt it, drifting like a message in a bottle far away from us.

"It's like we're on two different trips." Cam said, and I nodded, knowing exactly what she meant.

"I feel that, too." I said, looking away again.

We were the quietist couple in New Orleans. Sitting there, sober and teary eyed and fully out of place. It was getting harder to look Cam in the eye without seeing everything I'd been ignoring. I knew, I *been* knew, this hurting she felt couldn't be fixed by me. I knew the solution to her pain lived somewhere beyond us. So, I could only look away. But in that away were my own questions, all rising to the surface from murky waters I'd tried drowning them in. The whats and whys for my continued stay in this relationship. The now almost 3-and-a-half-year promise of my faithful devotion now feeling more like stubborn posturing. I felt almost silly if not so sad. Almost laughing if not for the crying that would come first.

"This just...isn't working." She said.

I nodded. It felt like letting go, or the beginning of it. Tears filed like an army ready for battle. They wanted to fight for me.

I wanted to fight for myself, but there is no fighting in a war like this. I hadn't been honest with myself. Hadn't acknowledged this push I called our New Orleans trip, together. The final push shoving her right on off the edge of us. I would have ignored it forever had she let me. I still tried.

"What are you saying?" I asked her, fighting as if it made any good sense.

"Jaz."

Even now, she was trying to protect me. Saying it would be our end, for real. She'd never said it, never fully. I'd always let half-assed commitment be enough, when it was never really enough and oh, had I been lying to myself.

"What are you saying?" I asked again because I told myself I needed to hear it. That none of this was real until she said it was over all the way.

"I don't want to be with you anymore." She said, her face cold and still. Her eyes staring deep into mine, like a laser.

It's like she was protecting herself behind an icy wall. And so, I searched like hell to find a way to warm her up to me. Me, always, always searching for a way to warm her up *to me*.

"You can't mean that." I was hot as the sun.

Still, she showed no signs of warming. None.

"It's fucking over, Jaz."

My tears multiplied. I cried as quietly as I could but even my silent tears are so, so loud.

"Cam. Cam."

Cam stood. I stood with her. She walked. I followed behind. And she walked, and walked,

"Cam."

She kept walking. I moved behind her, driven by the sun and I could scream but I didn't and holding it in hurt. And I saw myself in my mind's eye, pulling again. Chasing, again. As if this time were any different, as if this weren't the worse it'd been between us. As if I hadn't already learned that together did not mean love. None of what I was doing was love. I stopped walking. I watched her from the sidewalk check her phone and wait for a Lyft and then, drive away. I was still as a tree and not nearly as wise, but wise enough to know that this, my part of us, was not love. I waited long enough to wipe my tears. I walked more, but this time alone, down Decatur Street. Floated into French Market like a ghost but moving slow and salient. So human and exposed. My stomach grumbled and I bit into a tasteless salmon crepe I was told would be quite savory. None of this was real. It couldn't be. I had nightmares of this moment that felt more real than this. I kept walking. Watching smiling faces as if through a shield that made them blurrier than usual. Like the start of a lucid dream that never quite drives into focus. Pinching myself would not help me wake up, nor screaming, because none of this could be real. I wouldn't let it. I was the one standing in the way of this reality. Still. Still. Still. Hours passed. I walked the bulk of French Quarter, and back around again in a meaningless circle like I was searching for something. A buzz from my pocket shocked me into being,

How's New Orleans?!

Leesie texted. She'd visited only months before, and years before that on an architecture student trip. She had no idea how weighted such a question was. I ignored my everything and said,

Amazing so far!

New Orleans was amazing. It was Cam and me that were a mess. If only I were around enough to experience it. I couldn't walk anymore. It felt strange to pretend to explore. I texted to see if Cam was in our hotel. She wasn't. I returned to it and closed my eyes for hours. Opened to find her glancing at me and not meaning to and a pang shuddered within my nerves, and I told myself it was her love.

"Hi." I said to her. So casually, almost flippantly what with all that happened.

"Hey." She said, sitting on the edge of her bed and removing her shoes.

Her lips were that bright red they'd turn when she'd bitten them too much. Her cheeks were flushed. Eyes heavy. But she was still beautiful.

"How was your day?" I asked her. Why, I don't know. I didn't want to know if her day was good or bad. I shoved down this steady beat of wanting brewing in my fingertips to reach for her.

"Stop." She felt it. She had to have felt it, too. Or why would she have pushed it away, because she always pushed it away when she felt it.

"Cam."

"No. Don't do this to yourself, it'll only make it worse."

I forced my hand back to me.

She continued, still not looking my way, "This is the right choice for both of us. You don't see it now, but you will."

"You can't know that." I told her.

"Yes, I can."

"Cam, you're literally always running. You've been running this entire time even when we've been so fucking good, so why now? Because my brothers dragged you? Because—"

"Yeah! What if that is a part of it? Why should I be okay with that?"

"I never said you should!"

"Why would I wanna be a part of a family like that?"

"What the fuck does that mean?"

I knew what it meant. Being a part of a family that doesn't accept you. A part of something that doesn't fit yet you force it to fit...

"I'm not explaining shit to you, it's over, okay?"

"You're gonna regret this. I know you are. You're gonna look back and wish we were still—"

"Still what? Still like *this*? Because fuck this. Fuck this!"

This. Cam, seated facing the wall on the edge of the bed in front of me. Me. Legs crossed on a bed too big for just me, staring ahead at the shaved head of a woman I still love.

"Do you even love me anymore?"

We were both quiet. She turned then to look me in the eye. No tears, not like the ones flowing down my face.

"Yeah, I love you."

She said it like it hurt coming out of her mouth. I wanted to reach for her again, but not in the same way.

"I love you. But I'm not *in love* with you," she finished.

I turned away from her this time. Shook my head and wiped tears as if rebuking the truth, I'd just experienced. It was a cliché sentiment I'd heard so many times that meant nothing real to me. *I love you. But I'm not in love with you.*

Until now. Now it felt like a tsunami enveloping me. There is no pulling hope out of this sort of wave. This wave of finality. *I'm not in love with you.* It didn't matter how much I still chose us. She did not choose us. But then I heard my own thoughts as if outside of myself and the whispers like a question, lingering,

Why would you even want her to? Don't you want to be happy? Don't you want to be whole?

Trying to hold on for dear life to something unreal is the best way to fall. Yet, I'd done it and still tried even when real freedom stared me in the face and said, *grab hold.* Because freedom can look different than you think it would.

It hurt to sleep in the same bed. Even though we slept as far apart as we could, it hurt to know we were still together and not together. I kept my eyes closed almost the whole night, but I did not sleep. There was not enough money between us to take separate flights. And so, like relics to a love affair, we sat beside each other for three long hours to New York City. Back to our one-bedroom Flatbush apartment and to Bear, and to what was once all the things between and about "us."

I emailed Dr. Patel. Told him the thing I said couldn't happen, did. And I was still here. That I felt like a tsunami hit me, but that I somehow survived. I have not drowned. *I'm still here*, I said. But I was hurting. He told me he was proud, and that he was available to meet Monday.

Child:

How do you love yourself?

Mother:

Start with the sky

Then love on the trees

The ocean

The clouds

The bees

And soon you'll find

Loving You

Is easy

LOVE INTEREST #4

Dr. Patel's office, Winter 2018

"So straight to D.C. after this, huh?"

I nodded, "Yup, I'm all packed, all I need to do is go back to my apartment."

"One last time." Said Dr. Patel.

I nodded, "One last time."

Jess would meet me there. She'd take one of my three suitcases and we'd both hop on a train back to D.C. along with everything I could afford to keep. It had been three weeks since Cam and I ended. One week since I'd seen her. In those three weeks I'd sold my bike. Planned to sign off our apartment to a coworker, because Cam could not afford to pay for it on her own. I didn't know where Cam was. I didn't need to. I was proud of that.

"That's very good to hear. I hope you feel the significance of that, Jasper." Dr. Patel affirmed.

I tried to smile. I wanted to cry. A good cry this time. I'd have to say goodbye to Bear for the last time when I got home. I dreaded the thought. When I'd leave, Cam would pick him up to stay with her friends in the Bronx till she got situated. It felt like part of my life was ending, but Dr. Patel was right when he said,

"You made it. You're still here."

I told him it felt strange to leave New York. I still loved it, deeply. Once, I thought I'd end up like Fran Lebowitz in a brownstone full of eight thousand books in forty years. But I knew, though I'd grown past many of my demons, life only made sense to me if I truly started over and left this gorgeous funky chaos called NYC behind.

"And that's okay. Trust the instinct that tells you where you're happiest," Dr. Patel said.

It was risky. To sneak off to Centreville, VA for the foreseeable future, and then hopefully New Orleans, while working remotely, under the guise of a soon return. But my supervisor, who was now a good friend, promised not to say a word,

"My lips are sealed." Matt laughed. I knew he was serious.

He cared less about the higher ups than I did. He'd just been promoted after Sven moved to a different department and I declined the raise, citing a preference for the flexibility in my current position.

"Totally understand. I just wanted to bring it to you first. People like us rarely get the chance to excel in these spaces."

I nodded. I appreciated them. Thanked them for constantly being a beacon of light in a land of hungry corporate sharks. Told them, what I really wanted was to be an author full time. An artist, too. They understood. And with Dr. Patel's help I was starting to believe that dream was truly possible for me.

"I ordered my copy, by the way." Dr. Patel told me.

I blushed. The thought of my therapist reading my book seemed the most bizarre compliment. But I was excited. I'd worked hard over the past year, with Cam and Jess and an editor that I hired on Upwork with my side work money, to try and make *Juniper Leaves* something I could be proud of.

"Jasper, I can't begin to tell you how proud I am. I can't wait to read it." He told me.

Heart said the same, "I'm so proud of you, friend."

We'd spent most of the past two weeks together, when she wasn't with her new boyfriend, a guy she met at work with whom she now lived with. I liked him. I liked him for her. I invited him to the bar the night before, along with some of my Dyke March committee friends. Later, I met with Belle and some of my old roommates I'd grown close to. Went to one last bklyn boihood party to say goodbye to AJ and everyone else.

"I wish you weren't leaving, but like, I also love New Orleans sooo...I'mma see you!" AJ laughed.

I laughed with them. The train ride to Centreville was quiet. Simple. Smooth, almost like a dream.

"It'll all feel real eventually." Jess told me.

I believed her. Thanked her, asked her how she was doing. We talked about her life for a while.

"You wanna watch *The Flash* when we get to your place?" I asked.

It made her laugh. I was serious.

Dr. Patel and I had long since written an exit plan involving almost every step I'd taken these past few weeks. But I'd never answered his initial question, about what life looked like without Cam. I knew now.

Said to him, "Freedom, I guess."

Such a big word for such a small sentence, as if the world I live in offers freedom to someone like me, but I meant different.

He almost chuckled at the simplicity of it. Asked me, "What does that look like for you?"

"It looks like me loving myself? Like, finally killing that cop in my head? Full guillotine. 'Off with her head!'"

He smiled gently, never one to entertain my jokes in sessions so as not to encourage my chosen defense mechanism. I nodded. I was still working on me. He asked what ways I might go about doing that, "finding freedom." I told him I'd stop dating for a while. That'd I'd focus on other kinds of love: platonic, familial, communal, self...I told him I wanted to be the sort of person whose love for themselves bubbled over into others, that I had so much to give that I could be that solid someone in other people's lives like many had been for me.

"And romance is overrated." I added.

"You joke, but you're really onto something, Jasper. "He said, "Something we've discussed a lot is this idea that romantic relationships don't have to, nor do they need, to be the most important thing in your life. We're a fascinating species, humans, and we can love and value more than one thing at once. Including ourselves!"

Dr. Patel and I had been starting our sessions in brief meditation or quiet mindfulness. This would be our last meeting together, so I asked him if instead, we could end our time with a poem I wrote that I felt set the tone for my new journey. He said of course.

He bowed his head, waited. I began to speak...

Intro
everything

is breathing

we are

alive

all of us

black

we are

eternal

now

close your eyes

and

get acquainted

It's just a feeling. It's like how you tell someone what it's like to be in love. Are you going to tell anybody who has not been in love how it feels to be in love? You cannot do it to save your life... That's what I mean by free... I'll tell you what Freedom is to me. No fear.

Nina Simone, New York, 1968

ACKNOWLEDGEMENTS

To my ancestors. Thank you for your continued guidance and love. For living through me so that I may continue our story. Thank you endlessly to my mother, who pushed past her own inner dissidence to meet me again, arms outstretched and ready to love. Thank you to my big sister, Jess, who's always, always been my ally and greatest role model. I cannot thank you enough. For Jalisa, who accepts me, no matter how odd or strange. To my brothers who helped me see the light and laugh the laugh. Thank you to my dearest friend, Lezlie. Without their friendship and inspiration, I'm not sure I'd have reached this version of *Pansy* y'all just read. To Joi, my partner, whose righteous rebellion, and glowing being are a boundless gift for all lucky enough to encounter. I'm so endlessly inspired by you and honored to move through this life together. To Aunt Patrice "Treacy" Joyner, who sowed a seed so poignant it would lead me to the most necessary resolve. I love you so much, and your honesty is forever appreciated. Thanks to Jalisa for your critical eye, making sure I didn't release a cover full of graphic design faux pas. Thank you to my cousins Ashley, KeKe, April, Nicky, Vita, for loving my core and knowing my heart. To the wonderful few folks who donated to the little IndieGogo for this book, some of whom are already listed. You believed in this work when many others didn't, or did but not enough, and that is something I'll cherish forever. To Cydney Humphrey, oh my goodness, Cydney! The diligent care with which you offered edits to *Pansy* helped smooth out parts of this book I never would have caught otherwise. Thank you to the incomparable Stanley Fritz for giving me my first official writing gig those many years ago. Your kindness and ability to navigate beyond the gatekeeping tendencies of this media and publishing landscape are still examples I follow today. Thank you to the folks at Gotham Writers Workshop for offering me the opportunity to take one of your workshops at no cost. And for connecting me with Dani, a smart and wonderful literary agent, for an invaluable review of an earlier version of *Pansy*. I am so glad we got to meet before I called this thing "complete." Thank you to Killens Review of Arts and Letters for including "san.ko.fa" in your Spring 2024 issue. To Mojo, my dog, my homie. We are each other's mutual guardians and ain't that sweet. And to Isobel, I've never looked up to a cat more. To Belle and "Casey" for our dear friendships, which began in that magical chaotic city. To Heather, and "Tey," and "Ra" and all you beautiful New York friends with whom I'll share lifelong memories. We had an adventure, didn't we? To all my internet friends whose bonds have been just as deep as any other. To Penn, love you! To Professors Jonathan Rattner and Alice Randall for guiding me in the most interesting, fun, and right direction for my creative journey. And to all the teachers out there who continue to dedicate their lives to fostering brilliance in young folks who may not have seen it in themselves otherwise. To "Camelia," for those several years of love and lessons together. Thank you, Audre Lorde. If not for you and your biomythography, *Zami*, there'd be no *Pansy*. Thank you for the questions you asked yourself out loud so folks like me could hear them, and then ask ourselves. To all of the writers and poets, living and ancestral, young and older, who've made me a better writer once I finally picked up your books. Thank you to every person who might share some of the same words or shapes I call myself. To all the ones who came before us, who, post-colonialism, weren't allowed the right words that gave validity to what existed anyway, and always. I am so grateful for you. For the beauty that is Us. Thank you to the bold ones, like Jessie, my dear chosen family, who have lived freely despite the consequences, and have saved lives like mine just existing because of your bravery. Thank you to those spirits who've guided me since I've existed on this earth. Leading me with dreams of better days, and whispering truths for my stubborn ears, even when I wanted not to listen. Thank you so much to my late great Dad, THEE Philip Joyner, Jr., who journeyed with me through pain, then understanding, then love. I love you Grandmother Joyner, Grandma Palm, Aunt Jackie, Uncle Jessie, Uncle Johnnie. To all the names of ancestors I'll never know. I love you. I'll see you when I see you.

ABOUT THE AUTHOR

Jasper Joyner (they/them) is a Black trans author, editor, and poet. Their chapbook *A Flamboyance* with Bottlecap Press and indie YA fantasy novel *Juniper Leaves* are out now. Jasper lives in Memphis, TN with their partner Joi, cat Isobel, and dog Mojo. jasperjoyner.com

Printed in the USA
CPSIA information can be obtained
at www.ICGtesting.com
LVHW031015021024
792472LV00004B/26